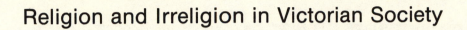

Religion and Irreligion in Victorian Society

R. K. Webb (Photo: Tim Burns)

Religion and Irreligion in Victorian Society

Essays in Honor of R. K. Webb

Edited by R. W. Davis and
R. J. Helmstadter

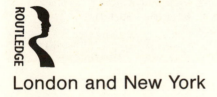

London and New York

First published 1992
by Routledge
11 New Fetter Lane, London EC4P 4EE

Simultaneously published in the USA and Canada
by Routledge
a division of Routledge, Chapman and Hall, Inc.
29 West 35th Street, New York, NY 10001

Typeset in 10 on 12 point Garamond by
Witwell Ltd, Southport
Printed in Great Britain by
T J Press (Padstow) Ltd, Padstow, Cornwall

British Library Cataloguing in Publication Data
Religion and irreligion in Victorian society:
essays in honor of R. K. Webb.
  I. Helmstadter, Richard J. II. Davis, R. W.
  III. Webb, R. K.
  274.1081

Library of Congress Cataloging in Publication Data
Religion and irreligion in Victorian society: essays in honor of R. K.
  Webb / edited by R. W. Davis and R. J. Helmstadter.
    p. cm.
  Includes bibliographical references and index.
  1. Great Britain—Religion—19th century. 2. Irreligion—Great
  Britain—History—19th century. I. Webb, R. K. (Robert Kiefer),
  II. Davis, Richard W. III. Helmstadter, Richard J.
BR759.R42   1992
274.1′081–dc20   91–40384

ISBN 0-415-07625-0

Contents

Contributors

Jeffrey Cox is Professor of History at the University of Iowa. He is the author of *The English Churches in a Secular Society: Lambeth, 1870-1930*.

R. W. Davis is Professor of History at Washington University in St Louis. He is the author of *Dissent in Politics, 1780-1830*; *Political Change and Continuity, 1760-1885: A Buckinghamshire Study*; *Disraeli*; and *The English Rothschilds*.

Ainslie T. Embree is Professor of History Emeritus at Columbia University. He is the author of *Charles Grant and British Rule in India*; *India*; and *India's Search for National Unity*; and editor and author of numerous other works in Indian history.

Peter Gay is Sterling Professor of History at Yale University. He is the author of numerous books on socialism, the Enlightenment, Freud and bourgeois culture in the nineteenth century. His *The Rise of Modern Paganism* won the National Book Award in 1967.

R. J. Helmstadter is Professor of History at the University of Toronto. He is the co-author of *Religion and Victorian Society*, the co-editor of *Victorian Faith in Crisis*, and the author of articles and chapters on Victorian religious and intellectual history.

Sandra Herbert is Professor of History at the University of Maryland, Baltimore County. She is the editor of *The Red Notebook of Charles Darwin* and the co-editor of *Charles Darwin's Notebooks, 1836-1884: Geology, Transmutation of Species, Metaphysical Enquiries*.

David C. Itzkowitz is Professor of History at Macalester College. He is the author of *Peculiar Privilege: A Social History of English Foxhunting, 1783-1885*. His current research is on the history of Anglo-Jewry.

Patricia S. Kruppa is Associate Professor of History at the University of Texas at Austin. She is the author of *C. H. Spurgeon: A Preacher's Progress*.

I. D. McCalman is Senior Lecturer in History at the Australian National

University. He is the author of *Radical Underworld: Prophets, Revolutionaries and Pornographers in London, 1795–1840.*

Reba N. Soffer is Professor of History at California State University, Northridge. She is the author of *Ethics and Society in England: The Revolution in the Social Sciences, 1870–1914* and a forthcoming book, *The University and National Values, 1850–1930.* She has also written numerous articles and chapters on nineteenth- and twentieth-century intellectual, social, and institutional history.

J. M. Winter is Fellow and Tutor of Pembroke College, Cambridge. He is the author of *Socialism and the Challenge of War: Ideas and Politics in Britain, 1912–18* and *The Great War and the British People.*

Acknowledgments

The Hibbert Trustees and the University of Maryland have made generous grants towards the publication of this book. Their support is highly valued.

The Editors also wish to thank Elisabeth Davis in St Louis and Andrea Smith in Toronto for helping them put this volume into final shape. They have caught and corrected many errors.

Introduction

Fashions in history come and go, and religion is once again fashionable among historians of modern Britain. For some it has never been out of fashion. Among these one of the most influential is R. K. Webb. Originally drawn to the history of religion by his interest in Benthamism, and struck by the unusual prominence of Unitarians among the master's disciples, Professor Webb began his study of Unitarian history with *Harriet Martineau: A Radical Victorian* (London, 1960). That book both provided a beautifully clear explication of the tenets of Necessarianism, as Joseph Priestley's philosophy was called, and established its importance, quite independent of Benthamism, in the growth of British Radicalism. It also revealed the existence in the late eighteenth century of a quite remarkable Unitarian elite, centered in Norwich, but with extensive provincial connections, as well as ties to the metropolis.

In the three decades since 1960, in scores of articles and papers, Professor Webb has pursued his interests in Unitarians and their origins and influence over three centuries. In his *Modern England* (New York, 1968 and 1980), a general history widely acclaimed on both sides of the Atlantic, he has emphasized for students the primary importance of religion in shaping British policies and attitudes over the same period. And, especially in his years of teaching at Columbia University from 1953 to 1970, he has exercised a strong personal influence over a large number of scholars and teachers, including several represented in this book.

The first essay in this volume deals with the period Professor Webb studied in his first book, *The British Working Class Reader 1790-1848: Literacy and Social Tension* (London, 1955). For many this period was the age of proselytism; men and women persuaded that they knew the truth were optimistic that they might be able to persuade the masses to join them in that knowledge. Webb has examined how a liberal intellectual elite organized the Society for the Diffusion of Useful Knowledge in order to educate working-class readers to become progressive citizens committed to Ricardian economics and a program of peaceful political reform. In his essay on Andrew Reed, Richard Helmstadter looks at another variety of evangelism, that associated with the great revival of religion. He shows how the evangelical revival embodied some of the patterns that we have come to identify with the Industrial Revolution – innovations in practical techniques, an inherent drive for expansion, an emphasis on usefulness, and, above all, an overarching dedication to mass marketing – and he sets out the successful career of Andrew Reed in the Congregational ministry as a case study in religious entrepreneurship. Andrew Reed's entrepreneurship is emphasized in this essay not only to establish an abstract link between the religious and economic worlds, not merely to suggest the cultural unity of the period, but also to point out that successful nonconformist ministers could achieve material as well as spiritual rewards. The roles of women in Reed's family and in his congregation are noted, serving in a small way to recognize the importance of women's history, a thread that links a number of the essays in this volume, and a theme that is certainly appropriate in a work that honors the biographer of Harriet Martineau.

Appropriate also is the central concern of the second essay, which examines an issue of religious liberty that bedeviled British politics in the half dozen years before Victoria's succession to the throne – and long afterward. This was the question of the Irish Church, and of its relation to the great majority of Irish men and women who resolutely maintained their allegiance to the old religion and rejected the Protestant usurper that had seized the Catholic birthright. The Whigs who came to power in 1830 had long been the champions of the rights of Irish Catholics, as had the Whigs' allies, the Protestant Dissenters (at least officially) under such leaders as the Unitarian MP, William Smith. Recently, historians have demonstrated considerable confusion over both Whig policy on religious questions in the 1830s and Unitarianism. Richard Davis examines recent interpretations and questions their validity, arguing instead for the essential continuity of Whig policy and positions.

There were, it is true, large new problems for those, such as the Whig and later governments, that wished to maintain an alliance with Protestant Dissent, or at least to gain its acquiescence in vital legislation. At the root of these problems was what became fully apparent only in the 1830s, the triumph within the Dissenting movement of a vigorous and aggressive new evangelical and trinitarian Dissent over an older, more rational, and in many cases more heterodox Dissent of the sort that had accepted the lead of William Smith. The new Dissent proved a puzzle to politicians, as it has to historians since.

Another puzzle for politicians, and one that Iain McCalman has done more to unravel than any other historian, is that posed by those self-indulgent, wild, and unrespectable early nineteenth-century radicals who are so dramatically different from the earnest men and women who figure in Edward Thompson's *Making of the English Working Class* (London, 1963) or in the works of R. K. Webb. In his essay on popular irreligion, Iain McCalman focuses on the spectacular career of the Reverend Robert Taylor, the star performer at the Blackfriars Rotunda in the late 1820s and early 1830s. Taylor, once an Anglican clergyman, packed the Rotunda with his splendidly theatrical presentations of astronomical atheism, his appearance as "the Devil's chaplain" who caused Satan himself to materialize on stage, and his extravagant, unrestrained espousal of Radical political reform. A hard drinker, a womanizer, and an irresponsible spendthrift, Taylor was as much a problem for Richard Carlile, the serious-minded proprietor of the Rotunda, as he was for the authorities. McCalman makes a case for Taylor's representing an important and little-recognized stream in popular radical culture.

Religion and irreligion greatly complicated nineteenth-century politics. Equally certainly, serious scientific thought, whether its intention was hostile or not, complicated religion. Drawing on work undertaken since Charles C. Gillispie published *Genesis and Geology* in 1951, Sandra Herbert discusses the strategic developments in geological theory during the second, third and fourth decades of the nineteenth century. She shows how the synthesis that Georges Cuvier achieved between geological science and biblical interpretation, a synthesis publicized in Britain by Robert Jameson and William Buckland and supported by them for a time, was gradually eroded before it was overwhelmed by Charles Lyell's *Principles of Geology* in 1830. Charles Darwin was a student at Edinburgh and Cambridge when geological theory was a hot subject, particularly as it related to the flood. Darwin took a considerable interest in geology as a young man, and the geological debates of his youth played an important role in his development as a scientist. By the end of the 1830s, after the *Beagle* voyage, Darwin had rejected the biblical account of the catastrophe, and was already engaged in an exploration of the origins of mankind that was set within the framework of his evolving ideas about geology.

The development of religious pluralism in nineteenth-century British society presented minority groups with new problems as well as new opportunities. Over the course of the century, many of the traditional privileges of the established church were done away with, and many legal disabilities were removed from those who were not Anglicans. Progress in the direction of liberty was welcomed by those who had been discriminated against, but this progress also threatened the identities of communities that had gained strength and cohesion from their legal separateness. Protestant nonconformists, especially, found their sense of separate purpose eroded as they were increasingly drawn into the mainstream of national culture toward the end of the century. Less ambivalent about their relation to the British national community, the leaders of British Jewry in the second half of the century developed strategies for the promotion of cultural pluralism within which the distinctive customs and beliefs of Jews might be recognized within a legal context of liberty. In his essay on the Board of Deputies of British Jews, David Itzkowitz shows how the political aspirations of the Jewish community shifted away from an agenda that emphasized removal of legal discrimination toward a more positive agenda that requested legal privilege for distinctive Jewish needs. He builds his case with particular reference to Sunday trading legislation in the third quarter of the century and the efforts of the Board of

Deputies to gain exemption for Jews from the regulations preventing work on Sunday.

Some years ago, before the changes in society and scholarship that give the word its current rich combination of overtone, implication, and political nuance, G. S. R. Kitson Clark pointed to the central role played by "manliness" in Victorian rhetoric. In his contribution to this volume, Peter Gay explores the meaning of "manliness" for the Victorians through an examination of *The Manliness of Christ*, a little-remembered book published in 1879 by Thomas Hughes. The muscular manliness we associate with Thomas Hughes's passion for boxing, or Charles Kingsley's love for the hunting field and the battlefield, is, Gay demonstrates, an exaggerated simplification of the Victorian ideal. Animalism and athleticism fade in Hughes's discussion of Christ's manly character, and softer virtues emerge, virtues perhaps more harmonious with Hughes's Christian Socialism, qualities certainly more consonant with trad-itional Christian ideals. Hughes and Kingsley both are shown to embrace within their ideas of masculinity a good deal that might be considered feminine. Their mature, manly ideal was richer and psychologically more complex than that embodied by the young Tom Brown in the Eden of boyhood at Rugby.

The tenderness and compassion of manly Victorian Christianity are highlighted in the fascination felt by nineteenth-century men and women for Mary Magdalene. That fascination is detailed by Pat Kruppa in her wide-ranging exploration of the variety of ways the Magdalen was treated in Victorian art and literature. Mary Magdalene provided a focus, legitimized by ecclesiastical tradition, for interest in female sexuality and the quality of feminine virtue. Her powerful sensuality and her redemption by Christ's love, an attractive parallel to the surprisingly strong nineteenth-century interest in prostitutes and their reform, helped make Mary Magdalene a compelling figure in the mythic pantheon of the Victorians. The Magdalen was certainly not Everywoman; she was not an angel in the house. Was she the dark shadow of that domestic angel? Was she what Everywoman might have been?

The pantheon of eminent Victorians has no place for Everyman, but a strong case might be made for nominating J. R. Seeley to that select company. His life of Christ, *Ecce Homo*, published anonymously in 1865, created a sensation. It was without doubt the most important British contribution to that popular nineteenth-century genre. Without the dissolvent skepticism of the German historical critics of the Bible, Seeley wrote for an audience of educated men and women whose religious needs were not satisfied by a conventional Christianity that seemed timid and slow in its confrontation with modern science and historical scholarship. His *Expansion of England* (1883), another work with a large readership, invested imperialism with both practicality and moral grandeur. His *Life and Times of Stein, or Germany and Prussia in the Napoleonic Age* (1878) constituted a liberal argument for the high place of the state in the progress of modern civilization. Seeley, moreover, as Regius Professor of Modern History, set his stamp on the tone and style of the history program at Cambridge for a generation. Reba Soffer draws the various strands of Seeley's life, work, and ideas into a coherent picture of a man suffused with the optimistic doctrine of progress. Only toward the end of his life did Seeley begin to think that the laws, as he considered them, of historical development might have a dark side.

The history of empire seems darker today that it did in Seeley's time, and religious confrontation sometimes lies at the heart of the darkness. This is dramatically illustrated in the Indian Mutiny of 1857, which was at least in part a revolt against an alien culture and an alien religion. Ainslie Embree treats the development of an official policy on government support of religion, or religions, in British India. He concludes that, though there was an effort to be fair and evenhanded, by the lights of the time, Victorian administrations in India were never impartial where the interests of Christianity were concerned, and that this made an impression on the Indian mind that continues to influence the religious struggles of the present day.

Jeffrey Cox is also concerned with religion in Victorian India; his subject is the roles that missionary work provided for women. In 1878 the Cambridge Mission to Delhi, operating in cooperation with the Society for the Propagation of the Gospel, began sending out to India young high-church priests committed to clerical celibacy. In Delhi these men organized St Stephen's Community of Anglican sisters in order to carry on zenana work with highly placed Indian women. The Cambridge Mission soon became predominantly female, and the sisters soon moved beyond the zenana visitations to set up schools and to provide medical care. By the 1890s St Stephen's Hospital in Delhi was at the center of the women's missionary presence in Delhi. Their schools, their medical work, and the administration of their well-organized institutions provided the women missionaries with opportunities for status and for visible positions of responsible authority in India that perhaps outran those available in England. Jeffrey Cox suggests that these Christian women provided role models for young Indian women, models in which their brisk efficiency and independence counted for more in the end than did their Christianity.

While the culture of British governing officials and missionaries in India was certainly affected by their experience abroad, it remained essentially British, in continuity with life at the imperial center. The First World War also raises questions of continuity and discontinuity. Without doubt, the war had a profound impact on British society and culture, but J. M. Winter argues that emphasis on the birth of "modernism" tends to make us lose sight of the multitude of traditional cultural forms through which men and women attempted to accommodate their experience of Armageddon. In the later nineteenth century, as faith in conventional Christianity diminished for many, some sought in spiritualism an alternative mode through which to deal intellectually and emotionally with death. Spiritualism, with its optimistic mixture of science and emotional commitment, was a thoroughly Victorian phenomenon. During the Great War, spiritualism, in a variety of forms that had been established while Victoria still reigned, flourished as life and death in the trenches moved beyond the margins of ordinary everyday comprehension. At least in this area of cultural life, the war, for a time, acted conservatively to encourage interest in a form of religiosity drawn from the Victorian past.

The essays in this book range freely about the modern British world; they deal with a variety of themes, times, and places. In this they reflect the spirit of the man in whose honor they are written. With striking generosity, R. K. Webb has shared his many ideas and interests with his students, colleagues, friends, and readers. He has helped to widen many minds. At Columbia, at the *American Historical Review*, at the University of Maryland Baltimore County, and latterly as a roving senior statesman of British history, he has impressed many with his commitment to broad horizons and open-minded scholarly integrity. He has never tried to narrow and shape his own work, or that of anyone else, to fit a Procrustean frame. And yet, his historical concerns and those of the men and women he has influenced most profoundly tend, as do these essays, to be anchored in nineteenth-century England and to be connected, in one way or another, with religion. It is our hope that this Festschrift, in concert and in parts, embodies to some degree the historical interests and professional virtues that R. K. Webb has taught us all to respect.

R. W. Davis, R. J. Helmstadter

Chapter 1

The Reverend Andrew Reed (1787–1862): evangelical pastor as entrepreneur

R. J. Helmstadter

With England at war with Napoleonic France and the Industrial Revolution transforming society at home, James Sedgwick, the Tory barrister, thought that changes in the religious world partook of revolution as well. The evangelical revival, he wrote in 1808, was weakening the bonds of civil order. Religious Dissent was undermining respect for the social hierarchy. Dissenting ministers were "blockheads, tainted with the mania of preaching, [who] turn religion into a trade."[1] Sedgwick's opinion has ambiguous validity, but his language is suggestive.

In every historical period, the great dominating events of the time give rise to a descriptive and analytical language. The international democratic movement of the late eighteenth and early nineteenth centuries encouraged the creation of a vocabulary and a set of ideas through which political aspirations and changes of unprecedented structure and form could be discussed and understood. With time, the leading metaphors within the discourse of democracy and revolution have been used by students of the period whose focus is on areas of life that are not overtly political. Economic historians have drawn on the language of politics in their effort to comprehend those interrelated social and technological changes that we now call the Industrial Revolution. Over the last one hundred years, the Industrial Revolution itself has come to be considered by historians as a phenomenon of primary influence and importance. Analyses of economic growth have stimulated productive intellectual debate, and the central metaphors and leading concepts of economic history have become familiar to all students of industrial society. The boundaries between economic life, politics, religion, and other forms of social behavior have become blurred, as Harold Perkin has demonstrated in *The Origins of Modern English Society* (London, 1969), where he makes a compelling case for considering the English Industrial Revolution as the product of a wide variety of elements in eighteenth-century English society. Perkin, however, in common with other scholars since the days of Max Weber, has conceived the connection between religion and the rise of capitalism in terms of the influence of religion on economic ideas and activity. This is also the case even with the most recent scholarship. Drawing on assumptions about cultural unity quite similar to Perkin's, Boyd Hilton has elaborated in *The Age of Atonement* (London, 1988) a considerable structure of connections between evangelical religious ideas and the ideas of economists and politicians who made economic policy in the first half of the nineteenth century. Hilton, like his predecessors, assumes that religion is prior to economics and more fundamental. For him the direction of influence is from religion to economics.

In this essay I wish to suggest that it might be productive to revise the scholarly pattern and use some of the metaphors and idea clusters that have arisen through investigation of the Industrial Revolution in order to further our understanding of the great evangelical revival of the eighteenth and early nineteenth centuries. More specifically and in more detail, I will try to show that the revival, like the industrial expansion of the same time, created opportunities for ambitious young men and that the successful ecclesiastical career of the Reverend Andrew Reed can fruitfully be seen as a case study in entrepreneurship. The argument is not that business methods influenced religious attitudes, though such might indeed be the case, but, rather, that the evangelical revival and the Industrial Revolution developed within the same cultural context and that their shared characteristics can be studied in similar terms. Andrew Reed is not approached so much as a businessman in the Congregational ministry, though he sometimes fits that picture, but, rather, as an ambitious nonconformist clergyman whose assumptions, goals and habits of mind are similar in many ways to those we have come to recognize in the entrepreneurs of the business world of the same period.

The revival of religion, roughly coterminous with the era of constitutional and industrial revolutions, is another element in the history of the period that is a contender for overarching importance. Thus far, however, very few studies of the revival have gone far toward integrating our understanding of evangelicalism into the mainstream history of the period. Elie Halévy, whose genius and insight seem to glow more brightly with the passage of time, made a serious effort at integration in part III of *England in 1815* (London, 1924; published first in French: Paris, 1913). In what has come to be called the Halévy thesis, he argued that the evangelical revival, particularly the growth of Methodism, was the most important explanation for why there was no violent political revolution in England akin to that experienced in France. In a splenetic variation on this theme, Edward Thompson in *The Making of the English Working Class* (London, 1963), pours vitriol on the spiritual terrorism and sexual repressiveness of a Methodism that, he contends, helped make wage slaves of freeborn Englishmen. Bernard Semmel makes a full-scale attempt to show that the religious revival shared many of the aspirations of the democratic movement, and that it was part of the same general cultural current, in his important study of *The Methodist Revolution* (New York, 1973). Semmel's work, which draws heavily on the rich pamphlet literature of the revival in the late eighteenth century, reveals a Methodism abounding in ideas of liberty and equality despite the conservatism of its official face. W. R.

Ward's *Religion and Society in England 1790–1850* (London, 1973) comes closer to a view of the revival as an integral part of the general history of its time. Ward locates the revival in its social and political context, and he proceeds to argue that the expansive, unified evangelicalism of the end of the eighteenth century was fractured into defensive denominational factions by the pressure of the politics of social class.

While it is not a theme that he pursues with any insistence, Ward's treatment of the revival suggests at times that it shared some features with industrialization. Just as new industrial centers were developed to escape the conservatism of the old, Ward points out that the revival had its greatest successes in those areas where the church was weakest in what he calls "plant and manpower." He is keenly sensitive, moreover, to the fundamental importance of the growth of population as a stimulus to evangelical activity. There is a clear parallel here with the growth of the domestic market that helped fire the ambitions of the industrial entrepreneurs. The foreign market, too, played a major role in the development of evangelicalism, just as it did for the cotton magnates, and almost at precisely the same time. The great missionary societies established in the 1790s had visions of converting the world, with a concentration on Africa and Asia. Manchester had visions of clothing the world, and its marketing campaign looked toward the apparently limitless populations of Africa and Asia. One might suggest that the revival is similar to the Industrial Revolution in that mass marketing was an essential feature. In each case, moreover, supplying the mass market required new methods that broke to some extent with the traditions of the past. The technological innovations of the textile industry have a parallel in the two fundamental innovations of the revival, field preaching and itinerancy. Preaching outside established churches or chapels, often in the open air, enabled John Wesley and George Whitefield and the other early innovators to reach a new and expanding market. So did itinerancy, a technique adopted and systematized by a number of evangelizing organizations in order to save more souls with less cost. Most itinerant preachers were in effect low paid traveling salesmen who could reach some areas of the market more efficiently than did their stationary brethren in their relatively expensive establishments. Improved means of transportation, so important to the material economy, helped move along the spiritual economy as well. The utilitarian pattern of thought embodied in these innovations and in countless others – one thinks for example of the monitorial system that made mass education cheap and therefore possible – is a pattern that marked the progressive areas of British life during this modernizing period. That is why "useful" became a term of commendation applicable to many different sorts of efforts and achievements. In the first half of the nineteenth century "useful" was one of the key words of praise in the evangelical movement. For evangelicals, "useful" always related, at the bottom line, to "usefulness" in saving souls.

The major organizations of the evangelical movement, the great national nondenominational societies – the London Missionary Society, the Religious Tract Society, the British and Foreign Bible Society, – the multitude of local and county evangelizing societies, as well as many denominational organizations, were created primarily to be useful; only secondarily did they embody theological ideals. They were conceived as pragmatically as was the Manchester Chamber of Commerce. All of these organizations operated in ways their members thought utilitarian, and some of them operated very much like business firms. It is not surprising that the production techniques and marketing strategies of contemporary businessmen were sometimes useful to evangelicals in furthering their spiritual cause. The British and Foreign Bible Society, for example, whose mission was to distribute Bibles "without note or comment" as widely and as cheaply as possible, attempted at times to calm its own internal denominational factionalism by the argument that it was more a business institution than a religious organization. One of the directors, John Owen, claimed that

> The line of business is, with few exceptions, as direct at the Bible Committee as it is at Lloyds; and there is little reason to expect the peculiar tenets of Calvin or Socinus to enter into a debate for dispersing an edition of the Scripture, as there would be if the same men met to underwrite a policy of insurance.[2]

Like the Bible Society, the Religious Tract Society mass-marketed spiritually improving literature to an enormous audience. Now the Lutterworth Press, the Religious Tract Society had become by the middle of the nineteenth century a great publishing house with a list of 4,363 titles, some with massive circulations.[3]

Andrew Reed was not a clergyman in business, like the Reverend Legh Richmond, author of *The Dairyman's Daughter*, who became in 1812 secretary of the Religious Tract Society. Nor was he a businessman in religion, like his son, Sir Charles, who earned his living through his printing and type-founding businesses and spent his time lavishly on the Sunday School Union, the London Missionary Society, and other religious causes. When Mr Alderman Abbiss remarked, toward the end of Reed's life, "I have been associated with many men, and have sat on many committees; but, I say it honestly, I have never met a man of such business capacity as Dr Reed," he referred to qualities of mind and temperament that might have made for success in any of a variety of callings.[4] His sons write that

> though specially trained to the work of the ministry, Dr Reed has been said to have been the model of a business-man. Decisive in all his acts, punctual to all engagements, and methodical in the conduct of his many great enterprises, he performed with comparative ease, as those who knew him best are well aware, a daily pressure of work wonderful to contemplate.[5]

Andrew Reed's calling was emphatically the nonconformist ministry, and his career centered on his own chapel in east London and on the five important philanthropies he created. And yet, in some ways, the results of his career for himself and his family were very similar to the results of a successful career in business. Samuel Courtauld in silk, Samuel Greg in cotton, Edward Baines in newspapers, George Stephenson in railways, Daniel Macmillan in publishing – the list could be extended to great length – each laid the base of fortune that enabled his family to leap ahead in prestige and status and move up onto a social plane that offered an entirely different sort of life from that in which the founder of the family had begun. Each of these entrepreneurs, moreover, accomplished his success outside the traditional arena of patronage, politics, and royal favor. Andrew Reed did the same for his family. His father had been a clockmaker of no particular financial success. But his own daughter married well, into the Spaling family of wealthy stationers. His oldest son, Andrew, became a successful Congregational minister. His second son, Charles, married the youngest daughter of Edward Baines, prospered in business, and became a distinguished antiquary, an MP, and chairman of the London School Board. Charles was knighted in 1874. Three of Reed's grandsons earned places in the *Dictionary of National Biography*, and the family, still flourishing, continues to provide board members for the charities Reed created in the early nineteenth century. Andrew Reed, like many successful businessmen of his time, managed to raise the fortunes of his family through his career in which he was successful in gaining for himself a great deal of prestige and enough money to mark him as a worldly success and to enable him and his family to live comfortably and in gentlemanly style. The character of his ambitions, moreover, his central values, and the ways he thought about his achievements were very like those of men we think of as entrepreneurs. The balance he sought between concern for his own advancement and that of his family, on the one hand, and his commitment to the good of the wider community, on the other, makes him at home in the company of those useful people who are studied by Leonore Davidoff and Catherine Hall in *Family Fortunes: Men and Women of the English Middle Class, 1750–1850* (London, 1987).

When Andrew Reed decided in 1806 to make a career in the Congregational ministry, he took a calculated risk. He gave up a safe and certain life as a watchmaker and began preparations for an occupation that he knew very little about. Failure would mean a considerable financial loss and the need to start over again in business; success would mean a higher social status, more money, and more prestige. In 1806 Reed was 18 years old and already on the way toward success in his father's trade, but a number of factors encouraged him to sell his tools and begin to study for the ministry. Family tradition was one of those factors. Reed's father, also called Andrew, had been born and raised in Maiden Newton, a Dorset agricultural village.[6] The Reeds of Maiden Newton were agricultural laborers, but Andrew was apprenticed to the village watchmaker. From Maiden Newton he moved to Weymouth in 1769, and sometime later to London, where he set up shop as a watchmaker in Cloth Fair, near Bartholomew Close. His success as a watchmaker in London seems to have been modest. In London he married Mary Ann Mullen, an orphan, and the first of their children to survive infancy, Andrew, was born on 27 November 1787. From his earliest years, Andrew lived in an environment suffused with evangelical religiosity.

Somehow, sometime around the middle of the eighteenth century, the Dorset Reeds had been caught up in the early fervor of the evangelical revival. Several became unpaid itinerant lay preachers, taking the gospel to the benighted villages near Maiden Newton. Reed the watchmaker became a lay preacher in London, where he itinerated up the Lea valley every Sunday.[7] Mary Ann shared her husband's enthusiasm for religion. In 1800 she opened a Staffordshire china shop in her house so that her husband could give up his trade and devote his whole time to spreading the word. At about this same time Andrew became a Sunday school teacher at one of his father's preaching stations at Ponder's End.[8] None of this religious activity earned money for the Reeds, however, and neither young Reed nor his parents seem to have contemplated any occupation for him except watchmaking before the Reverend Matthew Wilks of the Moorfields Tabernacle and the Tottenham Court Road Chapel recruited him for the ministry in 1806.

Matthew Wilks was one of the great men among the Calvinistic Dissenters in later eighteenth- and early nineteenth-century London.[9] He was trained for the ministry in the Countess of Huntingdon's college at Trevecca where he learned his Calvinism and developed an appreciation for itinerancy. For half a century, from 1780 to 1829, he was George Whitefield's successor in the two great London chapels that were known as the Tabernacle connection. Wilks was only one among a number of influential ministers who, in those days of fluid denominational boundaries, served to carry the methods and spirit of the evangelical revival into the old-established Dissenting communities of London. One thinks of Rowland Hill at the Surrey Chapel, for example, or William Bengo Collyer at Peckham, or George Ford and Joseph Fletcher at Stepney, J. Pye Smith at the Gravel Pit, or John Clayton at the King's Weigh House Chapel in East Cheap. Clayton, one of the men whom Reed particularly admired, is an interesting case in point.[10] John Clayton was educated at Trevecca, and became a Dissenter because he was refused ordination in the Church of England by bishops who considered itinerating disorderly. His first regular job was at the Weigh House, where a member of his congregation in the 1780s referred to him as an "Independent Presbyterian Methodist." Under Clayton, the Weigh House moved from Presbyterianism to Independency in order to escape the shadow of Unitarianism that was growing in many Presbyterian chapels. Because the old Dissent had a Calvinistic ancestry, it is not surprising that the Calvinistic stream within Methodism should have had more impact on Dissent than the Arminian stream associated with the Wesleys. The Calvinistic arm of the revival brought a new energy and expansionist dynamism to Dissenting life throughout the kingdom. London, however, attracted by far the greatest concentration of ministerial talent. This was not because Londoners were especially religious; the opposite would be closer to reality. London was at the center of much in national life, and London offered more prestige and more money to ministers of religion just as it did to bankers. The Dissenting world in London, moreover, was dominated by the Calvinist Independents or Congregationalists. *The Protestant Dissenters' Almanack and Annual Register for the Year of Our Lord 1811* lists 232 chapels in the metropolis, of which 108, including the two chapels of the Countess of Huntingdon's connection, are Calvinist Independent. This is 47 per cent of the list. The Methodists come next, with 46 chapels or 20 per cent, and the only other large group are the Baptists with 40 chapels or 17 per cent of the whole.[11] After the Unitarians, who had 9 chapels in London in 1811, and the Quakers, who had 6, the Congregationalists were considered the most wealthy and best educated among the nonconformists. London Congregationalism and the ministry offered promising opportunities to young men who sensed there was room, if not at the top, at least several rungs higher up the social and economic ladder.

Reed met Matthew Wilks at a time when Wilks was particularly interested in encouraging men to go into the ministry. Wilks was very active in the central, London-based institutions of the revival, including the London Missionary Society, the Religious Tract Society, and the *Evangelical Magazine*. He had long been involved with recruiting and training young men for the ministry, and for some time before 1803 he had supported the Congregational Academy at Hoxton. In that year he became the first secretary of the Village Itinerancy and switched his support to the college at Hackney that was associated with the Itinerancy. He met the Reeds through the Village Itinerancy, and invited young Andrew in 1806 to join a group with whom he met weekly in the Tabernacle with an eye toward finding suitable candidates for Hackney. Reed, then 18 years old, promptly joined his mother's church that met under the high Calvinist Samuel Lyndall in the New Road, St George's in the East, where he declared that he had been converted by reading a life of Whitefield. After a few months of meetings with Wilks, Reed sold his tools and devoted his time to reading in preparation for Hackney College. He delivered the required test sermon before the college committee, was admitted early in 1807, and spent the next four years in training for his new career.

The risk that Reed took when he determined to sell his watchmaker's tools and read for Hackney should not be exaggerated. The British population was growing rapidly, and the nonconformist world was expanding at an unprecedented rate. The number of nonconformists would increase by 50 per cent over the first decade of the nineteenth century, from 211,000 to 312,000.[12] A growing number of ministers was needed to maintain and accommodate the revival. The Congregationalists, in keeping with their Calvinist tradition, laid heavy emphasis on an educated clergy.[13] At the time Reed was preparing for Hackney there were two other Independent theological colleges in east London, Hoxton and Homerton, and each of the three wanted more students.[14] Hoxton at this time was rejecting one out of every three applicants, but it was not likely that Reed, with his family history, would be denied admission to Hackney.[15]

How Reed paid for his four years at Hackney is not clear. He lived in the college residence, and his annual costs must have been at least £30.[16] Francis Barnett claims that Reed's mother, at considerable sacrifice, found money for him, neglecting her younger son Peter and reducing her daughter Martha to servility at home, and that Reed borrowed and received gifts from his friends.[17] It is possible that Wilks personally and the Village Itinerancy helped as well, but there is no record of this.[18] The investment and sacrifices clearly seemed worthwhile to Reed and his family, as they did to numerous other men of similar background.[19] The potential rewards of the ministry outweighed the costs of preparation.

Riding the crest of the revival, men entering the Dissenting ministry in the very early nineteenth century did not have to fear unemployment. Jobs were plentiful. But most of the jobs were in the provinces, in villages or the poorer parts of towns, and most did not provide very high incomes. The average income was, however, not bad when compared to the prospects of a clerk or an artisan. In 1830 the statistically minded John Blackburn, himself the annual recipient of £600 from Claremont Chapel, calculated the average income among Congregationalist ministers at £100 per year.[20] At the middle of the century the Congregational Union boasted that 90 per cent of its ministers received more than £70.[21] For an ambitious and self-confident young man like Reed, it was not the average or the bottom that counted, but rather that the enormous variety of incomes among the Dissenting clergy opened the possibility of serious financial success. George Ford was said to earn £1,500 per year at Stepney, and incomes in the £200-to-£400 range were not considered unusual in London.[22] Francis Barnett claimed that when Andrew Reed was at Hackney his strongest ambitions were for money and the prestige that the ministry offered.[23] It must be kept in mind that when Barnett wrote he was embittered toward his former friend for having cast him as Lefevre, the antihero of *No Fiction*; his judgment of Reed's self-concern is certainly too harsh.

It is abundantly clear, however, that Reed did indeed hold the ministry in high esteem. For him the ministry, Anglican or nonconformist, was one of the learned professions that implied a level of culture and a style of life worthy of general respect. By virtue of their office and education most ministers were gentlemen. Grammatically correct eloquence, an acquaintance with Latin and Greek, and a polished style of behavior were, for Reed, marks of gentility.[24] Medicine and law, moreover, he saw as inferior professions because they deal with earthly cares, while the clergy looked toward eternal salvation.[25] According to the convention of the time, Reed, throughout his career, denounced "vanity and pride" and "temporal interests and worldly honours" as perils of the ministry.[26] On the other hand, he embraced with enthusiasm a theological glorification of the ministry that underpinned its general attractiveness to an upwardly mobile young man.

The doctrine of the ministry taught at Hackney College derived from the way Calvinists came to terms with the evangelical revival.[27] In the late eighteenth century the old Calvinism of the Independents, which was exclusivist and dryly intellectual, moved to the "New System" or "Modern Calvinism" and became expansionist, active, and much more emotional. R. Tudur Jones gives credit to Edward Williams, principal tutor at Rotherham Academy 1795–1813, for the formulation of the "New System," but that view discounts the earlier influence in London of George Whitefield and the Countess of Huntingdon.[28] Within the "New System" the commitment to predestination is retained, but "human agency" is given an honored place. God uses men to bring the means of grace to other men, and while all men are free to use those means, some are predestined to accept them and others are not. No one can know until the final day who is predestined to salvation and who to damnation. Therefore, as a working assumption, in order that souls should not be lost through inattention or neglect, everyone should be considered a candidate for salvation.

The "New System" harmonized Calvinism with the energy, optimism, and new techniques of the revival. Reed never questioned the basic elements of this moderated Calvinism and he welcomed the high place it accorded the ministry. He saw the "ministerial commission" as coming directly from God, and the minister's duty as "whatever has a tendency to meliorate the sufferings of humanity, to disperse the darkness of the mind, to subdue the vices of society, to restore man to a divine obedience, and to attach his hopes and his thoughts to an unseen eternity."[29] Over and over again he explained to ordinands that theirs was a role of peculiarly high importance, and that by virtue of their profession they stood closer to God than did other men. "A minister, more than others," he told the people of his own chapel,

> should possess a living and realizing conviction of Divine truth. Religion is his employ; the cure of souls and the honour of the Redeemer are his charge. He is a priest in the sanctuary, to him the holy mysteries are revealed; he is a prophet of the Most High, to him the visions and inspirations of an eternal world should be familiar.[30]

"Prophet" is a key word here. The minister's special duty, for which he was responsible to God, who was in a sense his employer, was to bring the truth to the masses. "If the few only are taught," he asked his oldest son, "what is to become of the million?"[31] The status of the ministry was buoyed up by its great responsibilities. "Magnify your office," he urged an ordinand, "that you may humble yourself to nothing."[32]

Reed's years at Hackney were very successful. With a strong sense that he was more able than most of his fellow students, he studied hard and to good effect. He told Francis Barnett that some of the Hackney students had "acceptable talents," but that none had "very remarkable ones." Most did not work much, many were insufficiently serious.[33] Reed's evaluation of the

Hackney students is echoed in the comments of other high achievers about their classmates in other nonconformist colleges.[34] At Hackney, Reed impressed his teachers. He studied Latin and Greek, and he developed a lucid prose style. He preached on the weekends in London, and in the summer vacations in the provinces. When he left the college in 1811 he had a number of job possibilities.[35] His own chapel in the New Road invited him to succeed Samuel Lyndall. He accepted that call, and remained as pastor of that congregation for the next fifty years.

The cause at New Road had not prospered under Lyndall, and the membership was down to 60 when Reed took the pastorship. The chapel had accommodation for 800, and there was clearly scope for improvement. This part of London, on the borders of Whitechapel and Stepney, was to become depressed and impoverished before the end of the century, but in 1811 it contained a flourishing middle class. The New Road congregation had never attracted families as wealthy as the Hankeys at George Ford's chapel in Stepney, or the Morleys, Flowers, or Fullers at the Weigh House, but the New Road people were solidly affluent.[36] It is unlikely that John Clayton's charge to the congregation at Reed's ordination, in which he urged paying a good salary and paying it promptly, was occasioned by a poor financial record on their part.[37] Reed was equal to the challenge that New Road presented. His pastorate was a success, and one of the measures of that success was the income that he was able to take from the chapel.

In their *Memoirs* of their father, Andrew and Charles Reed draw a modest veil over money issues. They report no specific figures when they write of his income, and they are at pains to insist that he had little interest in such matters. This is to some extent a matter of family reticence, and partly due to the convention of the time that supported the notion that the clergy should be concerned with higher things. Nonconformist clergy, however, protested so frequently that they were not in it for the money that one detects a certain amount of unease on their part. Reed wrote of his first salary raise in 1818: "I would rather have relinquished it for ever than have incurred the reproach of being avaricious. Nothing weakens a minister's character more than that vice."[38] Ten years later when he was thinking about a new building, he found it desirable "to satisfy the people that I was not seeking greater wealth for myself in requiring a larger chapel."[39] The pattern of Reed's income is clear, however, and for the last twelve years of his pastorate we have precise knowledge.[40] When Reed began at New Road Chapel, the congregation was £2,000 in debt and membership and attendance had fallen to a low level.[41] Also the burial grounds around the chapel, a potentially lucrative part of the operation, had been nearly filled up. Within seven years Reed increased the membership by more than 350, and the chapel was generally full for two Sunday services. A full chapel was the straight route to increased income, for New Road Chapel, like most others in the denomination, received most of its money from pew rents. Seats, rented for the year with quarterly payments, went at varying rates, with 10 shillings per annum a common price in London. Usually a minister's salary was a fixed annual sum, although in some cases he received a percentage of the pew rents and the collections. At New Road, Reed got a fixed sum. His sons report that in 1818, with the chapel free of debt for the first time in forty years, his salary was doubled.[42] They claim that this was the only increase that he ever accepted. In 1839 *Grant's Metropolitan Pulpit* claimed that Reed got £500 per annum.[43] While he sometimes took less, the chapel records indicate that for the last twelve years of his pastorate Reed's official salary was £500. If the sons are correct, and the 1818 raise was his only increase, Reed must have been offered £250 at the beginning in 1811. This is possible, but that figure seems high. If all the seats were rented at 10 shillings, the chapel could only produce £400 a year. We know they were not all rented at the beginning, and, further, that between 1811 and 1818 the chapel was able to discharge a debt of £2,000. It seems likely that Reed got less than £250; £150 seems more likely.[44]

In 1828 Reed and his deacons began to think about a larger chapel. A larger chapel meant more pew rents, and those who planned the move from New Road certainly thought in those terms. Reed hoped that for an investment of between £7,000 and £8,000, a new and more commodious chapel might produce a surplus of £200 per year.[45] The new chapel, called Wycliffe, was built in spacious grounds behind the London Hospital, not so far from the old chapel that members would find the move inconvenient. Wycliffe, built in the porticoed classical style then favored among the nonconformists, could seat 2,000 people, and there was plenty of burial space in the grounds. At midcentury it generated just over £600 in pew rents, nearly £200 per annum in burial fees until the grounds were filled up in 1854, and about £75 in collections.[46] After 1853 pew rents declined to just over £300 by 1861. Responding to this financial difficulty, Reed accepted only £425 in 1854, £400 in 1857 and 1858, £200 for the next two years, and £100 in 1861. After Reed's death his sons made a row and tried to collect the salary arrears.[47] The decline in revenues in the 1850s may have reflected the migration of the middle classes to the suburbs, but part of the cause was Reed's diminished effectiveness in the pulpit. Under a talented preacher, Reun Thomas, 1868–75, Wycliffe's income from pew rents rose again to nearly £600. Thereafter income, membership, and attendance steadily declined, until in 1904 the congregation moved to Christ Church, Ilford, which was renamed Wycliffe.[48] It is possible that Reed was paid £150 to start, £300 after 1818, and £500 sometime after Wycliffe opened in 1831. In any case, his salary was £500 per annum for at least the last twenty-two years of his career, a figure that put him comfortably in the top 1.5 per cent of incomes, according to the calculations of Harold Perkin.[49]

Reed's income, moreover, was more than his salary. How much more it is impossible to tell. In addition to his house near the chapel, he was able to buy sometime after 1816 a small country house in Cheshunt in which he installed his parents and his ailing sister, Martha. From time to time he made charitable contributions of £100. His sons say merely that "while Mr Reed was not entirely dependent on his ministerial salary, it must not be supposed that he was wealthy enough to make the large donations occasionally referred to without considerable sacrifice."[50] While it cannot be documented, it is likely that Reed's additional income came from his wife. He married in 1816 Elizabeth Holmes, daughter of Jasper Holmes, a wealthy City merchant living in retirement near Reading. The Holmes family had been major supporters of the Countess of Huntingdon's Chapel in Spa Fields. It is possible that Elizabeth Holmes brought a substantial amount of money into the marriage. Barnett said she did, and he accused Reed of searching for a wealthy wife from the time he left Hackney College. Matthew Wilks, he claimed, insisted that Reed concentrate on women of fortune.[51] Barnett tells a long tale of Reed, abetted by Wilks, courting Mary Cave, a wealthy widow from Petersfield who died young in 1814 and left, he says, £1,000 to Reed and £2,000 to the Village Itinerancy.[52]

There may be something to the charges Barnett brings on this point. Young ministers with places in respected chapels were in a position to make advantageous matches.[53] Their authority and status within the chapel world made them seem suitable choices for pious young women, even young women from quite wealthy families. The very thrust of the revival itself, moreover, may have made ministers attractive to women. It was just at this time that women of the middling classes were moving toward their separate sphere, which laid heavy emphasis on personal virtue, private feelings, and values associated with realms that transcended commerce and public life. "As daughters, sisters, wives, and mothers," wrote John Bowdler in 1808, "they have continual occasion to improve and exercise their knowledge of the heart."[54] In common with other popular ministers of the revival period, Reed conceived his preaching in terms that appealed to the domestic sphere in which the emotional bonds among family members had come to supplant more severely rational economic considerations. He did not consciously aim his sermons at women, but he certainly believed that preachers should speak to the heart rather than to the head. "Our business," said Reed, "is not to sit in judgment on the truth; but faithfully to publish it."[55] Those ministers who "look towards the philosophical and rational" were deluded. His own practice was to make his sermons "practical," by which he meant emotionally persuasive.

One of the high points of his trip to North America in 1834 and 1835 was a sermon he delivered to unrestrained, rapturous response from a group of black slaves at a camp meeting in Virginia.[56] Reed's emotionally charged sermons, delivered with a fair degree of grammatical precision and eschewing all that might be considered "vulgar, ignorant and methodistical," went over well with the people at New Road and Wycliffe. While he thought that a preacher without emotion must fail, he denied that emotion could be employed consciously as a technique. Manufactured fervor was worse than frigidity. Nevertheless, he cast an admiring eye on professional actors who succeeded with fiction in creating a greater effect than most ministers did with the truth.[57] While he was in the United States he made a study of revivalist innovations such as the "anxious seat," which he did not like, and the system of visitations developed in Northampton, which he did. Reed, like all good platform performers, had the ability to reach his audience and stir their feelings. He was good at creating effects; he specialized in describing the Day of Judgment.[58] Much of what he said from the pulpit seems open to parody now, just as, for example, does the melodrama of the contemporary popular theater. But in his own lifetime he was considered a gifted preacher by both his own people and his brother ministers. When the ministerial organizers of a professional lecture series asked Reed to speak in 1829 they urged him to talk about the Final Judgment.[59] The emotional sermon was his principal stock in trade; it was the key to his professional success.

His success, as measured by the membership of his chapels, was greater with women than it was with men. The membership rolls of New Road under Reed, and Wycliffe up through 1861, show that women outnumbered men in a ratio of more than two to one.[60] In most years Reed enrolled twice as many women as men; in no year did men constitute more than 44 per cent of the new intake. Without more studies of other chapels it is impossible to know if Reed's pattern is eccentric. One suspects that it is not, and certainly it was not remarked as unusual at the time. Nor is it clear that women outnumbered men in Reed's chapels because they were more susceptible to his revivalistic emphasis on feeling and the heart. Nonetheless, the record of his general success with women is certain. It is possible, moreover, that the skills that permitted him to touch the hearts of the many who rented pews and supplied him with an income of £500 might well have enabled him to touch the heart of one with similar effect.

If Elizabeth Holmes was indeed a wealthy match, Reed was following the footsteps of at least two of the ministers who took part in his ordination in 1811. Among the eight ministers who participated in that service, at least three possessed considerable private incomes that freed them from dependence on their salaries. John Clayton, who had no money when he entered Trevecca College, married a young woman from the congregation a year after he was appointed minister of the Weigh House. She was an heiress from both her father, a Flower, and her mother, a Fuller.[61] George Clayton inherited his father's good fortune. The wealth of the Claytons became legendary in Dissenting circles. Matthew Wilks also had no money when he was sponsored by the Countess of Huntingdon at Trevecca, and he also found his wealthy wife through the revival. Both he and his wife, a Shenstone and a cousin of the poet William Shenstone, had been converted by the same man, the Reverend W. Percy of West Bromwich.[62] These instances of fortunate marriages seem more concentrated than one would expect from the mere changes and chances of this fleeting world. Upward mobility via a good marriage was certainly nothing new in the late eighteenth and early nineteenth centuries. These cases are interesting, however, because each took place within the frame of the revival; each was made possible by ministerial status; and each represented what might be called an occupational opportunity.

Andrew Reed took advantage of another occupational opportunity, and, employing very impressive talents for administration and fund-raising, became a philanthropist of genuine importance. This was an extraordinary accomplishment. He managed to create five charities of national significance without using his own money, or that of his wife. The first of the charities was the London Orphan Asylum conceived and launched by Reed in 1813.[63] Inspired by the example of Whitefield's orphanage in Georgia, and perhaps by the fact that his mother had been orphaned, Reed persuaded some of his congregation to back his scheme. He then promoted a fund-raising campaign in the City of London that succeeded brilliantly after he personally sought and received support from the Duke of Kent. This was a formula for raising money that he continued to use with success for five decades; a carefully considered proposal with royal approval publicly expressed brought out money from the City merchants.[64] Reed always tried to maintain religious neutrality in his charities; he realized from the beginning that sectarianism would alienate the royal family and narrow the range of his fund-raising.

When the London Orphan Asylum was well established, Reed began in 1827 the organization of the Infant Orphan Asylum which would accept children under the age of 7. He received support from the Dukes of Gloucester and Clarence, from the Duchess of Kent and her orphaned daughter, from the Duke of Wellington, and eventually from Prince Albert. In 1843 Reed was driven from the Infant Orphan Asylum by its Anglican chaplain's intransigence over the catechism.

Thereupon he founded the Asylum for Fatherless Children in 1844, an institution that was eventually located on an estate renamed Reedham, near Coulsden in Surrey. This was probably his most impressive philanthropic monument. Next came the Asylum for Idiots, begun in 1846, and last the Royal Hospital for Incurables, instituted in 1854. Each of these institutions was a major accomplishment. Each required an enormous amount of his time and energy. Not only did Reed organize the initial planning and secure the funding for these projects. He also, particularly with the first two orphanages, superintended their operations in fine detail. No wonder that his doctor once told him that he was "living too fast for his strength."[65]

Reed's ministerial status made his philanthropic career possible, and Reed himself believed that the charities enriched and deepened his pastorate. At his son Andrew's ordination in 1841, commenting on the "decided usefulness of the ministry as a profession," he spoke of the importance of acting beyond the official pastoral sphere: "you must go forth in spirit and in act from the Chapel to the city, the city to the county, the county to the nation and the nation to the world."[66] In the early days of the London Orphan Asylum he noted in his diary that his philanthropic work had developed and strengthened his own character, making him a more useful minister in New Road Chapel.[67] Thirteen years later, in 1827, with more calls on his time he was more ambivalent. "The concerns of the orphan," he confessed,

> from engaging too much of my time, engross too much of my affections. I am resolved particularly to watch and pray against this. May I remember that I am a minister of the New Testament! What is equal to this? The pursuits of the philosopher, the patriot, the philanthropist, are nothing compared with the minister of Jesus Christ.[68]

The orphanages certainly stole time from the chapel, but they also did much to make Reed an eminent person. To some extent, his highly visible philanthropic profile must have helped attract those men and women who filled the seats in New Road Chapel and in Wycliffe.

Toward the end of the 1820s, when the unseemly controversy created by *No Fiction* and Francis Barnett's *Memoirs* had faded, when New Road Chapel was thriving and about to expand, when the London Orphan Asylum had become a spectacular success, Andrew Reed came under heavy pressure to serve his denomination on a multitude of boards and committees. For the next twenty years he acceded to many of those demands and played a prominent role among the leaders of Congregationalism.[69] He was one of the active founders of the Congregational Union in 1831. Along with James Matheson of Durham, he visited North America for eight months in 1834 as a delegate from that body.[70] In 1836 Reed laid the groundwork for the foundation of the Colonial Missionary Society, and early in 1837 he experienced a major embarrassment in connection with this society. Speaking for the London Missionary Society in Exeter Hall in 1835, Reed created a sensation by suggesting that the ministers on the platform should volunteer as missionaries, and he offered himself. If a committee of ministers should decide, he said, "that I could better serve the cause of Christ by going to Malacca, or India, or Greenland, or to Iceland, *I am ready to go.*" Subsequently his offer was emulated by others throughout the country, and five of his nine deacons at Wycliffe Chapel declared their willingness to go with him. Shortly after the formation of the Colonial Missionary Society an urgent application came for an experienced minister to go to Toronto, and a group of distinguished London ministers formally urged Reed to accept. This caused a time of elaborate wriggling for Reed, while he sought an acceptable excuse. He might have been tempted, according to his sons, by China; Toronto was definitely not on his list.[71]

Like almost all other Congregational ministers of his generation, Andrew Reed was consistently liberal in his politics, but not radical.[72] His political interests were almost exclusively concerned with the status of nonconformity. Lord Sidmouth's notorious 1811 bill, which threatened the revival through its attack on itinerancy, drew a little fire from him, and he supported the Protestant Society for the Protection of Religious Liberty. Unlike many members of the Protestant Society, however, in the 1820s he favored Catholic Emancipation as well as repeal of the Test and Corporation Acts. In the following two decades he spoke out on the problems of Dissenting marriages and he put some little effort into organizing opposition to compulsory church rates. He denounced the corn laws, more privately than publicly, and he was involved in some of the early efforts to put together a nonconformist political pressure group that would be more effective than the Dissenting Deputies. He disapproved of anything that looked like a hostile attack on the Church of England. The Evangelical Alliance, which included both churchmen and Dissenters, received his support in its early years, while he was intensely suspicious of the Anti-State Church Association that Edward Miall formed in 1844.[73]

Compared with the leading ministers of the following generation, men like R. W. Dale, C. Newman Hall, J. Baldwin Brown, J. Guinness Rogers, or Edward Miall himself, Reed's political activity was negligible. This is because he, like many of his contemporaries, saw his career and his status as a minister in terms that pushed politics to the margin or beyond. Busy as he was with his congregation and with his philanthropies, Reed had little time to spare for politics. But time is a matter of priorities, and he did find time to write the two-volume novel, *No Fiction*, in the hectic early years at New Road when he was expanding his congregation and setting up the London Orphan Asylum. His philanthropies, of course, encouraged him to avoid political controversy. He was sensitive to the possibility that he might offend potential givers. Time and time again, over his career, he felt it necessary to explain to his donors that his Dissent carried with it no antipathy to the Church of England.[74]

Another ground, perhaps even more imperative than fund-raising, persuaded Reed to avoid sectarianism and the politics of democracy. He was profoundly committed to the religious core of the ministry. He never doubted that his first duty was to serve the Lord in helping to save souls from everlasting torment in the fiery pit. "Eternity is at hand! The Judge is at the door! Prepare to meet your God! By all that is awful – by all that is sacred – by all that is dear – by all that is dreadful – I beseech you – I entreat you – PREPARE TO MEET YOUR GOD!"[75] Preaching for salvation, praying for salvation, encouraging the anxious many toward the mystical experience of conversion, these, for him, were the privileged duties of the ministry. In his sermon for the London Missionary Society, he pressed the theme that the role of the churches should be "not so much the civilization of men as their regeneration."[76] Revealed truth, he taught, was the only remedy for human woe. "As it blesses the individual, so it is prepared to bless the family, the village, the city, the nation, the world."[77]

Reed's attitude toward politics, moreover, was established at a time when political activity might call down upon Dissent the wrath of the state. At his ordination in 1811, George Collison, Reed's tutor at Hackney College, had said, "Sincerity will prevent us from mingling *worldly politics* with our instruction." This was a matter of prudence "in seasons of ferment and commotion." Also important was the consideration that politics would lead away from the central purpose of the revival. Political involvement "will pollute your own mind; it will introduce a worldly spirit into your ministry, and make you much more like a political demagogue than a wise, prudent, and holy minister of the gospel." "Eminent piety," Collison concluded, was the key to success for a minister.[78] Every year on the anniversary of his ordination, Reed reviewed what had been said on that day. The phrase "eminent piety" stuck with him throughout the rest of his life and became his motto. Long after the Napoleonic wars were over, Reed retained the idea that a minister's calling was to something higher than politics.

In the year following the passage of the great Reform Act, when the political hopes of the Dissenters ran high, Reed published his one sustained political tract, *The Case of the Dissenters, In a Letter Addressed to the Lord Chancellor*. Characteristically, he opened with a call for Dissenters to put evangelical considerations first: "Let them rise above sectarian views into those which are strictly religious; let them seek not the good of their separate communities, but the good of the land in the welfare of religion at large."[79] He goes on to catalogue the usual list of Nonconformist political grievances, and concludes with a passionate cry for a sort of social equality. As long as the church is established, Dissenters will be injured by Anglican arrogance. Dissenters suffer "in estate, in reputation, and in good fellowship" by virtue of the prestige associated with the monopoly granted the church by the state. The inferior social status assigned to Nonconformists operates as a "subtle and malignant influence, through every path and every hour of life; when it gives a lower place in the settled opinion of one's fellow citizens; when it dishonours us at the exchange, at the college, in the senate, in the pulpit."[80] Reed's political interests centered on equality for that middle or upper-middle class group of Dissenters that he had himself joined. His concern was not so much with how the poor might move up into the middle class, but with how those who were already successful might become more so by removing the ceiling he thought the Anglican monopoly created for aspiring Dissenters. This is a very soft-edged form of social revolution. Insofar as it was typical of the most successful Dissenting ministers, it certainly did not warrant the near-hysterical attacks launched against religious Nonconformity by men like James Sedgwick early in the century.

By the middle of the nineteenth century it was easy to see that Sedgwick and the other Cassandras of pre-Waterloo days had been wrong to castigate Dissent as an enemy of civil order. But Sedgwick's comment that Dissenting ministers turned religion into a trade did not lose its force. Andrew Reed's success made him atypical among ministers, but his values and opinions and his entrepreneurial approach to the ministery were not unusual for men of his time.

G. J. Holyoake, the radical secularist, noticed similar qualities in John Angell James, minister of Carr's Lane, Birmingham, and one of the bright stars among evangelical Nonconformists in the first half of the nineteenth century.[81] Like the Reeds, John Angell Jones came from Dorset where his father was a maker of wire buttons. James himself served an apprenticeship as a draper before he attended theological college on a bursary. The period of his pastorship at Carr's Lane, and its character also, corresponded almost precisely with those of Reed's at New Road and Wycliffe. At Carr's Lane he married the independently wealthy daughter of a physician; after her death he married a rich widow. He became an eminent person in Birmingham. His political quietism and sense of the ministerial profession were very similar to Reed's. They both represented the prevailing views and pursued the prevailing goals of their generation. Many years later, when reflecting on his experience in the Carr's Lane Sunday Schools during the early years of the Chartist movement, G. J. Holyoake wrote:

> Once the Rev. John Angell James, the pastor, delivered a week-night public address, in which he counselled young men to be content with the lot which Providence had assigned them. Dissent was no better than the Church as regarded social progress. When I heard Mr James' counsel, I believed it. It was logical Christian doctrine I knew, and I could see that if acted upon, the Political Union was an organized sin – as its object was to alter and raise the condition of the people. Had Mr James himself acted upon his own principle, he would not have been a preacher.[82]

If Holyoake had sat under Reed, he might have said the same of him. The class of self-made men, in religion or in trade, that seemed a threat to conservatives at the beginning of the century had become a target for radicals by the end.

The evangelical world within which Andrew Reed lived and thrived offered clearly visible opportunities for ministerial success in the early nineteenth century because it was an expanding world. Just as the growing markets for consumer goods encouraged ambitious young men to seek their fortunes in commerce and industry, the prospect of almost limitless numbers of souls yearning for salvation attracted talented men to the ministry. During the lifetime of Andrew Reed, there were many patterns shared between the worlds of business and religion, many crossovers and many connections. Men fired with the entrepreneurial spirit played major roles in both the Industrial Revolution and the evangelical revival. The career of Andrew Reed, who might have been a successful businessman if he had not chosen the ministry, illustrates some of the ways in which evangelical culture reflected the commercial spirit.

Notes

1 Quoted in Erik Routley, *The Story of Congregationalism* (London, 1961), p. 70.
2 J. Owen, *A Letter to a Country Clergyman* (London, 1805), p. 50. Quoted in Roger

H. Martin, *Evangelicals United: Ecumenical Stirrings in Pre-Victorian Britain, 1795-1830* (London, 1983), p. 88.

3 Martin, *Evangelicals United*, p. 156. See also R. K. Webb, *The British Working Class Reader 1790-1848* (London, 1955), pp. 26-8.

4 Andrew Reed and Charles Reed, *Memoirs of the Life and Philanthropic Labours of Andrew Reed, D. D., with Selections from his Journals* (London, 1863), p. 577.

5 Ibid., p. 377.

6 See ibid., pp. 1-6. The *Memoirs* draw heavily on Reed's unpublished journals and letters, which have subsequently disappeared. The other most important sources for this essay are Reed's published sermons and political articles, his autobiographical novel *No Fiction* (London, 1819), the critical commentary on that novel by Francis Barnett, *Memoirs of Francis Barnett, the Lefevre of "No Fiction": and a Review of that Work, with Letters and Authentic Documents* (London, 1823), and the few remaining manuscript records of his chapel, which are deposited in the Greater London Record Office.

7 Reed and Reed, *Memoirs*, p. 18. Reed the elder worked with the Itinerant Society, set up in 1796, and participated in the establishment in 1797 of the Congregational Society for Spreading the Gospel in the Dark Parts of England. This society became the famous Village Itinerancy in 1803. For Dissenting itinerancy, see Deryck W. Lovegrove, *Established Church, Itinerant People: Itinerancy and the Transformation of English Dissent, 1780-1830* (Cambridge, 1988).

8 Reed and Reed, *Memoirs*, p. 21.

9 Very little is written about Wilks. He has no biography and he left no papers. The most useful source for information about him is the sketch of his life in John Morison, *The Fathers and Founders of the London Missionary Society, a Jubilee Memorial* (London, 1844), pp. 444-61.

10 For John Clayton and his three sons, all of whom became Congregational ministers in London, see T. W. Aveling, *Memorials of the Clayton Family, with Unpublished Correspondence of the Countess of Huntington, Lady Glenorchy, the Revs John Newton, A. Toplady: Etc.* (London, 1867).

11 See "London Nonconformity in 1810," *Transactions of the Congregational Historical Society* (London, 1913-15), VI, pp. 126-34. It is estimated that at this time there were approximately 800 Congregational chapels in all of England: R. Tudur Jones, *Congregationalism in England, 1662-1962* (London, 1962), p. 168.

12 Robert Currie, Alan Gilbert, and Lee Horsley, *Churches and Churchgoers: Patterns of Church Growth in the British Isles since 1700* (Oxford, 1977), p. 25.

13 See J. Harris, *The Importance of an Educated Ministry: A Discourse Preached Preparatory to the Opening of the Lancashire Independent College* (London, 1843).

14 See Kenneth D. Brown, *A Social History of the Nonconformist Ministry in England and Wales, 1800-1930* (Oxford, 1988), ch. 3, "Training, 1800-c.1860," pp. 56-79.

15 Ibid., p. 68.

16 Homerton at this time charged £20 for tuition alone. Room and board at £10 is probably too conservative an estimate. Ibid., p. 86.

17 Barnett, *Memoirs*, pp. 24-30, 62.

18 Brown concludes that most students in the theological colleges in the early nineteenth century were "self-financed," and he thinks this was one of the reasons the college authorities had problems with discipline: *Social History of the Nonconformist Ministry*, p. 73.

19 Ibid., pp. 20-5. Brown, working principally with the records of Hoxton Academy, finds that the majority of Congregational ministers in the early nineteenth century came from artisan families or white-collar families. Reed's friends before he went to Hackney were clerks and artisans.

20 Albert Peel, *These Hundred Years: A History of the Congregational Union of England and Wales, 1831-1931* (London, 1931), pp. 26-7.

21 See *Congregational Year Book*, 1853, pp. 34-46 for a discussion of ministerial incomes.

22 Tudur Jones, *Congregationalism in England*, p. 292.

23 Francis Barnett, *Memoirs*, pp. 62-5. See also Francis Barnett, *A Reply to Mr Reed's Advertisement to the Seventh Edition of "No Fiction", with a Review of "Martha"* (London, 1823), p. 21. Barnett consistently charges Reed with "ambition," "selfishness," "vanity," and "avarice." See *A Threatening Letter from Douglas (The Self-Acknowledged Author of "No Fiction") to Lefevre: with Lefevre's Reply* (2nd edn, London, 1822), pp. iii, 11, 12.

24 See Reed and Reed, *Memoirs*, pp. 356-7, for a discussion of Reed's views of the superiority of Latin and Greek over a commercial education. Hackney and the other training colleges provided the rudiments of a classical education. The inclination of successful businessmen toward polite, ornamental learning has been explored by Arnold Thackray, "Natural Knowledge in Cultural Context: the Manchester Model," *American Historical Review* (June 1974), pp. 672-709.

25 Andrew Reed, *Ministerial Perseverance. A Charge Delivered at the Settlement of the Rev. Arthur Tidman, over the Church Assembling in Barbican, London, on the 8th January, 1829* (London, 1829). This statement of his view of medicine and law may have been exaggerated. Matthew Wilks's only son, John, was a lawyer of some eminence. One of the sons of J. Pye Smith, the principal tutor at Homerton, became a famous doctor.

26 Andrew Reed, *Eminent Piety Essential to Eminent Usefulness. A Discourse Preached at the Anniversary of the London Missionary Society, at Surrey Chapel on the Eleventh of May, 1831 (London, 1831).* See his *An Efficient Ministry. A Charge Delivered at the Ordination of the Rev. Joseph Elliot, over the Congregational Church, Bury St Edmunds* (London, 1837), for a warning against ease, reputation, and applause as ministerial temptations.

27 George Collison, the resident tutor, was the principal teacher at Hackney. He delivered the charge to the minister at Reed's ordination, and that charge contains the central idea of the ministry to which Reed continued to subscribe. See *The Ordination Service of the Rev. Andrew Reed, to the Pastoral office, over the Congregational Church of Christ Assembling in the New Road Meeting, St George's in the East, November 27, 1811* (London, 1812), in which Collison holds up Whitefield as the model for young ministers. "How I pant," Reed wrote a few years later, "for Whitefield's ardour, talents and success." Reed and Reed, *Memoirs*, p. 55.

28 Tudur Jones, *Congregationalism in England*, pp. 169-71.

29 *The Man of God. A Charge Delivered at the Ordination of the Rev. Ebeneezer Miller, over the Church Assembling in Old Gravel Lane, 22 February, 1828* (London, 1828).

30 *The Pastor's Acknowledgments. A Sermon Occasioned by the Occurrence of the Ninth Anniversary: On Sunday, November 26, 1820* (London, 1820).

31 *The Work and Reward of the Christian Minister. A Charge Delivered at the Ordination of the Rev. Andrew Reed, A. B., over the Church Assembling in the Old Meeting, Norwich, March 2, 1841* (London, 1841).

32 *The Sacred Trust. A Charge Delivered at the Ordination of the Rev. Thomas Atkinson, over the Church Assembling in Hounslow, Middlesex, October 2, 1832* (London, 1832).

33 Barnett, *Memoirs*, p. 25.

34 See Brown, *Social History of the Nonconformist Ministry*, p. 79.

35 See Reed and Reed, *Memoirs*, p. 45.

36 Ibid., pp. 50–1.

37 *The Ordination Service of the Rev. Andrew Reed, to the Pastoral Office, over the Congregational Church of Christ Assembling in the New Road Meeting, St George's in the East, November 27, 1811* (London, 1812).

38 Reed and Reed, *Memoirs*, p. 60.

39 Ibid., p. 68.

40 The financial records of his chapel, by then called Wycliffe, exist from 1848 and are deposited as N/C/40/13 in the Greater London Record Office.

41 Reed and Reed, *Memoirs*, p. 61.

42 Ibid., p. 60.

43 Tudur Jones, *Congregationalism in England*, p. 292.

44 At the height of Reed's drawing power in the late 1840s, Wycliffe, with more than twice as many seats as New Road, generated only £600 to £650 from pew rents: Greater London Record Office, N/C/40/13.

45 Reed and Reed, *Memoirs*, p. 68.

46 Greater London Record Office, N/C/40/13.

47 Deacons' minutes, 30 May 1862, Greater London Record Office, N/C/40/3.

48 Greater London Record Office, N/C/41.

49 Harold Perkin, *The Origins of Modern English Society* (London, 1969), p. 420.

50 Reed and Reed, *Memoirs*, p. 164.

51 Barnett, *Memoirs*, p. 55.

52 Barnett, *A Reply to Mr. Reed's Advertisement To the Seventh Edition of "No Fiction"*, pp. 20–1.

53 See Elie Halévy, *Victoria Years, 1841–1895* (London, 1951), pp. 350–1, for the notoriety of the mutual attraction between evangelical preachers and women, rich widows particularly.

54 John Bowdler, *Thoughts on the Proposed Improvement of Female Education* (London, 1808). Quoted in Dale Johnson, *Women in English Religion 1799–1925* (New York, 1983), p. 57.

55 *The Work and Reward of the Christian Minister*, see note 31 above.

56 Andrew Reed and James Matheson, *A Narrative of the Visit to the American Churches, by the Deputation from the Congregational Union of England and Wales* (London, 1835), Vol. 1, pp. 282 ff. It was "the most remarkable service I have ever witnessed. I shall never forget that time – that place; and often as I recur to it, the tear is still ready to start from its retirement." Reed was so moved by the weeping of his listeners – always a sign of success for him – that when the general shout went up, "Pray, brother, pray," he could not speak.

57 *An Efficient Ministry.*

58 See, for example, his own short sermon on the occasion of his ordination, or the high-prestige sermon for the London Missionary Society that he preached by invitation in 1831, *Eminent Piety Essential to Eminent Usefulness*: "The voice of prophecy; the finger of Providence; the wickedness of the wicked; and the strange expectation in the heart of all men; tell us that He is coming. Are we now ready? Prepare, prepare, O Israel, to meet thy God."

59 *The Final Judgment. A Discourse Delivered at the Meeting House, Old Gravel Lane, before the Monthly Association of Congregational Ministers* (London, 1829).

60 Greater London Record Office, N/C/40/10.

61 Aveling, *Memorials of the Clayton Family*, p. 69. Her mother disapproved the union with a "penniless parson."

62 Morison, *Fathers and Founders*, p. 446.

63 Only a summary account of the charities will be offered here, drawn from the

relevant chapters in Reed and Reed, *Memoirs*. All five charities continue, although in changed form. Their histories have not been written.

64 For an earlier example of a similar pattern of fundraising, see Ruth K. McClure, *Coram's Children: The Foundling Hospital in the Eighteenth Century* (New Haven, 1981), pp. 27–9, 179–89.

65 Reed and Reed, *Memoirs*, p. 158.

66 *Work and Reward of the Christian Minister.*

67 Reed and Reed, *Memoirs*, p. 104.

68 Ibid., p. 123.

69 See Peel, *These Hundred Years*, pp. 48, 64, 94, 97–9, 105, 169.

70 Matheson wrote the second volume and Reed the first of *Narrative of the Visit to the American Churches*. Reed's volume is a minor masterpiece, beautifully written in simple direct language and without those passages of high-flying rhetoric that marked his sermons. This compelling account of his encounter with American life is earthy, remarkably humorous, and full of human interest. It was deservedly popular in its day and reads well still.

71 The story is told in Reed and Reed, *Memoirs*, pp. 285–96.

72 John Clayton of the Weigh House was said to be the only Congregational pastor in early nineteenth-century London who was a Tory: Aveling, *Memorials of the Clayton Family*, p. 352.

73 Reed and Reed, *Memoirs*, pp. 196–242.

74 Ibid., p. 112, for an example.

75 *Pastor's Acknowledgements.* One imagines that the words in capital letters were shouted.

76 *Eminent Piety Essential to Eminent Usefulness.*

77 *Work and Reward of the Christian Minister.*

78 *Ordination Service of the Rev. Andrew Reed*, pp. 49–55.

79 *The Case of the Dissenters, in a Letter Addressed to the Lord Chancellor* (London, 1833), p. v.

80 Ibid., pp. 25–6.

81 For James, see R. W. Dale, *The Life and Letters of John Angell James* (London, 1861).

82 G. J. Holyoake, *Sixty Years of an Agitator's Life* (London, 1893), Vol. 1, p. 33.

Chapter 2

The Whigs and religious issues, 1830–5

R. W. Davis

The Whigs are in danger of being analyzed to death. Ellis Wasson first brought the "young Whigs," as opposed to the "old Whigs," to our attention.[1] Though I think he presses his point rather too far, there is no doubt that it has validity. Younger Whigs, such as Lord John Russell, clearly did more to popularize traditional Whig issues in the 1820s than did the older leaders of the party, such as Lords Grey, Holland, and Lansdowne. Russell's larger role can be explained in part by youthful zeal; but at least equally important is the fact that while the older leaders of the party sat in the House of Lords, Russell and other "young" Whigs were in the Commons. If Whig measures were to get anywhere in the 1820s, they had to be introduced into the more liberal atmosphere of the Commons.

"Liberal," however, is a word that now, it seems, has to be treated with some care. When Grey wrote to Russell in December 1829 that "my wishes must naturally be in favour of liberal principles and opinions," he knew what he meant: "in the words of the old Whig toast, . . . 'the cause of liberty all over the world.' " He spoke with particular reference to the cause of liberty in France, but he went on to make clear that at home what he had in mind was "the repeal of the Test Act and the [Catholic] Relief Bill."[2] Such a straightforward – some might say Whiggish – usage of the word "liberal" is not, however, acceptable to recent revisionists. Either it does not apply to true Whigs at all, or it does not apply to the likes of Grey.

The latter position is taken by Richard Brent in *Liberal Anglican Politics: Whiggery, Religion and Reform, 1830–1841* (Oxford, 1987). Brent argues that the Whigs in the 1830s can be divided into three groups: "older Foxites (or Foxites)"; " 'young' Whigs"; and " 'liberal Anglicans.' " He admits that there was not much to distinguish the positions of the two latter groups. It is perhaps as well that, with the retirement of Lord Althorp in November 1834, there was no longer any representative of the "young" Whigs (as Brent understands them) at the center of politics. For Althorp's retirement, following his succession as Earl Spencer, put in train events that led to the dissolution of the Whig government, and set the stage for the triumph of the "liberal Anglicans." First in opposition to the Conservative government of Sir

Robert Peel, and then in power again after they successfully overthrew Peel in April of 1835, these "liberal Anglicans" were at last able to set forth their distinctive principles. According to Brent, it was not until then that "Above all, the Whigs emerged as sympathizers with Nonconformist religion, both Catholic and Protestant, willing to legislate in its interests, to encourage its adherents to participate in government and to admit them to a full share of national life." (Though undoubtedly original, the definition of "Nonconformist religion" is unfortunately none the better for being new; it would certainly have shocked the parties it yokes together.) What had mainly impeded the "liberal Anglicans" in making their position clear before this was the dominance in the cabinet of Lord Grey and other Foxites, who were unsympathetic to their liberal notions. Now, however, Grey was gone, and with him the Foxite dominance. Lord John Russell and the "liberal Anglicans" whom he led were at last unmuzzled, themselves the dominant element in Lord Melbourne's subsequent governments.[3]

Peter Mandler, in *Aristocratic Government in the Age of Reform: Whigs and Liberals, 1830-1852* (Oxford, 1990), agrees that a different kind of Whig became dominant as a consequence of the events of late 1834 and early 1835 – the Foxites led by Lord John Russell! Indeed, in Mandler's analysis, it appears that only the Foxites, primarily defined as the "Grand Whiggery" of the Holland House circle, really deserve the name Whig. As he describes Grey's government formed in 1830, it was a "coalition of whigs, liberals, moderates, and liberal Tories." Elsewhere, the three latter groups are identified as "Young Whigs, offspring of the Grand Whiggery who had shrugged off their Foxism for liberalism; the Bowood set, a group of moderates who followed the independent Whig Lord Lansdowne; and the Panshanger set, liberal Tories who made a somewhat cynical decision for Reform in 1832." What was common to all three was their liberalism, which Mandler equates with the *economic* liberalism of the liberal Tories. Most keen were the "Young Whigs"; of somewhat cooler disposition were the moderates who grouped themselves around Lord Lansdowne. Ironically, "the Panshanger set," most notably Lords Melbourne and Palmerston, seem to have been as cynical about economic liberalism as about Reform – and almost everything else. When, however, we are told that as the "Young Whigs" cut themselves off from the Whig tradition they cut themselves off from "what made their liberalism so liberal," our minds may begin to spin a bit.[4] At any rate, Mandler's contention is that it is "liberalism" that separates everyone else from the Foxites, "the whigs." Precisely where Fox's political heir, Lord Grey, fits in all this is unclear; as little as possible is said about him.

It is, of course, all too easy to dismiss the work of others in a couple of paragraphs. To dismiss these authors is not my intention. Yet that two such conflicting views of Whiggery should have emerged from two scholarly monographs published by the same press within three years of each other does suggest that a certain confusion exists in the scholarly community about the subject both treat. The basis of that confusion, I suggest, is in the failure to recognize that both books attempt the impossible. Brent tries to treat religious issues without relation to other political questions. Mandler, for his part, seeks to treat "political" issues with only passing (and rather misleading) reference to religious issues.[5] To attempt to separate religion and politics in the history of the Whig party is quite impossible.

In the limited relief bill that caused the ouster of the "Ministry of All the Talents" in 1807, the Whigs, by including Protestant Dissenters on the same grounds as Catholics, had intended to send a positive message to both groups. The message was not lost on the Dissenters. This is not surprising in the case of the traditional representatives of Dissent, the Protestant Dissenting Deputies, whose chairman from 1805 to 1832 was himself a Whig MP, William Smith. And, albeit sometimes only by fast political footwork, Smith managed to keep control of the official Dissenting movement and to keep it firmly in line with Whig policies.[6] The Dissenters' reward came in 1828, when Russell's motion to repeal the Test and Corporation Acts passed the House of Commons by a healthy majority. The Duke of Wellington's government thereupon conceded the case; but it was Holland, ably backed by Lansdowne and Grey, who managed the bill, which abolished the political disabilities of Dissent, in the Lords. Repeal was meant by the Whigs to be the prelude to Catholic Emancipation, and so it proved the following year. This time the bill was a government measure from the beginning; but Wellington and Peel would never have carried it without enthusiastic and united Whig support. Catholics, especially Irish Catholics, may sometimes have doubted the depth of the Whig commitment to the removal of their political disabilities. The Whigs themselves never did – Catholic Emancipation was the single most important issue that held the party together after 1807. It was also the main ground for the coalition that Lansdowne and other Whigs entered into with George Canning and continued with Lord Goderich after Canning's death in 1827.[7] The attachment of the Whigs to the cause of religious liberty before 1835 used to be a widely accepted fact. But in light of recent revisionism, it is perhaps a fact that needs to be emphasized again.

Did something strange happen between 1829 and 1835 that caused a division of principle on religious questions among the main body of the Whigs? The answer to that question is no, but it is clearly a question that needs to be addressed again. In doing so, I shall naturally be concerned with many of the same issues as Brent, and I shall attempt to place those issues in a broader political context. The question to be addressed first is the one Brent sees as the key issue in the achieving of dominance in the party by the "liberal Anglican Whigs," and the issue on which their distinctive religious attitude first displayed itself.[8] That issue is the appropriation of any surplus revenues of the (established Anglican) Irish Church to lay purposes. I shall argue that the basis of the difference among the Whigs over the issue of lay appropriation has been seriously misunderstood.

The fact that the first suggestion of lay appropriation came from Lord Grey appears to have been overlooked by historians of the question. In his journal entry for 15 August 1831, Holland records:

> Lord Grey left the Cabinet to meet the Archbishop, the Bishop of London and the Primate [of Ireland] on a suggestion he had made of curtailing the revenue of the Bishopric of Derry and appropriating part of it to Queen Anne's bounty or some ecclesiastical object. . . . All three prelates maintained the danger of such a step and would not acquiesce in Grey's view that a more reasonable distribution of the revenues of the Church would contribute to its safety.

An entry three days later makes clearer what was implied by the term "ecclesiastical object": "The surplus we thought might well be applied to the relief of the poor or to Queen Anne's bounty."[9] Queen Anne's Bounty, designed to supplement poorer livings in the church, fell easily enough under the conventional meaning of the term ecclesiastical, with its implications of the organization of the church and the clergy. The relief of the poor, however, stretched the meaning of ecclesiastical considerably, and stretched it in the interest of an evident case of lay appropriation. Grey's proposal was made in response to conversations he had had with the Bishop of London, which encouraged Grey to believe that the bishops would be responsive to a piecemeal reform of the Irish Church, dealing with reform diocese by diocese, as their bishoprics became vacant. This proved not to be the case, and no detailed plan was ever proposed. It is, however, significant that it was Grey who put forward the first suggestion of lay appropriation in the cabinet; and it is also significant that Edward Stanley was present at both cabinet meetings. In future Grey would lay great emphasis on a broad interpretation of the phrase "church purposes," and believe that much reform could be accomplished under that guise, with the cooperation of Stanley and others of like opinions.

There can be little question, then, of Grey's acceptance of the principle of lay appropriation. Why, therefore, at least until the final weeks of his ministry, did he oppose the public espousal of the principle? The usual explanation given is that he sought, above all things, to avoid the breakup of his ministry. As far as it goes, this explanation is true. A minority of the cabinet, led by Stanley, stoutly refused to accept the principle of lay appropriation (though not necessarily its practice). Rather inappropriately dubbed, in view of their flexibility, as "high church" by Althorp, four ministers would ultimately feel forced to resign over the issue in May 1834. (Besides Stanley, they were Sir James Graham, the Duke of Richmond, and the Earl of Ripon, briefly Prime Minister in 1827 as Lord Goderich.)

The issue first reached crisis stage in October of 1832 in the course of the discussion of a plan by Stanley, the Irish Secretary, for Irish Church reform. Stanley had already stated his general position in a letter to Grey in August:

If it be in the first instance broadly laid down that the property of the
Church is not to be diverted to other than Protestant Church purposes, I am
ready . . . to give a fair latitude to that expression, and am not only ready,
but anxious, to reduce the number of bishoprics and of sinecure dignities, to
dissolve unions, to abolish Church Cess, providing for it by making the First
Fruits a real tax on benefices; and still further to augment that Fund by the
suspension, on vacancies, of preferments without cure of souls. But I am *not*
prepared, and I cannot agree, to admit the doctrine of a surplus, disposable
for lay or Roman Catholic purposes.[10]

The plan Stanley finally produced fulfilled all his promises of reform, and
more. Church cess (the Irish equivalent of church rates) was to be abolished
and the burden shifted to a progressive tax on the incomes of the Irish clergy.
At least six bishoprics were to be suppressed and united to the adjoining see on
the next vacancy. Sinecures were to be assiduously sought out and either
attached to some inferior benefice or their incomes added to the general fund
for church purposes. There was a proposal for implementing the commutation
of tithes. But there was more. By an ingenious argument, Stanley, in effect, did
what he said he would not do – he proposed to find funds from church reform
that could be used for other than church purposes. He contended that long
usage had made the Irish bishops' lands more the property of the lessees than
of the church; and, by allowing the lessees to convert 21-year leases into leases
in perpetuity, he believed that he had found the way round a ticklish problem:

The purchase money which the tenant might pay for the exhange of a 21
years lease for a perpetuity, would be, it is conceived, applicable to *any*
purpose, unconnected with the Church, inasmuch as it would be the price of
a new value which would be created by an act of the Legislature, and which
does not at present attach to Church property.[11]

Stanley had made a considerable bow in the direction of lay appropriation,
but not enough to satisfy his critics. Both Althorp and Russell advanced the
same basic criticisms. What Stanley's plan did not do, and what he refused to
do, was to suppress any parishes. This basic element of the Establishment was
to remain inviolate. To maintain Protestant clergymen where there were few
or no Protestants seemed to Stanley's two colleagues the height of folly. As
Althorp wrote to Grey in proposing instead the utilization of less expensive
paid curates and the extension of unions of parishes to be served by such
curates:

it would . . . remove one great anomaly in the state of Ireland and one
which must and does produce a great deal of discontent, for I can conceive
nothing more irritating to a Catholic population than to feel that they are
paying a clergyman of a different persuasion apparently without benefit to
any individual but himself.[12]

But even more important than removing an obvious source of irritation,

Althorp and Russell hoped that the suppression of parishes would provide the basis of a surplus that could be used for the benefit of all Irishmen, Althorp suggesting education as a most appropriate object for such funds. As for the proposals before them, Althorp remarked: "Stanley's is a good and able plan on High Church principles but I really think that in the present circumstances of Ireland none but a High Church man can go through with him to the end of it."[13]

Grey's response to the latter charge was both strong and effective. "Though attached to the Church," Grey declared, "I certainly do not consider myself a *high* Church man." And he went on:

> . . . in supporting a plan which abolishes Church cess, reduces pluralities, diminishes incomes which are too great, abolishes sinecures, reduces the numbers and limits the emoluments of Bishops, and in one instance, whatever may be the soundness of the reasoning by which the conclusion is arrived at, admitting [*sic*] what is derived from a sale of the property of the Church to be applied to other than Church purposes – in supporting such a plan I cannot consider myself as acting upon, or favouring high Church principles.[14]

Althorp's characterization was clearly inappropriate, and its adoption by Brent is likely to cause at least as much confusion now as it would have then. For Stanley and his friends were clearly no high churchmen, which in the context of the time meant those who were unwilling to yield any of the church's position or property. Stanley was willing to yield a good deal.

Grey's more general reply to Althorp's letter ranged over several areas. "My mind," he said, "is overpowered with the thought of all the evils to ourselves, to the country, and to the peace of Europe, with which the breaking up at this moment, and upon such a question, of the present government would occasion." The reference to the peace of Europe was to the fact that the government was at the time engaged in a necessarily highly delicate co-operation with its old enemies, the French, to expel a Dutch army from a recently independent Belgium. It was an operation that involved sending a French army into Belgium, the danger of French domination of which it had been a cardinal point of British foreign policy for a century and a half to avoid. In domestic affairs, besides Ireland, there was the imminent first election under the Reform Act, and a whole range of issues on which a reformed electorate was likely to demand action. To himself, Grey said, retirement would be welcome:

> But I feel bound not to do so when the consequence would be to destroy the Whig Party forever, to give power in the first instance to those [the Tories] whose principles we have always opposed, and eventually perhaps, for such a government could not last, to produce a subversion of the government itself.

These were powerful arguments, for it was difficult to conceive a more dangerous time for a government crisis.

But it is the rest of Grey's letter that throws light on the fundamental reason for his delicate handling of the issue of lay appropriation over the next year and a half. The reason lay in his appreciation of the vast potential for an Anglican reaction, an appreciation that was earlier and keener than that of any other major politician, and certainly than that of Peel and Wellington, the leaders of the party that was to profit so greatly from the reaction. Grey argued that Althorp's idea of curates and unions would be "the same thing, if not worse than withdrawing them [that is, those revenues] altogether." (Worse presumably because it suggested a stipendiary clergy, reminiscent of the Civil Constitution of the Clergy of the first French Revolution, which was anathema to the supporters of an established church.) What Althorp's suggestions risked, Grey warned, was

> exciting an alarm that you were willing in this and all similar cases, to substitute another church for that of England; a principle that would apply to the Dissenters here, as well as to the Catholics in Ireland. I need not describe to you what would be the effect of this, in uniting all those who are sincerely attached to the Church, and whose numbers and influence in this country are most powerful, against the government by which such a measure would be attempted.
>
> Looking at the question, therefore, practically I cannot doubt that the consequence of this would be at once fatal to the government, and to all hope of present improvement. Surely no principle can make it necessary for us, with our eyes open, to expose the country, I will not say to the hazard, but to the certainty of such evils.[15]

While its stoutest friends were proclaiming doom and disaster,[16] Grey had no illusions whatever about the potential power of the Anglican Church.

Althorp and Russell, though they obviously did not share Grey's keen appreciation of the possibility of an Anglican reaction, were persuaded by his arguments of the danger, and of the inexpediency for the cause of reform, of breaking up the government in this critical period, and they withdrew their threats of resignation. Another crisis was avoided when Grey and a majority of his colleagues successfully resisted efforts by Stanley and Richmond to adopt a declaration that the government would not divert church revenues to any but church purposes, though it was agreed that the bill in contemplation would not do so. (Technically, this was correct, as the bill left to the discretion of Parliament the disposition of the increased revenue expected from the sale of the leases of bishops' lands.) Grey was optimistic about the result, writing to Holland that "I really believe we may have the means of effecting a very large measure of reform by giving a very liberal construction to the phrase 'Church purposes'." At the same time, he expressed his continuing apprehension that "if we attempt to carry any measure further which I am afraid Johnny is inclined to do we shall infallibly break up and throw the whole weight of the Church and all the Protestant feeling of the country into the arms of our enemies."[17]

Grey, however, was equally concerned to keep Stanley in check and leave him under no illusion that he supported the latter's theoretical position. The prime minister had already assured Russell in their October exchanges that "whatever difference there may be between us, is not a difference of principle, and arises only on a question as to what is most expedient and practicable, under all the circumstances of the time."[18] Understandably, Grey was not quite so explicit with Stanley, but he wrote to him in November to clarify the compromise that had been agreed on:

> This measure . . . I have no hesitation in saying does not contemplate any alienation of Church property. It was, however, agreed as I understood in the Cabinet not to press the abstract principle, to which, though I think this measure wisely abstains from any interference with it, I could not assent, to the full extent of saying that at no time, and under no circumstances, could Church property be applied to other than Church purposes.[19]

Grey may have been discreet, but there was never any question about his continuing basic adherence to the principle of lay appropriation.

The general election of December 1832, though it produced a large majority of Reformers and a significant strengthening of the Radical element, did not remove the fears of Grey and his friends of an Anglican reaction. In May 1833 Holland was still explaining the compromise bill in terms of the apprehension that "a larger and better plan, however preferable in reason and policy, could not be obtained, and possibly would be revolting not only to bishops and aristocracy but a considerable portion of the English public."[20]

In the event, much of the expected benefit of the bill was lost. In the middle of June while it was still being discussed in the Commons, it became clear that the measure would face powerful opposition in the Lords. Particularly objectionable to its opponents in the upper (as well as the lower) house was clause 147, which left open to Parliament's future decision the question of the disposal of the increased revenues from the sale of the leases of bishops' lands – and thus left open the question of lay appropriation. The opposition was not reassured by Stanley's ingenious argument that, since the new value of the bishops' lands as a source of revenue had been created by Parliament, the proceeds could be disposed of by Parliament for any purpose it chose.[21]

The prospect of the Lords' opposition caused panic among some in the cabinet, but Grey was not, initially at any rate, among them. "Some of our friends," Holland recorded, "and among them John Russell and Duncannon are for striking out the most obnoxious parts of the bill. At this I am surprised."[22] In view of Russell's earlier intransigence on the issue of lay appropriation, it does seem surprising; Lord Duncannon shared Russell's opinions, and was another of Brent's "liberal Anglicans." On 18 June another proposal was made in cabinet, this time to divide the measure into two parts, with the issue posed by clause 147 to be separated from the rest of the bill. No one could have been in any doubt of the fate of that part in the Lords; but once again Russell was "earnest" in espousing such a course, though this time with the support of Lords Melbourne[23] and Brougham, and of Holland himself. Grey and Althorp, however, opposed, and the latter successfully argued instead for amending clause 147. Now, rather than leaving the disposal of the expected increased revenue to Parliament's complete discretion, it was to be used for such "religious and charitable" purposes as Parliament deemed fit.[24] Such phrases of compromise were, as we have seen, favorites of Grey and Stanley;[25] but Althorp, too, obviously appreciated their advantage on occasion. Though the situation remains cloudy, Grey's most recent biographer accepts that he took the decision that led to dropping the clause altogether three days later, and took it without consulting a number of his colleagues.[26] There may have been grounds for complaint about the method, but not many of his colleagues would have had any basis for complaint about the substance of the decision. Whigs, old and young, had all been among the supporters of dropping the clause in one way or another.

The final breakup of the government, which Grey had so long struggled to avoid, came the following spring, occasioned by a bill to implement the commutation of tithes in Ireland. In the course of the debates early in May an Irish member gave notice of his intention to move a series of resolutions, the last of which endorsed the principle of lay appropriation, and Russell announced his determination to vote for it.

Russell was reaching the end of his tether. Already in February he had written a furious letter to Holland:

> I have read your long lecture and will only say in reply, why not preach to Stanley? Why not endeavour to convince him? Why try to make me act in a way contrary to your opinions and my own, and not endeavour some little to turn him? Why abandon a measure which Lord Grey, the Chancellor, Lord Lansdowne, Althorp, yourself, and others approved, and make me yield to an opinion which is not theirs or yours? I will tell you: because Stanley is determined, because he says that if such a measure is pressed, the sooner the ministry breaks up the better; and you, none of you *dare* to urge him to change his opinion. I am very sorry to be obstinate, but if the ministry is broken up, it is not my fault, but that of those who forget their principles in their fear of venturing to ask Stanley to reverse from the speech he made when he was one and twenty.[27]

What Russell referred to was Stanley's opposition to a motion of Joseph Hume's in 1824 to look into the services and revenues of the Irish Church. The actual measure under consideration in the cabinet in February 1834 was similar, a commission for the same purpose. What was involved, therefore, was not a direct commitment to lay appropriation. Few would have doubted the implication. As Holland said of Stanley's reaction: "he had too much sagacity not to perceive and too much spirit not to avow, that inquiry into the revenues and uses of such anomalies was equivalent to a prospect of subverting them."[28] Russell's letter gives an indication not only of his own state of mind, but also of his support by older Whig leaders, Lansdowne and Brougham, as well as Grey and Holland – support in principle. But once more they gave way to Stanley in the interests of unity.

In May, Russell could no longer be contained. In reply to a conciliatory speech by Stanley to the effect that he would not discuss lay appropriation because it was not a part of the bill before the house, but that naturally Parliament could do as it wished in future, Russell felt compelled to leave little doubt of what *he* would do. Further attempts to calm the situation within the government ultimately came to nought. The final straw was notice of a resolution by H. G. Ward, a Radical, that would state explicit approval of the principle of lay appropriation. The cabinet agreed to oppose the resolution; but, because of the evident strength of support for the principle in the House of Commons, not without announcing a commission of inquiry, the idea of which had been rejected earlier in the year. Stanley found this no more acceptable now than he had then, and by the end of May he and his three supporters had gone.

Grey was anxious to go too, but the efforts of his colleagues and the king, and a strong show of confidence from the government's supporters in the House of Commons, persuaded him to carry on.[29] Yet, however reluctant he may have been to stay at the helm, he had no hesitation in avowing the implications of the action the government had taken in deciding to appoint the commission. On 8 June he wrote to the king, using the formal third person:

> The Commission, which your Majesty has been advised to issue, is to ascertain and to report facts and circumstances, on which may rest the expediency of further alterations in the establishment of the Irish Church and the mode in which such alterations may be best effected. If upon the result of such examinations it should appear that the revenues of the Church are greatly beyond what its maintenance in a just dignity, efficiency and usefulness require, Earl Grey has never concealed from your Majesty his opinion, and he has felt himself bound to declare it before his peers in Parliament, that those revenues may admit of a different distribution and appropriation, first to pious [he had scratched out "religious"] and charitable uses connected with the first interests of true religion, and next to other objects of national advantage, on which it will be for a Protestant Parliament to decide.[30]

The prime minister had been even more direct with the Lords two days earlier on 6 June, in response to a question from the Earl of Wicklow "whether the Cabinet is determined to advocate the principle that it is legal to seize upon the property of the Church, and to apply it under the name of religious and moral purposes, to purposes other than the Church of England?" Grey replied:

> I will fairly avow my opinions with respect to the property of the Church in Ireland. I think that if a considerable excess of revenue should remain beyond what is required to support the efficiency of the Church, and those other purposes connected, as Sir Robert Peel says, with the interests of true religion, I avow the principle that the state has a right to deal with that surplus, with a view to the exigencies of the state, and the general interests of the country.[31]

There could hardly be a clearer statement of the principle of lay appropriation than that.

In July, Grey resigned over a difference of opinion in the cabinet on an Irish coercion bill, which had been accompanied by considerable maneuvering behind his back; so thereafter he ceased to be a direct participant in events. Nevertheless, his reaction to the events of the next nine months further clarifies his thinking on the issue of lay appropriation, and on the reasons that he had taken so long to avow a principle he obviously supported.

Grey's concern about an Anglican reaction remained as keen as ever. At the beginning of the year he had been appalled by a new militancy among Protestant Dissenters, particularly by demands for disestablishment (a concern shared by even the most radical of his Whig supporters).[32] As he wrote to Holland about the Dissenters' activities: "They really must be reasonable for their own sakes. If they provoke the adherents of the Church, they will find how egregiously they are mistaken as to the extent of their own power."[33]

The establishment of the commission of inquiry in May had been an act of political necessity, required to control the government's supporters in the Commons. But the simultaneous emergence of evidences of strong Anglican opposition, lay as well as clerical, naturally strengthened Grey's long-standing concern about forcing the issue of lay appropriation. He wrote to the king's secretary, Sir Herbert Taylor, on 7 June: "The Church is evidently greatly alarmed. A cry will endeavour to be put up upon the ground of its danger. For the peace of the country I hope it will not succeed."[34]

These were the concerns that Grey had taken out of office with him, and they continued strongly to influence his position. Grey's fear of Radicalism is often, and rightly, stressed. But he remained, as he always had been, deeply fearful of Toryism as well. It had always been the business of the Whigs to maintain a middle position and to mediate between the two extremes; but events were leading Grey to believe that, rather than mediating between the extremes, the party was more likely soon to be crushed between them. He wrote of the likely outcome of the general elections certain to follow the dismissal of Melbourne's government and its succession by Peel's in November: "The more probable result is that the new House of Commons will be so divided between two extreme principles, as to render it hereafter unmanageable by anybody." The resulting situation would be disastrous, and he told Palmerston that "my fears . . . as to the future peace and security of the country, are greater than they ever have been at any former period."[35]

Grey was in no way reassured by the composition of Peel's new government. Though it was a judgment that events would disprove, he wrote to Holland, who had sent him a list: "We have it now, pure, unmixed High Church and Toryism."[36] He found no comfort, but rather what he expected, in the outcome of the 1835 general elections. He wrote to Lady Holland:

> The result of them seems to be that the Tories have a considerable addition to their numbers, that the Radicals also have gained, but that the moderate Whigs have lost. This may produce a state of things in which it may be difficult for the Tories to carry on the government; but will it be less so for those who may succeed them?[37]

Grey's general analysis of the election results was accurate enough – particularly significant for present purposes, the Tories, with 290, had come only 10 short of doubling their numbers and were now the largest single party in the house.[38] Few could, or would, have doubted that the church question was a significant part of the explanation. Grey's long-standing fears of an Anglican reaction and a Conservative revival were proving justified; and this was just the beginning. Grey's final question about the ability of any government to govern is a more complex one.

Grey himself addressed it in long letters of advice to his former colleagues, Melbourne and Holland, in February. In his letter to Melbourne, though he began by putting the elections in a rosier light, Grey made clear that his general position had not changed:

> The result of the elections seems to me to prove undeniably that the feeling of the country is decidedly in favour of the principle of Reform; in other words of the principles on which we acted. The necessity under which Sir Robert Peel and his adherents have felt themselves compelled, to a certain degree at least, to profess an acquiescence in these principles, would be decisive proof of this, were there no other. Here then I think we have a satisfactory ground for deciding in the first place . . . that our conduct out of government, should be the same as it was in office; to work out the necessary reforms, which the state of our institutions may require, upon safe and moderate principles; in accordance with the constitution of our mixed government, and with the Spirit of the Age.

As to Peel, Grey of course had in mind the Tamworth Manifesto, with its promises of municipal reform, church reform, and the meeting of Dissenting grievances. Grey's reference to "the constitution of our mixed government" is significant. Though others might sometimes like to forget that there was a House of Lords, Grey never did. And on the question he had proposed as to the future manageability of Parliament, the Lords as well as the Commons had to be taken into account. It was a fact of which his successors would be frequently, and unpleasantly, reminded.

Grey went on to recommend how the Whigs ought to proceed:

> On the measures, which would be required . . . I think with you there would be little difficulty, except, perhaps, with respect to the Irish Church. I doubt very much as to the way in which any proposition upon this question, if it comes to be made a subject of party contest, may be taken by the public.

Another reason for Grey's advice to hold back on this issue was that he continued to hope for a reunion with Stanley. Grey therefore strongly advised against any raising of this "very embarrassing matter" until it was absolutely necessary. It would be better to wait for the measures which he believed the government must necessarily propose upon it. And he urged that there was excellent justification for such a line in waiting for the report of the commission that the Whigs themselves had appointed, and whose findings ought to be taken into account before any final decision was taken.[39]

To Holland, Grey wrote much the same advice, but coupled with a retrospective justification of his own position:

> An amendment [to the address] asserting the principle of alienating Church property would be in my opinion, of all, the most objectionable. When the question comes practically before us, I shall have no objection to deal with it. But I say now as I said in the Cabinet that I see nothing but mischief in forcing on a question, on which there is a difference of opinion among ourselves, and on which it is to me by no means clear that the public are with us. This question being brought prematurely into discussion produced the first breach in the government which has led to all the unfortunate consequences that have followed. How much better we should have stood if Stanley remaining with us we had carried, as we should have done, the Irish Tithe Bill, and how much easier all further measures would have become. Nay there would have been some hope now that in these measures Stanley might with good management have been brought to acquiesce. He had made a large stride in agreeing in the first Irish Church Bill, to the alienation of the money to be produced by the sale of the bishops' lands in Ireland. I say this because we now appear to be in danger of repeating the same error: the certain effect of which would be to drive Stanley at once to vote with the Tories; and I need not remark to you how greatly this might assist future co-operation between them. Mooting abstract principles is always inconvenient and dangerous.

And he urged again the necessity, as well as usefulness, of waiting for the commission's report.[40]

How realistic was Grey's position? Since the Irish Tithe Bill that Peel introduced in 1835 was basically the same as the one that the Whig government had introduced the previous year, as was the Irish Tithe Act that

Melbourne's government finally carried in 1838, it seems highly likely that on this point Grey was correct.[41] It was also true that in the Irish Church Bill of 1833 Stanley had made a significant practical concession to the principle of lay appropriation. In the spring of 1835 he continued to suggest the possibility of practical compromise with his former colleagues.[42] In the event, such a compromise was not worked out; and it is difficult, and probably idle, to speculate whether it would have given the Whigs the support they needed in the House of Commons, if not to have turned Peel out, at least to have carried on a government of their own.

What is important for present purposes, however, is not what might have been, but what had been. What had guided Grey's actions until the spring of 1834 was not opposition to the principle of lay appropriation, which he himself had been the first one to moot in August 1831, but rather, political realities. His aim was to secure needed Irish reforms, without arousing the church and its supporters, of whose potential power he was painfully aware. The Irish Church Bill of 1833 had shown that even the most delicate handling of the question could raise serious problems. On that occasion, Russell – not Grey – had been one of the first to advocate jettisoning principle in the interest of passing the bill.

The open avowal of the principle got the Whigs no further in advancing the question. Two Irish tithe bills incorporating lay appropriation in 1835 and 1836 went down to inevitable defeat in the Lords. In 1836 Grey had excluded from his proxy the question of lay appropriation.[43] In November and December of the same year the cabinet discussed a strategy of Russell's for dividing the next year's Tithe Bill into two parts, one part to deal with converting the tithes into a rent charge, the other to establish a land tax to be appropriated to non-Anglican purposes.[44] It was the same kind of plan that Russell had advocated in 1833, and with the same purpose: to allow their opponents to throw out lay appropriation without throwing out the other part of the bill. Grey, whose advice Russell sought in January 1837, was triumphant:

> all that I can say is, that having objected to the unnecessary assertion of an abstract principle from the beginning, I should be very glad to see the difficulty got rid of. . . . Whether *you* can now give it up is . . . a question depending . . . on what you may think necessary for your personal character and honour.[45]

Quite how Brent attaches the importance to the cabinet's discussions he does is difficult to see. He argues that those discussions reveal "that the Whigs, independently of . . . immediate party gain, were committed to a reformation of the Irish Church." What they rather seem to prove is that the Whigs were anxious to settle the question of Irish tithes, and that Russell and some others were beginning to show a sense of political realism that Grey had rarely lacked.[46]

No one would deny that Russell and his colleagues were supporters of Irish Church reform. But in this they were hardly unique; so had Grey been since 1831. What divided the former from the latter was not principles but tactics. Brent has misread, from beginning to end, the significance of the Irish Church question in Whig politics.

There are other problems with Brent's interpretation that are closely related to the issue just discussed. One is his selection of Russell as the central figure in "liberal Anglicanism."[47] This may be partly a problem of definition, or lack of it, but it leads, at the least, to considerable confusion. The so-called "liberal Anglicans," we are told, "believed that there were Christian truths which were common to members of all Christian sects, and which were independent of dogma: the beliefs these groups shared were more fundamental (and more important) than those on which they differed."[48] But Brent's brief description of these beliefs, especially in view of his treatment of the same beliefs elsewhere, confounds understanding.

Unitarianism provides a prime example. Holland's Unitarianism is adduced as proof that he was an eighteenth-century skeptic.[49] But later, Russell's admiration of the rational Christianity of eighteenth-century divines such as Samuel Clarke and Bishop Hoadly, and the ideas he derived from them, is advanced as evidence of his "liberal Anglicanism." The main virtue of these divines was that they "distinguished the truths of Christianity from disputed sectarian dogmas, including the doctrine of the Trinity." And Brent goes on to quote Russell: "A learned and pious writer has said with equal ingenuity and truth, 'We do not know enough of the mysterious doctrines of religion to quarrel about them.' "[50] Hardly surprisingly, notions such as these left Unitarians in no doubt that Russell was at one with them in doctrine.[51]

Certainly his family's sympathies seem all to have been in that direction, as is illustrated by their long patronage of the Tavistock Unitarians. In 1805, upon the death of an even more ancient predecessor, Joseph Rowe, a substantial tradesman and "a very zealous Unitarian Christian" became the senior and most influential member of the congregation of the Abbey Chapel, Tavistock. Ill himself, Rowe clearly acted with the proverbial impatience of an old man. In the same year, the hymns of Isaac Watts were banished "on account of his Calvinistic and Trinitarian Tenets," an organ was installed, and the chapel received a thorough repair. At the time, the list of contributors to the chapel was headed by John, Duke of Bedford, Russell's father. The duke would continue his support until his death; and it would, in turn, be continued by his eldest son, Russell's older brother Francis, the seventh duke, probably until his own death in 1861.[52] Furthermore, in an appreciation of the Countess Russell in 1898, W. Copeland Bowie, the secretary of the Unitarian Association, records that about ten years before (also ten years after her husband, by then Earl Russell, died) Lady Russell, "always . . . a liberal thinker on religious questions, . . . determined to throw in her lot with the small body of English Unitarians, whose best teachers and writers she held in the highest esteem: Dr

Martineau's genius and character especially evoked her warmest appreciation." Bowie went on to praise a book the countess had written for family worship, which "contains many of the readings and prayers which she prepared for the morning services at Haslemere and Pembroke Lodge." The "religious" atmosphere at Pembroke Lodge, which the second Earl Russell remembered, and of which Brent makes much,[53] clearly existed. The question is, what does it prove? Judging, among other things, from Brent's remark on John Cam Hobhouse two pages earlier, that though brought up a "Unitarian" Hobhouse's education at Westminster School and Trinity had made his religion "temperate Anglicanism,"[54] it appears that Brent believes that the "religious atmosphere" of the Russell household establishes a similar religious position for Russell. In fact, it establishes absolutely nothing. It was Joseph Priestley, in his *Discourse on Habitual Devotion*, who advised "by no means to omit stated times of worshipping God by prayer, public and private. Every passion and affection in our frame is strengthened by the proper and natural expression of it."[55] Piety was no proof of churchmanship. Doubtless Russell thought of himself as an Anglican. This would have caused James Martineau no difficulty either. One historian of Unitarianism has described Martineau and his followers by saying that they "sighed for comprehension within an enlarged Church of England and found friends among Anglican Broad-churchmen."[56] It would be quite safe to describe the Russells as "Broad-churchmen" – a term that makes up in clarity what it lacks in novelty. Lady Russell and her children[57] went further, but it is unlikely that they considered themselves apostates from the faith of Lord John.

We have already encountered Brent's strange assertion that it was not until 1834–5 that the Whig party became concerned with the political and civil rights of those of "Nonconformist religion, both Catholic and Protestant." Only relatively late in the book do we discover that when Brent talks of what he appears to consider the Protestant branch of "Nonconformity," he has trinitarian Dissent primarily in mind. And he seems to assume that Whigs of the stamp of Grey and Holland were both unwilling and unable to deal with the concerns of the great majority of Dissenters: "As might be expected from their rationalist religious views, the Foxite generation of Whiggery primarily associated with the Unitarianism of Belsham and Aspland, and it was through these Unitarians that the old Whig alliance with Dissent was organized."[58]

This statement, though partly true, is misleading. In the 1820s, as in the 1830s, on matters affecting Dissent generally, the Whigs worked primarily with their official representatives. In the earlier decade these representatives were the Dissenting Deputies and the United Committee organized for the repeal of the Test Acts, many of whose leaders were Unitarians, such as William Smith, chairman of both bodies. It is true that Holland had a strong admiration for Unitarians, but this was more than a matter of personal preference. As he told Russell, in advising him in the autumn of 1828 on the organization of public support for Catholic Emancipation, in this case a Kent meeting: "Unfortunately Dissenters are not strong at Maidstone, and the majority of such as are there are neither Independents nor Unitarians. Of the latter, however, there are some – and one of that stamp is generally in talent and always in stoutness a match for ten of any other denomination."[59] It was a matter of fact that, as a denomination, the Unitarians were the most ardent for religious liberty. Holland's admiration was based on the most solid of Whig grounds.

There is no evidence that the proposals for the relief of Dissenters in 1834 divided Grey's government or were the monopoly of any particular group in it. In 1833 the Dissenters had formed a new United Committee, once again dominated by the Committee of the Dissenting Deputies, whose chairman was now Henry Waymouth, a Baptist. In May the United Committee advanced a list of six grievances, identifying three as the most pressing: the fact that only Anglican marriage ceremonies were legal; church rates; and the subjection of Dissenting chapels to the poor rate. On 25 May a deputation from the United Committee called on Lord Grey, "met with a very courteous reception and held a very long and interesting conversation with that liberal and enlightened statesman." Grey suggested that the government could be expected to support "any reasonable measures."[60] He agreed immediately to accept a bill moved by John Wilks, who was also the secretary of the Protestant Society, the main representative of evangelical Dissent, to exempt Dissenting chapels from the poor rate. This bill passed in July, so one of the three main grievances identified by the United Committee was quickly removed.[61]

In its legislative program the following year, the government attempted to meet the two primary grievances remaining, and to support the removal of one of the three subsidiary ones, the exclusion of Dissenters from the universities. Grey took a personal interest in both the Marriage Bill and the Universities Bill, himself introducing the petition for the latter to the Lords and thus giving it official government sanction.[62] Althorp moved the Church Rates Bill, and Russell the Marriage Bill. Both bills had to be dropped because of strong opposition from the Dissenters. They objected to the former because, though church rates were to be abolished, an annual charge on the land tax was to take their place. The latter was unacceptable on the grounds that the calling of banns was still to take place in the parish church. Thus the Dissenters spurned the legalization of their marriage ceremonies, as Russell complained to Grey, for "no other hardship than having their names called three times in church."[63] What is more, a meeting of the United Committee and country representatives in May not only condemned the principles of the government's abortive bills, but went on to declare for a complete separation of church and state. No Whig would have that, as Grey's son-in-law, the Radical Lord Durham, as well as James Abercromby, tried to persuade the meeting.[64] The Universities Bill was rejected by the Lords. But none of these defeats can be laid at the door of the older Whig leadership.

Nor did Whig policy magically change with the accession of Melbourne's government in July. In a committee of four, chaired by Russell, to draw up a plan to meet Dissenting grievances, Russell placed his main reliance for advice, as he always had, on Holland. Indeed, Russell was delighted when Holland offered to approach the champion of trinitarian Dissent, John Wilks, replying: "I can see no objection to your communicating with Mr Wilks; on the contrary, I think your intercourse with him is more likely to be beneficial than mine."[65] As a consequence of the dismissal of Melbourne's first government by the king in November, nothing came of the negotiation and planning. It does, however, reveal that Russell realized as well as anyone else the difficulty and delicacy of the problem of trying to satisfy the Dissenters.[66]

It is true that in 1836 the Dissenting Deputies were rebuffed by Holland, who declined his usual role of presenting one of their petitions to the House of Lords, "on the ground of its purporting to be a Petition from the Presbyterians as well as from the Independent and Baptist denominations."[67] Long since, Presbyterianism in England had become the stronghold of Unitarianism (though by the 1830s a new, Scottish-based, English Presbyterianism was beginning to emerge). For two decades there had been an onslaught by trinitarians on chapel and other trusts, which Unitarians had inherited from their Presbyterian forebears, and which the trinitarians claimed was a misuse of endowments originally intended for trinitarian purposes. In the 1830s these disputes had spread to London, where they also included the questioning of the right of Unitarians to play their traditional Presbyterian role in the Deputies. In 1836 the Unitarians felt it necessary to secede from that body; thus reducing, they claimed, the Deputies of the "Three Denominations" to the Deputies of only two. The Unitarians believed that they had been driven out by trinitarian intolerance,[68] and Holland clearly sympathized with them.

Holland, however, as events were to prove, was not alone in his sympathy. This was demonstrated by the strong support given by the Whigs to the Dissenters' Chapels Act of 1844, which had the effect of confirming the Unitarian title to the properties in dispute. Naturally, the Whig advocacy of the Unitarian position did not endear them to the Deputies, who played a prominent role in the violent opposition to the measure, nor to the trinitarian forces throughout the country to which the Deputies helped to give the lead.[69] The argument advanced by Russell, that "changes of opinion and of doctrine must constantly be taking place,"[70] might have been particularly unsettling. It was a fine old Unitarian principle.

On the central religious issues of Irish Catholicism and Protestant Dissent, the party's positions were firmly grounded in the Whiggery of Grey and Holland. And, though Russell's religious observances were certainly more conventional than Holland's, changing times and fashions are the likely explanation; the evidence suggests that their religious beliefs were very similar. Brent is, of course, right that the Whigs had to try to take account of the burgeoning power of trinitarian Dissent; and from Grey's ministry onwards, they did try – with about as much success as might have been expected, and more than they are usually given credit for. They did not, however, ever attempt to distance themselves from their friends in the powerful Unitarian elite; they did not want to, and they would have been very foolish if they had. On the Whig connections with Unitarianism, Brent is once more confused from beginning to end – to demonstrate adequately just how confused would take at least another, and longer, essay.

What has been argued in this one is not to deny the likelihood of Brent's basic contention that the theologians he discusses helped to influence new dimensions and emphases in Whiggery and to provide, if there were any Whigs who needed it, a new justification for the older political principles of "civil and religious liberty." But to suggest that those principles, and their development in the 1830s, were the invention of "young" Whigs or "liberal Anglicans" is a distortion of the truth. In these principles, at least, there was a clear continuity with the Whiggery of Fox and Grey; and they continued to bind together such diverse figures as Holland, Lansdowne, and Melbourne. Only two with long allegiance to the Whig party, Stanley and Graham, left Grey's government in May 1834. They were joined by Canning's political heir, Ripon, and Richmond, who reverted to his own eccentric form of ultra-Toryism. The rest of the government, whatever political provenance may be assigned to them, remained. A common attachment to "civil and religious liberty" provided a bond of party that no historian of the Whigs can ignore. Russell, as Mandler convincingly demonstrates, was at the center of political developments of immense significance for the party's (and indeed the country's) future. But to understand the party's future properly, it is necessary also to understand its past.

NOTES

1 Ellis Wasson, *Whig Renaissance: Lord Althorp and the Whig Party, 1782–1845* (New York and London, 1987), esp. pp. 45–56.
2 British Library, Add. Mss 38, 080, ff. 43–5, Russell Papers, Grey to Russell, 13 Dec. 1829.
3 Richard Brent, *Liberal Anglican Politics: Whiggery, Religion, and Reform, 1830–1841* (Oxford, 1990), esp. opp. p. 1 and p. 22.
4 Peter Mandler, *Aristocratic Government in the Age of Reform: Whigs and Liberals, 1830–1852* (Oxford, 1990), esp. pp. 123, 86–7, 96.
5 As this essay will demonstrate, Mandler's version of the Irish Church Bill of 1833 and the issue of lay appropriation provides one example. And in view of the events of the spring of 1834, his remark that lay appropriation was "not particularly a Radical cause" seems quite inexplicable: ibid., pp. 152-3, 159.
6 R. W. Davis, *Dissent in Politics, 1780–1830: The Political Life of William Smith, MP* (London, 1971), *passim*.
7 Public Record Office 30/22/1A/188–9, Russell Papers, Lansdowne to Russell, 14 Apr. 1827. Nor did Lansdowne forget about the Dissenters. A. Aspinall (ed.), *The Formation of Canning's Ministry, February to August 1827* (London, 1937), pp. 190–1. On the latter question, I was myself in error: Davis, *Dissent in Politics*, p. 238 n.
8 Brent, *Liberal Anglican Politics*, p. 65.

9 Abraham D. Kriegel, *The Holland House Diaries, 1831-1840* (London and Boston, Mass., 1977), pp. 31, 33.

10 Durham University, Grey Papers, Stanley to Grey, 4 Aug. 1832.

11 Ibid., printed paper endorsed "Stanley's Plan," p. 9.

12 British Library, Spencer/Althorp Papers H7, Althorp to Grey, 20 Oct. 1832.

13 Ibid.

14 Ibid., H8, Grey to Althorp, 21 Oct. 1832.

15 Ibid.

16 On 28 Oct. 1832, Wellington wrote to Lord Aberdeen: "I think that the country will be pretty evenly divided between Tories on the one hand; and Whigs in Government and Radicals, Unitarians and Quakers and Jews on the other. The latter will be the strongest": British Library, Add. Mss 43, 060, ff. 15-20, Aberdeen Papers.

17 British Library, Add. Mss 51, 556, Holland House Papers, Grey to Holland, 29 Oct. 1832.

18 Ibid., 38, 080, ff. 58-9, Russell Papers, Grey to Russell, 25 Oct. 1832.

19 Grey Papers, Grey to Stanley, 17 Nov. 1832.

20 British Library, Add. Mss 51, 869, ff. 569-70, Holland House Papers, Holland's diary from Mar. 1832 to July 1833, in a recapitulation of events that Holland wrote in May 1833 after his return to the cabinet following a long illness.

21 Norman Gash, *Sir Robert Peel: The Life of Sir Robert Peel after 1830* (London, 1972), pp. 49-50.

22 Kriegel, *Holland House Diaries*, p. 220, entry of 16 June.

23 Melbourne strenuously denied that he had ever been a Canningite, the designation usually assigned to him: University College, London, Brougham Papers, Melbourne to Mrs George Lamb, 24 Dec. 1838. There is good reason to believe him. On 23 Apr. 1827, Lansdowne had made it a condition of taking office that "an AVOWED Catholic" should be Irish Secretary: Aspinall, *Formation of Canning's Ministry*, pp. 156-7. Canning's response was to invite William Lamb (as Melbourne then was) to take the office. Lamb entered office as a Whig; and, though unlike Lansdowne and other Whigs, he did not leave office in Jan. 1828, the reason he had taken the Irish Secretaryship in the first place would have constituted a good reason for staying on with the Huskissonites until May. Melbourne was, of course, particularly close to Palmerston. On the other hand, he never severed his Whig connections at Brooks's and elsewhere.

24 Kriegel, *Holland House Diaries*, p. 222.

25 See above, pp. 33, 35.

26 E. A. Smith, *Lord Grey, 1764-1845* (Oxford, 1990), p. 301. See also A. D. Kriegel, "The Irish policy of Lord Grey's government," *English Historical Review*, 86 (1971), pp. 43-4.

27 British Library, Add. Mss 51, 677, Holland House Papers, Russell to Holland, 15 Feb. (1834).

28 Ibid., 51, 870, f. 716, Holland's diary, July 1833 to Apr. 1835.

29 On the whole May 1834 crisis, see Smith, *Lord Grey*, pp. 303-5.

30 Royal Archives, Add. 15/7086, Grey to William IV, 8 June 1834. The author was able to make use of the material in the Royal Archives by gracious permission of Her Majesty Queen Elizabeth II.

31 J. H. Barrow (ed.), *The Mirror of Parliament* (1834), Vol. 3, pp. 2077-8.

32 See below, p. 45.

33 British Library, Add. Mss 51, 548, Holland House Papers, Grey to Holland, 25 Jan. 1834.

34 Royal Archives, Add. 15/7083, Grey to William IV, 7 June 1834. In Feb. an address

of the clergy, bearing some 7,000 signatures, was sent to the Archbishop of Canterbury. This was followed in May by a second address, this time from the laity and signed by some 230,000 heads of families. As Professor Gash remarks: "This impressive mobilization of feeling, demonstrating a strength unknown to the anglicans themselves, powerfully affected the political situation." *Aristocracy and People: Britain 1815-1865* (Cambridge, Mass., 1979) p. 176.

35 Southampton University Library, Broadlands Mss, GC/GR/2320/1-3, Grey to Palmerston, 9 Dec. 1834.

36 British Library, Add. Mss 51, 557, Holland House Papers, Grey to Holland, 19 Dec. 1834.

37 Ibid., 51, 549, Grey to Lady Holland, 16 Jan. 1835.

38 Gash, *Sir Robert Peel*, pp. 101-2.

39 Royal Archives, Melbourne Papers 5/128, Grey to Melbourne, 1 Feb. 1835.

40 British Library, Add. Mss 51, 556, Holland House Papers, Grey to Holland, 10 Feb. 1835.

41 Elie Halévy, *The Triumph of Reform, 1830-1841* (London, 1961), pp. 186, 203.

42 Brent, *Liberal Anglican Politics*, pp. 84-5.

43 (J.) Morgan Sweeney, "The House of Lords in British politics, 1830-1841" (D. Phil., Oxford University, 1973), p. 102. It would perhaps be more accurate to say that Grey suspended his proxy on lay appropriation as part of Irish tithe bills.

44 Brent, *Liberal Anglican Politics*, p. 101.

45 Smith, *Lord Grey*, pp. 318-19.

46 Brent, *Liberal Anglican Politics*, p. 101. There are several peculiarities about Brent's treatment of this episode. But perhaps the greatest is that he chooses to leave the Whigs and the question of lay appropriation in early Dec. 1836, with the cabinet allegedly unanimous on the issue and firmly committed to the position it had taken in 1835. But in view of the maneuvering that took place in 1837, the cabinet discussions of 1836 appear rather to lead toward the decision to drop lay appropriation altogether in the successful 1838 bill, which Brent ignores completely. See also, Halévy, *Triumph of Reform*, p. 203; and Gash, *Sir Robert Peel*, p. 160.

47 Brent, *Liberal Anglican Politics*, p. 16.

48 Ibid., p. 28.

49 Ibid., p. 112.

50 Ibid., p. 60.

51 *Christian Life*, 1 June 1878. I owe this and the references to Unitarian newspapers that follow to the kindness of Professor R. K. Webb.

52 Devon Record Office, 1154D/A1, *passim*, and 1154D/M4, letter to E. C. Rundle, 21 Aug. 1904. Once again, I am indebted to Professor Webb for the reference to these papers.

53 Brent, *Liberal Anglican Politics*, p. 137.

54 Ibid., p. 135.

55 J. T. Rutt (ed.), *The Theological and Miscellaneous Works of Joseph Priestly*, Vol. 20 (1820), p. 112. Professor Webb will examine Unitarian piety at length in forthcoming publications.

56 H. L. Short, in C. G. Bolam, R. Thomas, J. Goring, and H. L. Short, *The English Presbyterians: From Elizabethan Puritanism to Modern Unitarianism* (London, 1968), p. 260.

57 Lady Agatha Russell, the youngest child and only daughter, died in 1933. Like her mother and brothers, she had become a member of the Richmond congregation, and for the last ten years of her life was a regular supporter of the Bournemouth church: *Inquirer*, 29 Apr. 1933.

58 Brent, *Liberal Anglican Politics*, pp. 255–7.
59 Public Record Office 30/22/1A, Russell Papers, Holland to Russell, 15 Oct. 1828.
60 Quoted in B. L. Manning, *The Protestant Dissenting Deputies* (Cambridge, 1952), p. 386.
61 G. I. T. Machin, *Politics and the Churches in Great Britain, 1832–1868* (Oxford, 1977), pp. 42–3.
62 Grey Papers, Grey to the Archbishop of Canterbury, 21 Feb. 1834; Brent, *Liberal Anglican Politics*, p. 190.
63 Machin, *Politics and the Churches*, pp. 43–4.
64 Brougham Papers, 10,015, Durham to Brougham, endorsed May 1834.
65 British Library, Add. Mss 51, 677, Holland House Papers, Russell to Holland, 24 Aug. 1834.
66 On the discussions as a whole, see the correspondence between Russell, Melbourne, Hobhouse, and Holland in the Melbourne and Holland House Papers, 15 Aug. to 26 Oct. 1834.
67 Quoted in Manning, *Protestant Dissenting Deputies*, p. 82.
68 Bolam et al., *English Presbyterians*, pp. 245–52.
69 Manning, *Protestant Dissenting Deputies*, pp. 87–93.
70 Quoted in Bolam et al., *English Presbyterians*, p. 252.

Chapter 3

Popular irreligion in early Victorian England: infidel preachers and radical theatricality in 1830s London

I. D. McCalman

The popular agitations of the early 1830s that are said to have put the finishing touches to the making of the English working class and to have laid the foundations of Chartism were partly masterminded from the Blackfriars Rotunda in London, headquarters and auditorium of an impressive range of radical leaders and orators, including the fiery National Union of the Working Classes. But historians have failed to notice that the radical orators of the Rotunda were overshadowed for much of this period by an unlikely co-tenant – a former Church of England clergyman, Reverend Robert Taylor, who delivered esoteric mythological sermons several times a week to capacity crowds. As a self-professed infidel, or popular radical freethinker, Taylor blended ultra-Radical politics with irreligion – a position that had traditionally appealed to an intellectual minority. How was this "earnest and scholarly man"[1] able to attract such substantial Radical audiences at this time of political crisis?

Robert Taylor has received little attention from modern historians; he is viewed as an eccentric, ephemeral figure who stands outside mainstream traditions of nineteenth-century Radical and freethinking history.[2] In this chapter I argue that his appeal rested on a self-conscious romanticism and theatricality, making him a more significant and representative early Victorian figure than has generally been allowed.

The notorious infidel-Radical publisher, Richard Carlile, decided in June 1830 to lease the Rotunda building south of the river at No. 3 Blackfriars Road so as to exploit the talents of his recently adopted partner, Reverend Robert Taylor. He admired Taylor as a dispenser of "really useful" and rational knowledge designed to liberate the common people from religious superstition and ignorance, and to transform them into rational and moral individuals. During the first half of the 1820s Carlile had himself been a nodal point of the Radical "march of mind," the artisan and lower-middle-class drive for educational and moral self-improvement, which collectively produced what Edward Thompson has called a Radical intellectual culture. Carlile's prison-orchestrated campaign for popular press freedom generated a country-wide network of Zetetic, or radical knowledge, circles, who read and debated rationalist theories and volunteered to cram the courts and prisons in defense of free thought.[3] But in spite of a triumphant release from prison in 1825, Carlile found himself eclipsed in the late 1820s by a new breed of deist preachers.

Men like Reverend Rowland Detrosier in Manchester and the Reverends Josiah Fitch and Robert Taylor in London were specialist teachers, preachers, and orators whose "useful knowledge" curricula encompassed a dazzling array of scientific, literary, economic, philosophical, political, and theological subjects. By the time Taylor moved to London in 1824 he had accumulated qualifications and experience as a surgeon, a BA graduate of St John's College, Cambridge, an ordained Church of England clergyman, and a schoolteacher, journalist, and deist lecturer in Ireland. Over the next four years he graduated from debating and preaching in low metropolitan alehouses to presiding over his own freethinking chapel, or "Areopagus," purchased at great expense by prosperous supporters. "Here we come to learn," Taylor declaimed to packed audiences of well-dressed and "respectable" men and women, ". . . to have new capacities of knowledge unbarred . . . and new treasures of intellectual worth supplied to fill those capacities."[4] But a twelve-month jail sentence for blasphemous libel in 1828 cost him his following and threw him into dependence on Carlile's matchless political and press skills. The indifferent success of a pioneering "infidel mission" to the North in 1829 convinced them of Taylor's need for "a well-dressed audience, and a respectable place of assembly, a splendid structure."[5]

If the splendor of the Blackfriars Rotunda had faded somewhat since its foundation as the Leverian Natural History Museum in 1787, Carlile's expenditure of the awesome borrowed sum of £1,275 on rent, cleaning, and minimal painting made the premises more than serviceable. From May 1830 Taylor preached in the same "small theatre" that Coleridge and Hazlitt had used a decade earlier when lecturing on philosophy and literature to capacity crowds of around five hundred. Taylor looked up from the podium to an emblematic statue of contemplation mounted on a marble-balustraded gallery for patrons willing to pay a silver sixpence. Seated in the pit below, in greater numbers but still moderate comfort, were the threepence admissions. Twelve zodiacal emblems painted on the ceiling of the overarching dome signified the theater's transformation into an infidel "coliseum" and provided practical illustrations for Taylor's astronomical discourses. Other visual aids included a large board carrying Greek "hierogliphs," a mechanical pointer, a costly illuminated globe, and a clockwork "orrery" to demonstrate the movement of the planets.[6]

As in Areopagus days, advertisements also offered "divine service" on Sundays. Even the most burlesqued Rotunda services opened with a properly reverential reading of the lesson, taken either from Matthew 2 or 3 or "the sublime pages" of Volney's *Ruins of Empire*, a work, claimed Carlile in 1830, whose visionary structure was "truly prophetic."[7] His willingness to use such religious language shows how far he had traveled under Taylor's influence. In early 1828 he was bankrupt; book sales had dwindled and few bothered to attend his free thought discussions, yet he despised the milksop deism of men like Fitch, whose published liturgies and "deist public worship" mimicked Christian superstition.[8] And though he admired Taylor's intellect, he likewise castigated the Areopagus "divine service" as a "performance of fiction" that degraded both performer and hearer.[9] All forms of imaginative art were, he believed, distracting and trivial at best; at worst, an insidious form of priestcraft that exploited "the syrens of human language."[10] Although it stared him in the face, he could not see that Taylor and his ilk represented an altogether new challenge. Aesthetic and vitalist currents had touched infidelity during the late eighteenth century through the poetic and prophetic sensibilities of artisan literati like William Blake. During the postwar years, however, the popular movement had taken its coloring from Carlile's mechanistic rationalism.[11] Taylor was the first metropolitan infidel in the nineteenth century to recognize and tap powerful romantic-religious impulses within the popular Radical milieu.

By education, personality, and style he was perfectly fitted for the task. As the pampered youngest son of a wealthy Birmingham ironmonger, he had shown early scholastic, dramatic, and "poetical promise," memorizing Gray's "Elegy" as a child, scribbling nature poems while working as a boy shepherd, and catching "the passion of liberty" when performing in a play as Gustavas Vassa. Throughout a four-year apprenticeship to a Birmingham surgeon, he saw himself as a romantic artist who "formed juvenile friendships – early loves – went to plays – shooting, fishing – wrote poems – and invented systems." The tedium and uncertainty of surgical practice, as well as the inspiration of evangelical preachers like Burn in Birmingham and Simeon at Cambridge, persuaded him to qualify for a clerical career. Here again his restless, self-indulgent temperament blighted dazzling prospects. He gave way to bouts of moody introspection, "irresistible waggery," melancholy contemplations of suicide and hereditary insanity, and a self-dramatizing belief that he was a Promethean genius tormented by envious and inferior talents.[12] Flirtation with deism and a succession of clashes with clerical superiors pushed him into an increasingly rebellious and marginal position until, in February 1819,

> it occurred to his mind, so forcibly, what a downright fool and idiot he must be, at 35 years of age, to be at the baby's game still, and not to have seen through the trick, by which fools and knaves of not half his natural gifts, had pushed him from his chance in the scramble of life.[13]

When Taylor transplanted his Christian Evidence Society from Dublin to London in 1824 he was still a sincere, even ardent, deist. His *Liturgy* of 1826–7 followed the Anglican order of service minutely, not – he stressed – in a spirit of ridicule, but because "its majestic rhythms, pointed sentences, and declamatory grandeur having often excited a wish to hear it performed . . . by our more popular tragedians as a specimen of oratory and poetry."[14] This merging of religious and literary forms typified Taylor's free thought. His discourses of the 1820s were steeped in the fashionable romantic influences of Shakespeare, Byron, and Shelley. *Queen Mab*, in particular, became his enchiridion: "It is the constant of my waistcoat pocket," he wrote to Carlile in March 1828, "and comes in as an ever ready meal to recruit exhausted thought in my walks."[15] Carlile approved of its atheistical notes, but failed to notice that his Zetetic shopmen were gripped by Shelley's wild imagery, "flights of ardent imagination," "allegorical complexity," and (borrowing from Coleridge) "esamplastic power."[16] He and Taylor differed still more fundamentally, "as the nadir from the zenith," in their evaluation of theater. Taylor thought it a powerful lever of social change that could ultimately replace the "savagery and melancholy . . . and mischievous excitement" of orthodox religion, and he criticized Carlile in 1828 for failing to appreciate the revolutionary potential of the medium: "I should anticipate the moral regeneration of the world, if we had twenty theatres and twenty thousand Keans and Kembles."[17]

Not surprisingly Taylor's mid-1820s infidel creed and cosmology were constructed from romantic ingredients. His *Thirteen Moral Discourses*, delivered to Dublin and London congregations between 1820 and 1828, set out to counter guilt-ridden Judeo-Christian ethics with a cheerful, sensual, and "natural" pagan morality derived from Socrates, Cicero, Catullus, Juvenal, and Ovid.[18] In Marlow at much the same time the young romantic rebels Shelley and Peacock were similarly immersing themselves in neoclassical pagan culture, including esoteric Eastern anti-Christian mythologies. Marilyn Butler's explanation of this Radical neoclassicalism as a displacement of blocked political impulses, a disguised affirmation of romantic intellectual exclusivity, and "an immensely potent cult of self"[19] fits Taylor in all respects. When the enforced discipline of an Okeham prison cell encouraged him in 1828 to compose a serious intellectual critique of Christianity, he drew on the oriental mythological researches of Volney, William Drummond, William Jones, and, above all, Dupuis. His resulting works, *The Diegesis* and *Syntagma*, echoed these precursors in arguing that all religions originated as personified allegories of solar myths, and so, as Taylor put it in one of his last published lectures, "are more or less cleverly constructed poems or tissues of fiction."[20]

And if Taylor embellished this essentially simple and unoriginal idea with a "phantasmagoria of misplaced erudition,"[21] that was part of his appeal. His contention that "Everything of Christianity is of Egyptian origin"[22] was genuinely original, but his audiences were probably more impressed by the welter of scientific, etymological, and theological references. Like most theories favored by early Victorian artisans, his astronomical critique also purported to demystify the conspiracies of a ruling-class elite. The "lazy monks and wild fanatics" who comprised the Therapeutae Essenes of Alexandria had, he claimed, "clubbed together in the University, concocting holy mysteries and inspired legends" that were elaborated and secretly transmitted by Christian priests in succeeding centuries.[23] With irresistible humor and zest, he showed how this arcane code could be cracked. In a letter of

1839 the freethinking scholar Charles Hennell described his style as "honest hating, reckless, witty, abusive, take-hold-of-anything special pleading. He gets the laugh on his side till you cry."[24] Taylor's astronomo-theological critique of 1828 contained, in fact, the same mix of ingredients that had contributed to the immense success of Byron's *Don Juan* exactly a decade earlier.

Carlile was among the many artisan and middling intellectuals who succumbed to this potent recipe. No doubt he was influenced too by pragmatic considerations such as Taylor's potential drawing power. But astronomical mythology became an enduring component of Carlile's free thought philosophy from 1828 and there is every reason to believe that Taylor's rich blend of rationalism, pseudo-scientific erudition, and romantic anthropology had worked its intellectual magic on the tough ex-tinmaker. Ardent testimonies from individuals who attended Taylor's Rotunda services show that his preaching could induce something like a religious conversion. An architect's clerk, William Knight, scribbled a passionate response to one of Taylor's sermons of 1830: "in vain my pen attempts to express the throbbing joys which fill my heart, no tongue can utter and no Christian's mind can imagine the pleasures which fill my soul."[25] Thomas Bull, surveyor, and "H.J.T." wrote letters in 1831 testifying that Taylor's "learning, science and truth" and beautiful "allegorical representations of the mysteries of religion" had freed their minds from the chains of superstition.[26] And a young law stationer was so moved by news of Taylor's imprisonment in 1831 that he proposed to erect a marble-pillared memorial temple containing a statue of the great infidel teacher.[27]

Added to the Rotunda's appealing program of moral and theological instruction was the promise of something altogether original in the sober history of free thought. In November 1830 the opening number of Carlile's new periodical, significantly named the *Prompter*, boasted that Taylor's Rotunda performances provided "all that is splendid in theatrical entertainment."[28] Taylor's deist preaching had always shown a histrionic flair, but the facilities and location of the Rotunda enabled him to develop an explicitly theatrical repertoire.

"Raising the Devil," the most notorious and successful of his performances in the winter of 1830, customarily began with a reading of the lesson, after which Taylor was summoned onstage under the titles of "The Devil's Chaplain, Archbishop of Pandemonium and Primate of All Hell." Dressed in full canonicals, he swept into the darkened theater, pledging solemnly to raise the Devil and put him down again without endangering his audience. Hell, he promised, would be turned into heaven, and every step of this cosmic inversion would follow true scientific principles. Satan himself was introduced by means of a dramatic materialization. After muttering the Lord's Prayer backward in accordance with English folk superstition, Taylor would incant the words, "Satan, Beelzebub! Baal, Peor! Belial, Lucifer, Abaddon, Apollyon, thou King of the Bottomless Pit, thou King of Scorpions, having stings in their tails to

whom it is given to hurt the earth for five months – Appear! – Appear!"
Instantly, the large globe lit up to reveal a hideous caricature of the Devil.
Then, with a flick of his wrist – "Behold Satan himself is transformed into an
angel of light." Both devil and angel, he later explained, had originally been
zodiacal representations of the seasons formulated as a teaching device by
ancient scientists, teachers, and poets. Gradually the physical allegory had been
obfuscated by the Christian priesthood in order to exploit and enslave the
common people.[29]

Audiences loved it. They crammed the larger theater to see twice-weekly
performances in numbers that rarely fell below 1,000, the surplus threatening
on one occasion to instigate a serious riot until Taylor promised a repeat the
following night.[30] His closest rival, a French Radical named Pierre Baume who
conducted Universalist services at a chapel in Finsbury, despaired of competing. Spies believed that Baume's political ardor failed to compensate for the
absence of extravagant special actions or dress at his services.[31] Taylor's cheeky
adoption of the nickname "Devil's Chaplain" and other Satanic variants also
carried a Byronic frisson of the tabooed and dangerous, tapping a folk
preoccupation with diabolism reflected in both evangelicalism and popular
melodrama. In 1829–31 the Surrey, one of London's most popular melodrama
houses situated only a block from the Rotunda, featured such attractions as *The
Devil's Walk, or Pluto in London,* Jerrold's *The Devil's Ducat,* Fitzball's *The
Devil's Elixir,* and an adaptation of Delavigne's *Robert le diable.*[32] The latter
specifically inspired Taylor's favorite nickname, "Robert, the Devil," while
melodrama in general gave him many compelling motifs and stage techniques,
including specter-raising (as in Byron's *Manfred*); Manichean contrasts
between good and evil, and light and dark; the *coup de théâtre* when evil is
exposed and virtue triumphs; the violent and emotional language; and even
the use of spectacular mechanical props.[33]

Melodrama, a "key modality" of early Victorian popular culture,[34] seemed
also to suit the charged political atmosphere of the winter of 1830–1. In
November and December the mounting popular excitement stimulated by
trade depression, foreign revolution, democratic political successes in Ireland,
and the prospect of a Whig reform, inflamed Taylor to greater linguistic and
gestural extravagance. Outside the Rotunda 6,000 people cheered excitedly as
he spoke from under the provocative symbol of a tricolor flag, promising that,
if the "madman" Wellington blocked reform, "the trunkless heads" of the king
and his ministers would "Roll on the Ground as Footballs."[35] Policemen and
government spies noted that the reputation of the Rotunda "had flown rapidly
through all the classes," even attracting young Julien Thistlewood from Paris
where he had been emulating his late father during the July Revolution.[36]
Government officials sent shorthand writers to note prosecutable statements
at the Rotunda, posted 100 special constables in nearby stables to deal with
Rotunda-led riots, and debated the legality and wisdom of indicting Carlile and
Taylor for sedition or blasphemy.[37] An imprudent, though not extreme, article

defending the "Swing" agricultural riots in the Southeast promptly earned Carlile the severe sentence of thirty months' jail, a £200 fine, and heavy sureties.

Taylor instinctively turned to theater. He helped stage mock trials to publicize the dubious court proceedings and reach a more satisfactory fantasy verdict. The need to counteract loyalist works like Charles Knight's *The Rick-Burners: A Tale for the Present Times* also inspired him to write a three-act "tragedy" entitled *Swing: or, Who are the Incendiaries?*, running in published version to 47 pages. Never short on pretension, he sent an inscribed copy of *"this specimen of what Drama should be"* to the famed actor, producer, and playwright Charles Kemble.[38] *Swing's* extensive use of blank verse was consciously Shakespearean, though the work reminded Carlile of the Restoration dramatist Otway's *Venice Preserved*, which also treated the subject of popular rebellion. Taylor's language was, he believed, equally lofty, but his plot was more subtle. "It admirably displays the three degrees of religious hypocrisy and wickedness in the fanatic rabble, in the priest, and in the mitred Archbishop."[39]

Despite this literary pretension, the play was really a pastiche of fashionable melodramatic themes. Echoing Jerrold and others, it placed the idealized hero, John Swing, in a village setting and burdened him with conventional childlike encumbrances – a naively innocent younger brother, credulous sisters, and an elderly, Bible-befuddled father. Against them was pitted the full panoply of melodrama villains. Judge Jeffries, Elijah Brimstone, and Ebenezer Sanctity represented the unremittingly fiendish "black villain" type, while the Archbishop of Cant was depicted as a craven, buffoonish "white villain" who – true to type – eventually deserted to the side of the good. The creaking plot also managed to incorporate a good-hearted poacher driven to crime by the desperate poverty of his family, and a conspiracy that culminated in the execution of the preternaturally innocent Francis Swing. The actions and emotions of all characters were typically extreme and volatile. Stage instructions had Jeffries gloating "very cruelly" and "chuckling" at a "horrible joke"; Brimstone "gnashes his teeth" and "exits in a violent rage"; the archbishop "faints," "shudders with horror," and has "violent hysterics"; John Swing himself almost succumbs to "an ecstasy of grief."[40] Interspersed with all this were relieving interludes of song and burlesque. *Swing* aimed, Carlile wrote, "to make you cry and laugh"[41] and, judging by its explicit political references and heroic revolutionary ending, to make you seize your pike as well.

The play's effectiveness cannot be gauged from the printed text alone. Both the political context and the actors' performances worked to enhance its impact. Taylor imitated the grandiose acting style of Kemble, as well as the passionate, brooding romanticism of Kean. Spies observed that he and his assistant Joseph Harris repeated numerous abbreviated performances of *Swing* in early 1831, invariably attracting audiences of two or three hundred who "applauded loudly."[42] Both the long shilling version and short threepenny edition were also reported to have sold well, to the extent that Taylor's followers – including Carlile in prison – gleefully anticipated an even more explosive sequel. It never came, or not at least in the form that Carlile hoped. Instead, Taylor produced in February 1831 a short biblical burlesque called *Balaam's Donkey*, which tilted mainly at the "Lord Mare's" attempts to close down the Rotunda.[43]

Balaam's Donkey signaled a change of emphasis that Taylor was to sustain for the remainder of his career as an infidel preacher. Melodrama began to be supplanted by burlesque. Sermons, services, and lectures were increasingly given over to ribald buffoonery. There are many possible explanations for this. Taylor's performances in the 1820s had always contained elements of burlesque, as did most melodrama productions in the early nineteenth century. Freed from Carlile's nagging asceticism and political seriousness, Taylor could indulge his natural levity, sensuality, and wit. Unlike Carlile, moreover, he genuinely believed in the demystifying force of satire and ridicule. His interest in Radical politics, as distinct from irreligion, had always been slight – all the more so because of the growing influence of the tough, committed leaders of the NUWC who shared the Rotunda premises from July 1831. And of course Taylor could never resist playing to the gallery. Reports of his services in the late winter and spring of 1831 show that the more he clowned, the more the pit and gallery cheered.

He now offered an elaborate theatrical burlesque of the "astronomical pantomime" of the Anglican service. The Rotunda stage was embellished "in derision of the protestant communion tables" with a white-clothed "altar," complete with six-foot crucifix, communion bun, and chalice. On entering dressed in the manner of a bishop or archbishop, "with white lawn sleeves," he would typically make three bows "and other silent motions to the cross," hold up "his hand wrapped up in a garment, before his face in mockery of the manner of the regular clergy," place his head in his hands in the posture of prayer, and pretend to be in a state of "holy ejaculation": all of this accompanied by roars of laughter or cheers from the audience.[44] His service of 3 April 1831 took this a step further by deconstructing the clerical rituals as he performed them:

> The Priest ought not to stand at all but to fall on one knee thus (placing himself in the attitude while describing it), stretch out his other Limb, shut his eyes and open his mouth exactly after the figure of Orion – you see him depicted in the very attitude of Prayer (pointing to the celestial Globe) as you may see him in the visible Heavens every night and having put himself in the Hoax position . . . he is in a drawling tone to utter the magical words to the Collect, Almighty and everlasting God . . . (falling on both his knees and singing the remainder with a whining nasal sound in derision amidst loud plaudits).[45]

He spiced this buffoonery with colloquial asides that produced "loud exclamations of approval," "theatrical applause," and "shouts of bravo." St Mark's "breeches" were included in "the divine beautification," the holy gospel was described as "altogether a book of Moonshine," Jesus was likened to "a quack doctor" who "pretended to have dealings with the Devil," and Noah was described as a "drunk" who "reeled about like a beer barrel and snored like a trooper." The association of the Eucharist with drink he found especially irresistible; Jesus was said to have asked: "Can you toss off a pot of porter because if you cannot . . . you will never do." Similarly, "the reason why the blood of Christ does induce God to forgive us our sins is that he liked a drop of the cratur, it puts him in a good humour and he is not so particular."[46]

If Taylor's sermons of spring 1831 were saturated in references to "blue ruin" and "Barley and Perkins ale," this was partly because he was consuming a good deal of both – off and on the stage. As a result, his private behavior became as outrageous as his public. Informers reported that he flaunted his torrid sexual affair with Georgiana Richards, a stay and corset maker whose coffee shop in the Rotunda was suspected by some Radicals of doubling as a brothel.[47] His "beastly intoxication" also induced violent and erratic changes in mood and behavior, as when he suddenly began dancing, swearing, and jumping over a broomstick in the passage of the Rotunda, pleading to be accompanied to "some brothel."[48] When Carlile's son failed to procure him a live pigeon to use in a Rotunda service, he shouted drunkenly: "Dam and bugger his bloody eyes. I never wish to see him again alive, goodnight . . . it is likely you will hear of my death tomorrow."[49]

From his Giltspur Street Compter cell, Carlile noted this public and private extravagance with mounting alarm. He was genuinely proud of Taylor's ability to draw larger audiences than political rivals, but he had long been concerned about the infidel preacher's self-indulgence and levity, chiding him for including "jests and sarcasms" on such a serious subject as the nativity of Jesus Christ[50] and wishing that he would "curb his witty faculty and reduce his philosophy to more gravity."[51] Taylor's histrionic response to a two-year prison sentence for blasphemous libel in early July only worsened the problem. Instead of behaving like a disciplined and dignified free thought martyr, he indulged in embarrassing "theatrical vaunting." In stronger moments he wrote narcissistic poetry, stimulated "by the romantic character of my situation"; more often, he issued a stream of maudlin complaints about the horrors of his Horsemonger Lane cell, his health-impairing deprivations of sex and brandy, and the plots against his life. To the great satisfaction of conservative newspapers he was caught trying to smuggle brandy into his cell, as well as masquerading Georgiana Richards as his legal wife. In a fit of drunkenness, he even attempted to stab a jailer with a penknife. Still worse from Carlile's point of view, he sent cringing letters to Lord Melbourne in the hope of a sentence reduction.[52]

It was the beginning of the end of a fruitful, if improbable, partnership. Personal jealousies exacerbated their squabbles, but ultimately the two infidels held incompatible views about both the form and substance of Radical irreligion. Carlile continued infidel lectures at the Rotunda for a short time; they featured the ex-Southcottian shoemaker prophet, John "Zion" Ward, and Eliza Sharples as "Isis," the feminist Lady of the Rotunda. Neither possessed Taylor's theatricality, notoriety, and crowd appeal. At the end of March 1832 Carlile relinquished the lease on the Rotunda with some relief. Without Taylor it had become a financial drain, and he was always uncomfortable with the elevation of the emotional, artistic, and humorous sides of the human psyche over the rational.

The contrast with Taylor could hardly be greater. Buoyed by money from marriage to a wealthy St Simonian widow, his infidel services of 1834 reached a zenith of romantic theatricality. While Carlile struggled to attract thirty listeners, Taylor, or "Talisiphron" as he now called himself, again drew large crowds to a new Areopagus at No. 8 Theobalds Street. Spies and observers reported that he more than ever resembled "a perfect fribble," "mountebank," or "coxcomb" in dandified clothes of satin adorned with brilliants. Rings sparkled on his fingers and he periodically touched a perfumed cambric handkerchief to his nose. His accent and tone were more "ludicrous" and "impious" than ever, his jokes coarser and more "excremental." Now a costumed thirteen-piece Swiss band and a guitar-strumming lady singer ushered him onstage to the tune of "See the Conquering Hero Comes," punctuating his service with renditions of the "Marseillaise" hymn, "Rule Britannia," and Mozart's overtures, each chorus being taken up rousingly by the audience. In short, concluded one spy on 14 April 1834, "during the whole time the place was a complete Theatre."[53]

Taylor would have thought this the highest possible praise. But what did audiences make of this infidel theater? Did they appreciate its revolutionary implications as Taylor hoped, or simply enjoy the entertainment as Carlile feared? The memoirs of bookseller Henry Vizetelly incline to the latter view, implying that many visited the Rotunda simply to see cheap theatrical entertainment. He himself had been lured by Taylor's notoriety as a dandy who sported bishops' robes, white kid gloves, an eyeglass, and fashionable curls. Vizetelly compared Taylor's "theatrical get-up . . . stagey manner and . . . ranting delivery" to the styles of professional actors like Malibran, Macready, and the Kembles.[54] The popular sporting and theatrical newspaper *Bell's Life in London* carried commentary on "Dandy Bob Taylor" alongside other theatrical intelligence,[55] and the ribald *Paul Pry* saw his act as a compound of the military, clerical, and cockney dandy.[56] The Blackfriars Rotunda had hosted circus and equestrian entertainments immediately before Taylor's advent and continued, under the name of the Globe, to provide popular theatrical and musical entertainment well into Victorian times. Its central location, excellent facilities, and proximity to a popular melodrama theater like the Surrey probably ensured a natural catchment of theater-loving artisans and costers.[57] Spies and shorthand writers confirm that Rotunda audiences would "applaud in theatrical manner," laugh uproariously, yell "Bravo," give vent to "tumultuous shouts of applause," and sing snatches of chorus from popular songs.[58] In short, they experienced all the expressive and cathartic satisfactions of participatory demotic theater.

Enjoyment need not, however, have ruled out political edification. Vizetelly might have been attracted by Taylor's sensational reputation, but he was also at this time under the spell of the "impassioned language" and republican-infidel ideas of Shelley's *Queen Mab*.[59] Taylor surely deserves some credit for reinforcing Vizetelly's lifelong commitment to romantic radicalism and free thought. I have elsewhere argued that the convivial theatricality of ultra-Radical alehouses and blasphemous chapels helped to carry plebeian traditions of countertheater and anti-Establishment populism into the newer, more class-conscious modes of popular politics in the 1840s.[60] Taylor's infidel theater perhaps exerted a parallel influence among the more prosperous artisan and lower middle class. At one level Rotunda audiences were automatically implicated in a political process simply through the struggle of popular theatrical outlets in the 1830s to break the monopoly of "legitimate" theaters. Modern analysts have also stressed melodrama's radical affinities, especially its utopianism, vilification of aristocrats, and commitment to absolute moral justice.[61] Taylor's brand of irreligious melodrama and burlesque gave such points an explicitly political slant – accentuated by the Rotunda's simultaneous hosting of London's ultra-reform movement.

Taylor drew no sharp distinction between serious modes of infidel discourse and his Sunday night theatrical entertainments. The dramatis personae of *Swing* were freely transposed onto political opponents; Reverend Osgood, an earnest missionary who debated at Christian Evidence Society meetings, became "Parson Brimstone," Justice Knowlys became "Judge Jeffries," and sundry established clergy were called "Archbishop of Cant."[62] Taylor rated *Swing* as highly as his *Diegesis* and *Syntagma*. He also believed that it had led Anglican bishops to plot his imprisonment on a false charge of blasphemy.[63] No wonder, then, that the prologue of *Swing* incorporated theater into the democratic constitutionalist mythology:

The ancient tragedy was first design'd
From slavish bonds to free th'insulted mind;
To speak the people's voice with magic art,
And launch keen satire to the tyrant's heart,
It was the people's tragedy. The stage,
The people's House of Commons was.

He valued burlesque equally. His *Third Moral Discourse* recommended the pagan ideal of *levitas* as an infallible solvent of melancholy tyranny, fanaticism, and crime, and the *Fourth Moral Discourse* made the still greater claim for popular theatricality that it could serve as a surrogate for religion,[64] thereby anticipating the French romantic Nodier's belief that melodrama replaced popular religious worship in the postsacral world of early nineteenth-century France.[65] Arguably Taylor's Rotunda theatricals continued the function of earlier deistic services of the mid-1820s, enacting a form of collective ritual that allowed his congregation to discharge powerful emotional yearnings.

The latter could include the darker, more dangerous sides of romanticism. Spies and police reporters were disturbed by the outward respectability of those who enjoyed Taylor's profane performances. Attendants in both gallery and pit were repeatedly described as "respectable," "respectably dressed," "of the middle class of society," "middling classes and well dressed mechanics," "surgeons, clerks," "decently dressed mechanics," and, most alarming of all, "youths and females of decent appearance" (up to 100 young women on occasion). Yet this cross-section of the self-improving classes roared with unseemly laughter when Taylor suggested that the Israelites ate manure rather than manna, or described the Virgin Mary as a young woman who had not been as prudent as she ought, or even implied that Christ had privately revived a sleeping but supposedly dead young woman, "by certain means of connexion with her."[66] The paradox of Rotunda bawdiness and profanity is as baffling to us as it was to Home Office officials, though it clearly represents another reason to question conventional views of early Victorian popular respectability. Perhaps the elevating architecture of the Rotunda, combined with Taylor's scholarly and clerical credentials, gave enough psychological reassurance for attendants to enjoy the Saturnalian elements of the proceedings. Perhaps theater attendance was automatically a moment of license for respectable early Victorians – it seems to have been for Francis Place.[67] Or perhaps, as Peter Bailey has argued, respectability encompassed an elaborate repertoire of roles that could be varied according to context and circumstance.[68]

Some of the high proportion of women attendants at Taylor's services no doubt resembled Eliza Sharples, who was attracted to Rotunda infidelity because it enabled her to discard a stifling regimen of provincial middle-class femininity in favor of exercising political talents in a public forum.[69] But Taylor seems also to have been a magnet for other kinds of feminine longings and frustrations. Carlile described him enviously as "a handsome fellow . . . [who] bewitches by his face and tongue some very smart ladies."[70] Carlile had to battle to win Eliza, whose "wild" and "romantic" nature responded initially to the sensual appeal of the Devil's Chaplain. Taylor's dashing good looks, dandyish style, brooding poetic sensibility, libertinism, and appealing vulnerability echoed the two great romantic heart-throbs of his day, Kean and Byron. If so level headed and respectable a young woman as Jane Austen could number herself among the thousands who longed to love the mad and bad Lord Byron,[71] we should not be surprised at the similar, if more modest, success of Robert, the Devil.

Robert Taylor's career as an irreligious preacher terminated abruptly and appropriately when he fled to Tours in 1834 to avoid paying breach-of-promise damages; thereafter he practiced medicine quietly until his death in

1844. What significance should we attach to this brief but spectacular episode in the history of popular irreligion? Are modern historians right to dismiss Taylor as a freakish figure who belongs outside the broad tradition of Victorian popular Radicalism and free thought? His intellectual contribution to free thought certainly seems to have been slight. The *Diegesis* became "a minor classic" among recondite Victorian freethinkers such as Charles Hennell and Godfrey Higgins in England, and Abner Kneeland and Judge Strange in America.[72] Taylor also helped to ensure that astronomical and mythological critiques of Christianity passed into the rich froth of ideas absorbed by Owenites and Chartists. He influenced Carlile to the extent that the redoubtable infidel spent the last years of his life as a licensed Dissenting minister preaching materialist moral astronomy. But Taylor's real significance lies in having been a conduit of popular Radical-romantic culture. A brief look at the parallel career of a more celebrated early Victorian preacher of irreligion, James "Shepherd" Smith, underscores the point.

Smith, whose growing modern reputation derives from having been a pioneering figure in Owenite–St Simonian feminist and social thought,[73] was undoubtedly a more original thinker than Taylor, but his resemblance and debt to the Devil's Chaplain have not been noticed. Their early lives followed the same romantic-rebellious trajectory. Smith had been similarly drawn to "imaginative literature," especially the works of Shelley, Wordsworth, Byron, Coleridge, and Shakespeare. He too took a university degree in theology, though as a Presbyterian in Glasgow.[74] He too worked for a time as an artist, teacher, and journalist, moving restlessly "with a religious mind dissatisfied and unsettled" through a variety of religious positions. According to an early biographer, the "Eastern tone of thought and expression" and "highly analogical views" of the prophet John Wroe's Christian Israelites enraptured Smith[75] until he came under more sceptical influences. Taylor was among these. Smith wrote to Carlile in 1830 claiming to have studied the Bible "astronomically" in the same way as Taylor for the past three years – "we adopt the same principles." He even endorsed "all [Taylor's] blasphemies," including the belief that the Bible was simply "a divine piece of waggery."[76] Carlile's reply is lost, but he must have encouraged the promising young disciple to join the Rotunda infidels in London.

The respectable-looking audiences of around 800 (100 of them women) who listened to Smith preach in Taylor's stead during November 1832 saw a Scottish incarnation of the Devil's Chaplain. He preached in a powerful Scottish brogue that "brandy, sugar and water" was the only genuine trinity, that Ezekiel was doomed by the Lord to eat dung, that God was to be found in excrement as much as anywhere, and that Christ was "a great bungler at miracle making." He decoded the hidden mysteries of the Bible using astrological "analogies," denounced kings, aristocrats, and priests, equated God and the Devil, denied the existence of Jesus Christ, and urged his listeners to put their trust in universalist principles. The ultra-Radical veteran and informer, Abel Hall, who had been listening to blasphemous sermons for more than twenty-five years, thought Smith's language "the most vulgar and blasphemous I ever heard."[77] Like Taylor, Smith relished "extravagant conceits" and "paradox," the exercise of wit, and the flouting of respectable taboos. He even possessed similar good looks. Smith's "piercing grey eye" and immense "charm," an early disciple tells us, ensured that "throughout his career women of refined minds with 'unfilled aspirations' drifted naturally within his sphere."[78]

Those who read Smith's first periodical, the *Shepherd*, which commenced in the year of Taylor's flight, would have found it as ardently romantic a work as the *Devil's Pulpit*. It quoted Shelley, Byron, and Shakespeare, delighted in astrological demystification, and presented much of its rationalism in the form of theatrical dialogues.[79] Like Taylor, Smith struggled throughout most of his life to make a living as a marginal intellectual, and the works of the Romantics spoke to his predicament. St Simonianism attracted both men in the mid-1830s perhaps because of the movement's idealization of the role of the artist and littérateur. And when Smith eventually became editor of the *Family Herald*, his opening editorial in the year of Taylor's death might easily have been borrowed from the Devil's Chaplain. Citing Coleridge, Smith argued that mankind was drawn to poetry and drama by the deepest laws of nature. Novels, romances, and dramas were the modern counterparts of the sacred parables and allegories of old; "the mystery is unriddled; the darkness is illuminated; vice is punished; innocence is acquitted or justified; and even the most trifling circumstances are discovered to have meaning." Passion for literature was inseparable from religious and political passion, and drama surmounted all. Life itself constituted a type of sacred drama in which "the final denouement and mystery will be dramatized and illuminated in the great consummation."[80] If so, one suspects that the incorrigible infidel trouper Robert Taylor will be there to take the last curtain call.

Notes

1 E. P. Thompson, *The Making of the English Working Class* (Harmondsworth, 1968), p. 844.
2 H. Cutner, *The Devil's Chaplain: Robert Taylor* (London, n.d.), p. 68; Joseph O. Baylen and Norbert J. Gossman (eds), *Biographical Dictionary of Modern Radicals*, Vol. 1: *1770–1830* (Hassocks, Sussex, and Atlantic Highlands, NJ, 1979), pp. 467–70; *Dictionary of National Biography*, Vol. 19, pp. 461–3; J. M. Robertson, *A History of Freethought in the Nineteenth Century* (London, 1929); G. D. H. Cole, *Richard Carlile* (London, 1943), pp. 22–3, 30. The best modern accounts are: Edward Royle, *Victorian Infidels* (Manchester, 1974), pp. 38–42; Joel H. Wiener, *Radicalism and Freethought in Nineteenth-Century Britain: The Life of Richard Carlile* (Westport, Conn., and London, 1983), esp. pp. 141–90.
3 See Wiener, *Radicalism and Freethought*, pp. 76–119; Thompson, *Making of the English Working Class*, pp. 781 ff.; I. D. McCalman, "Popular radicalism and freethought in early nineteenth-century England: a study of Richard Carlile and his followers, 1815–32" (MA, Australian National University, 1975).

4 Rev. Robert Taylor, *First to Thirteenth Moral Discourses* (London, Nov. 1833 to Apr. 1834), *Second Moral Discourse*, p. 18. On this deist milieu, see I. D. McCalman, *Radical Underworld: Prophets, Revolutionaries and Pornographers in London, 1795-1840* (Cambridge, 1988), pp. 188-91.

5 *Lion*, 7 Aug. 1829.

6 Public Record Office, Home Office Papers, "Rewards, pardons and secret service," 64/11, May 1831, f. 227, 9 Apr. 1831, f. 288; HO 40/25, 12 Nov. 1830, f. 262; *Prompter*, 30 Nov. 1830, 2 July 1831.

7 *Prompter*, 20, 27 Nov. 1830.

8 HO 64/11, n.d. [1828], ff. 78a, 80, 85-6.

9 *Lion*, 25 Jan. 1828.

10 Quoted in Wiener, *Radicalism and Freethought*, p. 62.

11 McCalman, *Radical Underworld*, pp. 189-90.

12 See "Memoir of Robert Taylor," *Devil's Pulpit*, 1 (1832), pp. vi-viii; "Life and opinions of Talisiphron," *Philalethean*, 5 Oct. 1833, pp. 6-8, 12 Oct. 1833, pp. 9-16, 19 Oct. 1833, pp. 17-23, 26 Oct. 1833, pp. 25-31, 9 Nov. 1833, pp. 36-40, 16 Nov. 1833, pp. 42-7; Robert Taylor, *Remonstrances addressed to . . . the Lord Chief Justice of Ireland . . .* (Dublin, 1822), pp. 21-3, 34-40.

13 *Philalethean*, 26 Oct. 1833, pp. 30-1.

14 Robert Taylor, *The Holy Liturgy, or Divine Service on the Principles of Pure Deism as performed every Sunday in the Chapel of the Society of Universal Benevolence* (London, 1827), pp. 4-5.

15 *Lion*, 21 Mar. 1828. For examples of other romantic influences, see 7, 14, 28 Mar., 16 May 1828.

16 *Newgate Magazine*, 1 May, 1 Aug., 1 June 1826.

17 *Lion*, 28 Mar. 1828; Taylor, *Fourth Moral Discourse*, pp. 63-4.

18 Taylor, *Third Moral Discourse*, pp. 42-7; *Fifth Moral Discourse*, 1, pp. 65-80, 2, pp. 87-95; *Seventh Moral Discourse*, p. 98; *Ninth Moral Discourse*, pp. 134-40; *Tenth Moral Discourse*, pp. 149-50; *Twelfth Moral Discourse*, pp. 181-91.

19 Marilyn Butler, *Romantics, Rebels and Reactionaries: English Literature and its Background 1760-1830* (Oxford, 1981), pp. 114-31, 182.

20 Robert Taylor, "The Fish," *Philalethean*, 21 Dec. 1833, p. 91; *Syntagma of the Evidence of the Christian Religion . . .* (London, 1828); *The Diegesis: Being a Discovery of the Origin, Evidences and Early History of Christianity* (London, 1829).

21 W. H. Oliver, *Prophets and Millennialists: the Uses of Biblical Prophecy in England from the 1790s to the 1840s* (Oxford, 1978), p. 172.

22 *Lion*, 10 Apr. 1829.

23 Quoted in Cutner, *Devil's Chaplain*, p. 46.

24 Quoted in Robertson, *History of Freethought*, 1, p. 65.

25 HO 64/18, 13 Nov. 1830, f. 4a.

26 *Prompter*, 13 Aug. 1831 [Thomas Bull]; Richard Carlile Papers, Huntington Library, California, H.J.T. to Robert Taylor, 17 July 1831.

27 HO 64/11, 15 July 1831, f. 347.

28 *Prompter*, 13 Nov. 1830.

29 *Prompter*, 4, 11 Dec. 1830; *Devil's Pulpit*, 13 June, 27 Nov. 1830.

30 For evidence of numbers, see HO 64/11, Nov.-Dec. 1830, ff. 151, 152a, 173, 212; HO 65/18, ff. 37-37a, 42a; *Prompter*, 11, 18, 25 Dec. 1830; HO 40/25, 4 Dec. 1830.

31 HO 40/25 [Dec. 1830], f. 281; HO 64/11 [Nov.-Dec. 1830], ff. 147, 152, 205.

32 Allardyce Nicoll, *A History of Early Nineteenth Century Drama*, 2 vols (Cambridge, 1930), Vol. 1, pp. 83, 228, Vol. 2, pp. 303-4, 322, 440.

33 Peter Brooks, *The Melodramatic Imagination* (New Haven, Conn., and London,

1976), esp. pp. 37–48; Michael R. Booth, *English Melodrama* (London, 1965), pp. 13–38, 190–9.

34 Louis James, "Was Jerrold's Black Ey'd Susan more popular than Wordsworth's Lucy?," in D. Bradbury, L. James, and B. Sharratt (eds), *Performance and Politics in Popular Drama* (Cambridge, 1980), p. 4.

35 HO 40/25, 10 Nov. 1830, f. 211.

36 HO 40/25, 9 Nov. 1830, f. 154; HO 64/11 [Nov. 1830], f. 253a.

37 HO 40/25 [Nov. 1830], ff. 154–8, 170, 211, 214a; HO 41/26, "Entry books: London disturbances, 1820–48," S. M. Philips to W. B. Gurney, 6 Nov. 1830, f. 44, R. Peel to Lord Mayor, 10 Nov. 1830, reverse of f. 49; HO 49/7, "Law officer entry books, 1817–31," various letters, ff. 406–8.

38 Cited in Cutner, *Devil's Chaplain*, p. 64.

39 *Prompter*, Jan. 1831, enclosed in HO 64/18, ff. 129–129a.

40 Robert Taylor, *Swing: or, Who are the Incendiaries? A Tragedy, Founded on late circumstances, and as performed at the Rotunda* (London, 1831), *passim*.

41 *Prompter*, Jan. 1831, enclosed in HO 64/18, ff. 129a.

42 *Prompter*, 5 Feb. 1831; HO 64/11 [Jan.–Mar. 1831], ff. 181, 197, 199, 206, 210–11, 231a–2, 235, 255, 291, 414; HO 64/18, f. 78.

43 No copy was printed. For a summary and report, see *Prompter*, 26 Feb. 1831.

44 HO 64/13, 20 Mar. 1831, f. 10, Apr. 1831, ff. 50, 69a–70; HO 64/11, Mar. 1831, f. 254a, Apr. 1831, ff. 291a–2; *Prompter*, 9 July 1831.

45 HO 64/13, 3 Apr. 1831, ff. 53–53a, 55.

46 HO 64/13, 20 Mar. 1831, ff. 10a, 19a; 3 Apr. 1831, ff. 61, 63–63a.

47 HO 64/11, 1831, ff. 231, 249, 252, 295. See also R. Carlile, *Scourge for the Littleness of Great Men*, 4 Oct. 1834.

48 HO 64/11, 1831, f. 225.

49 HO 64/11, 1831, f. 302.

50 *Prompter*, 8 Jan. 1831.

51 *Prompter*, 4 June 1831.

52 HO 64/11, Carlile to Taylor, n.d., ff. 337, 339a, 372; HO 64/18, f. 252 (*Devil's Pulpit*, 1832); *Prompter*, 9, 16, 13 July 1832; and the virtually daily correspondence between Taylor and Carlile, July–Aug. 1831, then more intermittently, Mar.–Apr. 1832, Carlile Papers.

53 HO 64/15, 14 Apr., f. 161; see also HO 64/15, Mar.–May, ff. 60–60a, 62, 64–64a, 67, and a separate set of reports from G. Ball, Feb.–Apr. 1834, ff. 144, 147, 161, 164; HO 64/19, "G. Ball," 26 Mar. 1834.

54 H. Vizetelly, *Glances Back through Seventy Years*, 2 vols (London, 1893), Vol. 2, pp. 98–9.

55 *Bell's Life in London*, 14, 30 Nov. 1830, 10 July 1831, 28 Sept., 5 Oct. 1834.

56 *Paul Pry*, 13, 20 May 1826.

57 C. Barker, "Theatre for the people," in K. Richards and P. Thompson (eds), *Essays on Nineteenth-Century British Theatre* (London, 1971), pp. 17–18, 21.

58 See, for example, HO 64/13, 20 Mar. 1831, ff. 24–5, 3 Apr. 1831, ff. 50–50a.

59 Vizetelly, *Glances Back*, Vol. 1, p. 121.

60 McCalman, *Radical Underworld*, chs 6–9.

61 Booth, *English Melodrama*, pp. 46–7, 61–2; Joseph Donohue, *Theatre in the Age of Kean* (Oxford, 1975), pp. 112–18, 181–2.

62 HO 64/11 [1831], ff. 192, 210b.

63 Taylor to Carlile, 31 July 1831, Carlile Papers.

64 Taylor, *Third Moral Discourse*, p. 42; *Fourth Moral Discourse*, pp. 63–4.

65 Brooks, *Melodramatic Imagination*, pp. 43–4.

66 HO 64/13, 13 Nov. 1830; HO 64/15, 30 Mar. 1834.

67 Mary Thale (ed.), *The Autobiography of Francis Place* (Cambridge, 1972), pp. 268–70.
68 Peter Bailey, " 'Will the real Bill Banks please stand up?' Towards a role analysis of mid-Victorian working-class respectability," *Journal of Social History*, 12 (1979), pp. 336–53.
69 I. D. McCalman, "Females, feminism and freelove in an early nineteenth-century radical movement," *Labour History*, 38 (May 1980), pp. 12–13.
70 Carlile Papers, Carlile to William Haley, 14 June 1825.
71 Rupert Christiansen, *Romantic Affinities* (London, 1989), esp. pp. 179–224.
72 Cutner, *Devil's Chaplain*, pp. 51–2, 65–6; Robertson, *History of Freethought*, Vol. 1, pp. 64–5.
73 John Saville, "J. E. Smith and the Owenite movement," in Sidney Pollard and John Salt (eds), *Robert Owen: Prophet of the Poor* (London and Basingstoke, 1971), pp. 115–44; Oliver, *Prophets*, pp. 197–217; Barbara Taylor, *Eve and the New Jerusalem* (London, 1983), esp. pp. 162–72.
74 Saville, "J. E. Smith," p. 115; Oliver, *Prophets*, p. 197.
75 W. Anderson Smith, *"Shepherd" Smith, the Universalist. The Story of a Mind: Being a Life of the Rev. James E. Smith, MA* (London, 1892), p. 49.
76 Carlile Papers, James Smith to Carlile, Ashton under Lyne, n.d. [c. 1830].
77 HO 64/12, Dec. 1832, f. 189; HO 64/11, Nov. 1832, ff. 170–1, 177, 180. See also HO 64/18, Sept. 1832, ff. 556–7, 560–3; *Cosmopolite*, 22 Sept. 1832.
78 Smith, *"Shepherd" Smith*, p. 205.
79 *Shepherd*, 30 Aug. 1834, 11 Apr., 16 May, 11 July 1835, 8 Jan., 15 Jan., 1 Mar., 1 July, 5 Aug., 12 Aug. 1837.
80 *Family Herald*, 6 Jan. 1844, pp. 553–4.

Chapter 4

Between Genesis and geology: Darwin and some contemporaries in the 1820s and 1830s

Sandra Herbert

In describing the time-reckoning system employed by the Nuer of Sudan, the anthropologist E. E. Evans-Pritchard concluded in regard to their long-term measures:

> What strikes one most about the time dimension of this Nuer world are its narrow limits. Valid history ends a century ago and tradition, generously measured, takes us back only to the beginnings of lineages, i.e. some ten to twelve generations. . . . Consequently, though it astounded me, it is in no way remarkable to Nuer, that the tree under which mankind came into being was still standing in Western Nuerland a few years ago and would still be standing had it not recently been burnt down.[1]

Keeping historical records has allowed literate societies to imagine a greater temporal dimension to their world than did the Nuer. Questions of origins, however, have not diminished. As the field of geology emerged into autonomy in the late eighteenth and early nineteenth centuries, primarily in France, Britain, and the Germanies, practitioners faced the task of integrating what was known of human history, much of it contained in sacred narrative, with what could be told from topography and the strata of the earth. Further, during the same period, and in the same countries where geology was establishing itself as a discipline, an enlightened skepticism cautioned against credulity in all areas of knowledge. On occasion skeptics challenged the opinions of geologists. Voltaire argued against the developmental view of the world: "Men have not been fish. . . . I cannot repeat too often that we are not gods who can create a universe with a word."[2] Other critics unjustly ridiculed the allegedly extraterrestrial origin of meteorites as "folk tales" and "fairy tales."[3] In the task of combining human history with geology, similar skepticism was expressed with regard to the use of ancient texts. Nonetheless, one strand of that skepticism called for subjecting such texts to scrutiny rather than disallowing them. On this basis, with Moses read as "neither prophet nor scientist, but *historian*,"[4] Genesis and geology might share common ground.

The classic formulation of the issue in the English-speaking world is Charles Coulston Gillispie's *Genesis and Geology: A Study in the Relations of Scientific*

Thought, Natural Theology, and Social Opinion in Great Britain, 1790–1850, first published in 1951.[5] The title of the present essay is intended to evoke that work, for Gillispie identified the dramatis personae of the story and its temporal boundaries. That there is anything new to be said on the subject arises largely from the attention given by scholars in the last forty years to various leading actors in the story, and on a growing appreciation of Charles Darwin's early achievements as a geologist.[6] The significance of the latter point is that Darwin can now be seen as entering the debate not in 1859, with publication of *The Origin of Species*, but earlier, in the 1820s and 1830s, when he was working as a geologist. To underline that point, this essay is organized around consideration of Darwin and some of his contemporaries. The chief figures to be treated include Georges Cuvier (1769–1832), Robert Jameson (1774–1854), William Buckland (1784–1856), Adam Sedgwick (1785–1873), John Stevens Henslow (1796–1861), Charles Lyell (1797–1875), Robert FitzRoy (1805–65), and Darwin himself (1809–82). All were Protestant in religion; all except FitzRoy made lasting contributions to the science of geology. Cuvier set the terms of the debate. Jameson, Buckland, Sedgwick, and Henslow were initially in agreement with Cuvier; Lyell broke with him publicly to the greatest effect. FitzRoy, Darwin's superior aboard HMS *Beagle*, is interesting as a counterpoint to the others. Darwin himself appears as a student, observer, and eventually, partisan.

Georges Cuvier was the author of what one commentator has referred to as the "Cuvierian compromise," but what I would describe in a more favorable light as the "Cuvierian synthesis."[7] Cuvier found a way of combining what he termed civil history, much of it drawn from sacred narrative, with his profoundly original understanding of the history of the earth. His synthesis is contained in the "Discours préliminaire" to his great multivolume work, *Recherches sur les ossemens fossiles* (1812). This *Preliminary discourse* was republished separately in English in 1813 and in French in 1825, both under new titles, and went through numerous editions and printings throughout the nineteenth century.[8] The message of the work remained constant, however, and its appeal is easy to see, even from the perspective of the present day. First, Cuvier's approach to Genesis is resolutely historical. The text is treated as one of the "histories of nations" that are useful for the "real facts" they contain among various "interested fictions."[9] The validity of such texts as Genesis rested wholly on the truth of empirical claims, which could be tested by comparison with other ancient writings. Thus Cuvier stressed that the Pentateuch was "received as authentic by the Samaritans as well as by the Jews" and that Egypt, whose history stood behind that of the Jews, was "universally allowed by all the nations of the west to have been the most anciently civilized kingdom on the borders of the Mediterranean."[10] Second, Cuvier judged that the text of Genesis was written by Moses about 3,300 years ago, which was centuries after the flood, but immeasurably long after the "history of thousands of ages which preceded the existence of the race."[11] Although he is not explicit on the subject, Cuvier seems to suggest that evils treated in the Bible can be dated only when they are events in human history for which there were human witnesses. The Bible, therefore, could not be used as a source through which to establish the age of the earth. Thus did Cuvier circumvent a subject that had troubled other authors. Finally, when Cuvier did introduce the subject of the biblical flood, he did so only in the most general terms. The flood appeared in the *Discours* as "an event of an universal catastrophe, occasioned by an irruption of the waters," with a date not "much farther back than five or six thousand years ago."[12]

On the geological side of the synthesis Cuvier drew upon the work that has formed his lasting scientific achievement, the evidence he provided for the extinction of species as a repeated occurrence in the history of life on earth.[13] His reconstructions of fossil quadrupeds provided the main text of the work to which the "Discours préliminaire" was the introduction.[14] In this context the deluge described in ancient literatures appears as but one of a series of violent episodes with the force sufficient to produce profound geological changes including extinctions of species. Evidence for the occurrence of such violent episodes might include overturned strata, "heaps of *debris* and rounded pebbles," and, in the most recent case, the preservation of "carcases of some large quadrupeds which the ice had arrested."[15]

Cuvier's synthesis appealed to the geologist who might wish to emulate him in serving as "an antiquary of a new order."[16] Such a geologist would seek to retain a unified view of history that encompassed traditional accounts and yet, on the geological side, absorbed the destabilizing notion of species extinction. There were weaknesses to Cuvier's argument in the *Discours* – the connections between biblical description and ascribed geological causation are loosely drawn, a perspective is taken on world history that is slighting of non-Western testimony, and Lamarck's transmutationism is pushed aside.[17] Nonetheless, the strengths of the synthesis were apparent to many.

We must next follow the appropriation of the Cuvierian synthesis by the British geologists Jameson and Buckland. Before doing so, however, it would be well to take note of recent work by Toby Appel on the subject of Cuvier's religious views. She has argued that the relatively greater prominence given to religion in the writings of Cuvier's British followers than by Cuvier himself is owing chiefly to the circumstances under which the scientists operated rather than to differences in belief. Appel has pointed to the unsympathetic attitude toward lay interpretations of scripture in Catholic France and to the tradition of natural theology operating in Protestant Britain, with its emphasis on adaptation and contrivance, which Cuvier shared. Appel has also drawn attention to the professionalism of French science and to the dominance in France of the physical sciences, in which area religious discussion was no longer welcome.[18] To her arguments against downplaying the importance of religion to Cuvier, it might be added that in later editions of the *Discours* Cuvier used the term "diluvium," which had been promoted by Buckland.[19]

In considering Darwin and some of his British contemporaries, it is helpful to divide the group in two: Jameson, Buckland, Lyell, Sedgwick, and Henslow on the one hand, FitzRoy and Darwin on the other. Members of the first group were older, all born in the eighteenth century, and their reactions to the issues addressed by Cuvier's *Discours* were fresher and more direct. FitzRoy and Darwin, born in the first decade of the nineteenth century, came on the scene as authors after the wave of reaction marked by publication of the first volume of Lyell's *Principles of Geology* in 1830.[20] Further, FitzRoy and Darwin are separable from the others through their common experience during the voyage of HMS *Beagle* in 1831–6, summarized in a joint publication of 1839.[21] In the discussion of the views of both groups, it must be emphasized that the issue summarized by the term "Cuvierian synthesis" was a complicated one. More people were involved than those whose names are mentioned here. Issues overlapped or came in chains: the deluge and its alleged geological traces, the antiquity of the human species, the fixity of species, and the rate of geological change. Then too, even for the prominent figures the reasons for shifting opinions are not fully known, though recent examination of lecture notes for several of them has proved illuminating. Yet, despite complexities, some salient points can be brought forward that suggest how the issue stood for Darwin and those around him by the end of the 1830s.

In 1813 Cuvier's "Discours préliminaire" was introduced to the English-speaking world in an edition for which preface and notes were supplied by Robert Jameson, since 1803 holder of the Regius chair in natural history at the University of Edinburgh. In the opening sentence of his preface Jameson demonstrated that he had not understood, or preferred to ignore, Cuvier's argument. Rather than following Cuvier in suggesting how the occurrence of the biblical flood might be inferred from the combined testimony of records of ancient peoples, Jameson appealed to revelation:

> Although the Mosaic account of the creation of the world is an inspired writing, and consequently rests on evidence totally independent of human observation and experience, still it is interesting . . . to know that it coincides with the various phenomena observable in the mineral kingdom.[22]

Although this sentence was dropped after the second edition, damage had already been done, for some of Cuvier's British readers continued to be ignorant of his subtle and scholarly method.[23] In any event, Jameson's five editions of Cuvier's *Discours* gave the work wide currency and provided Jameson the opportunity to expand his notes, which are particularly valuable to the historian for the record they provide of his changing opinions. Joan Eyles, Leroy Page, and James Secord have noted this fact, and in a fine piece of detective work Secord has shown how very far Jameson's opinions on species had changed by the date of the last edition.[24]

Still within the decade of the 1810s, however, William Buckland, reader in mineralogy (1813) and geology (1818) at Oxford, entered on a more significant engagement with Cuvier than Jameson had. Buckland's reputation in the history of geology has suffered from an obscurantist taint inevitably settled on an author, later Dean of Westminster (1845), who entitled one of his books *Reliquiae Diluvianae* – "Remains of the Deluge."[25] But Cannon has reoriented our view of Buckland by measuring his opinions against contemporary views within the Anglican Church. The evangelical John Sumner, later Archbishop of Canterbury (1848), was his foil. In Cannon's view:

> Buckland's insistence on the actual evidence of a deluge was partly an answer to Sumner's insistence that the Mosaic records were much more reliable than geological evidence. . . . For years one of Buckland's roles was to keep room clear for an independent evaluation of scientific evidence within the Anglican community, in spite of increasing pressures from Evangelicalism and, later, from Tractarianism.[26]

Further, in a major study, Nicholaas Rupke has reassessed Buckland's career against the background of university politics. In this light Buckland's bow toward historical knowledge, including biblical texts, is seen as a means to find a place for the fledgling science of geology in the Oxford curriculum, which was weighted toward the classics.[27] In any case, Cuvier and Buckland found in each other kindred spirits, Buckland pursuing Cuvier's paleontological leads and serving as his host in England in 1818.

The one feature in their relationship to which I should like to draw attention is that Buckland contributed to both sides of the Cuvierian synthesis. On the geological side Buckland's efforts are well known. In regard to the biblical flood, for example, he listed what he believed were its signs: rough gravels, valleys of denudation, and particular kinds of organic remains.[28] Indeed, his enumeration of signs was so empirical and his interpretation so sharp that they invited reaction. Buckland spoke straightforwardly in favor of a "transient deluge, affecting universally, simultaneously, and at no very distant period, the entire surface of our planet."[29] On the historical side Buckland's contributions have not been seen as clearly. Partly this is so because he did not follow Cuvier directly in arguing for the historical significance of the flood on the grounds of a comparison of ancient literatures. When speaking of texts he turned rather more comfortably to Bacon's contrast between the "Book of God's Word" and the "Book of God's Works."[30] Yet, in his practice over a lifetime, Buckland inclined toward Cuvier's intent to seek documentation for ancient human society and to integrate that history into geological understanding. Indeed, the very name Buckland chose for diluvian gravel – "diluvium" (flood, deluge, or inundation) – signaled in its Latin origin the union between historical and geological knowledge that he favored.[31] Also, Buckland hoped that one day human remains would be found in the diluvium.[32] There were other signs of Buckland's proclivities as a historian. In 1842 he suggested that the Regius chair of modern history be used to teach ethnography, and in 1844 he contributed a paper to the first meeting of the British Archaeological Association.[33] In sum, then, even when in 1832 a beleaguered Buckland fell silent on the question of the identity of the biblical flood with the last geological upheaval, and in 1836 retracted his previous position equating the two, he remained true to the balance of Cuvier's interests and to his program.[34]

Darwin enters this story in the 1820s, and as a student, first at Edinburgh (1825–7), where he attended the lectures of Robert Jameson, and then at Cambridge (1828–31), where he received training from Adam Sedgwick and John Stevens Henslow, both of whom were initially in accord with Buckland.[35] As Rupke has argued, there was a split between Edinburgh and the English universities on issues in geology including that surrounding the diluvium, and it is therefore of interest that Darwin's own movement traced the lines of the dispute. At Edinburgh, known for the strength of its medical faculty, he was a medical student. At Cambridge his declared vocation was for the church. His interests were therefore in harmony with the strengths of these institutions in the periods when he was in residence. While he did not leave behind full sets of notes from his student years, what he would have heard from his teachers can be inferred from their writings.

On 25 November 1826 Jameson signed the preface to his fifth and last edition of Cuvier's *Discours*. That same month Darwin signed the matriculation book for his second year at Edinburgh. One of the classes for which he enrolled was Jameson's in natural history, which included geology.[36] In notes to his fifth edition of Cuvier, and presumably also in lectures, Jameson described how opinion on the geological deluge was split:

> We have been frequently requested to give the two views, in regard to the universal deluge, namely, that which maintains that it is proved by an appeal to the phenomena of the mineral kingdom; the other, which affirms that that great event has left no traces of its existence on the surface or in the interior of the earth. M. Cuvier's Essay, and Professor Buckland's Reliquiae, are the best authorities for the first opinion; while numerous writers have advocated the second.[37]

While Jameson now clearly ranged himself with the latter group, it is interesting that he chose to present opinion as divided. When faced with a choice, he equivocated. Similarly, as Secord has shown, Jameson softened his shift on the concomitant issue of transmutation by publishing his views anonymously.[38] Jameson's own state of mind may well reflect his milieu, however, for on 26 December 1826 Georges Cuvier was proposed but blackballed for honorary membership in the Plinian Society, a university group devoted to natural history of which Darwin was a member.[39]

In Edinburgh the man from whom Jameson drew most considerably in his new views was John Fleming, a minister in the Church of Scotland (1806) and later Professor of Natural Philosophy at King's College, Aberdeen (1834). Fleming argued brilliantly against Buckland, and drew a rebuke from him for the immoderacy of his tone, but what is striking in much of Fleming's argument is his own biblical literalism.[40] What one finds in Fleming is a very different attitude toward text than in Cuvier. Cuvier had attempted to conciliate ancient traditions and had read loosely in order to do so. Fleming went back to a close reading of the biblical text, all the while professing against a union of geology and revelation as "indiscreet."[41] Thus, Fleming could argue against the Cuvier–Buckland notion of a violent flood on narrow textual grounds. In a passage later alluded to by Lyell, Fleming wrote:

> But if the supposed impetuous torrent excavated valleys, and transported masses of rocks to a distance from their original repositories, then must the soil have been swept from off the earth to the destruction of the vegetable tribes. Moses does not record such an occurrence. On the contrary, in his history of the dove and the olive-leaf plucked off, he furnishes a proof that the flood was not so violent in its motions as to disturb the soil, nor to overturn the trees which it supported.[42]

This same attitude on Fleming's part allowed him to choose a very low number – 6,000 years – in referring to the engagement between man and lower animals.[43] Thus, although Fleming's argument was effective against Buckland, he must not be taken to have supplied a substitute for Cuvier's synthesis between geological and human history.

In the later years of the decade of the 1820s resistance increased to the Cuvier–Buckland formulation on the flood. In his book on the geology of central France, George Poulett Scrope did not adopt Buckland's term "diluvium" in his description of surface deposits either in his text or in the exceptionally beautiful views and sections accompanying the volume. He also argued against the diluvial hypothesis as an explanation for the excavation of the valleys in the area he studied. On the historical side his primary contribution was to argue for "almost unlimited drafts upon antiquity" in geological reasoning.[44] The force of Scrope's work was magnified because of its adoption by Charles Lyell, who used it in constructing his arguments for present causes and against a universal flood. These arguments formed the cornerstone of the *Principles of Geology*. In a broad sense Lyell, like Cuvier and Buckland, was interested in forming a synthesis between human history and geology. But where Cuvier and Buckland sought to anchor their synthesis in a discrete event, Lyell's synthesis was methodological. To Lyell, just as the historian had to consider past society in understanding the present, so did the geologist have to consider former landscapes in order to explain present landscapes. As he wrote: "It is easy to imagine the general law by which the present course of Nature is governed, viz., that in each period, the earth's surface and its inhabitants should be influenced by their former existence."[45] More narrowly, as Gillispie wrote in a judgment that still stands, the *Principles of Geology* "administered the *coup de grâce* to the deluge."[46]

In addition to specific arguments, Lyell was important to the "Genesis and geology" debate for his ability to accommodate to change. On the scientific side he began as a student of Buckland's at Oxford, met Cuvier in Paris, and in his early years defended their position on the flood.[47] Within a few years he had developed his own opposing views. Further, over the course of a long life, he had occasion to alter his views on the antiquity of man and the transmutation of species. Bartholomew's analysis of Lyell's intellectual accommodation is most complete.[48] What is perhaps less well known is the extent of Lyell's accommodation in daily life. Raised an Anglican, Lyell joined the large number of men and women in Victorian Britain who sought in Unitarianism a middle ground of belief and practice. He eventually became part of the Unitarian congregation in London that assembled in Little Portland Street.[49] A member of the congregation recalled that "Sir Charles's pew at Portland-street was in full view from that in the gallery in which the Manchester College students sat, and my distinct recollection is that during my own undergraduate years (1868–1872) Sir Charles was regular in his attendance."[50] Thus, while Lyell was a modernizer by virtue of his campaign in the *Principles of Geology* against Mosaic geology and by virtue of his opposition to Anglican hegemony in such important areas of national life as education, he remained a religious man.

Unlike Lyell, Adam Sedgwick, Woodwardian Professor of Geology at Cambridge (1818), and John Stevens Henslow, Professor of Botany (1825), remained within the communion of their birth. Indeed, their Anglican faith brought them together as much as their science, as is evident from the tender affection shown by Sedgwick to Henslow in his final illness.[51] From their combined geological fieldwork on the Isle of Wight in 1819 through their activities on behalf of science at the university in the decades of the 1820s and 1830s, their interests remained mutual and sympathetic. The sequence of Sedgwick's positions on the flood has been established: his positive view of Buckland's treatment of the flood in 1825, together with his adoption of a distinction between diluvial and alluvial deposits; his backing away from Buckland's position in 1826–7; and his utter abandonment of a geological role for the biblical flood in 1830–1 following publication of the first volume of Lyell's *Principles*.[52] Henslow's views on the flood are less well known than Sedgwick's, but are of interest because of the greater intimacy between Henslow and Darwin than between Sedgwick and Darwin.

Like Sedgwick, Henslow had responded to Buckland's diluvialism with a corroborative contribution. In 1823 Henslow put forward a hypothesis of a nonmiraculous cause for the deluge, one that would employ the ordinary means of nature and also coincide with the account given in Genesis. He suggested that the nucleus of a comet composed of aqueous vapor might have fallen to earth, descending in the form of rain to create a flood. Water gained in this process might then have been partly absorbed by the solid portion of the earth; this last Henslow regarded as a key point in his argument.[53] So far as is known, Henslow did not comment again in print regarding the scientific aspect of Buckland's diluvialism; presumably he followed Sedgwick and other leading English geologists in altering his views on diluvium in the late 1820s and early 1830s.

Yet even if Henslow did not leave behind a record of the entire range of his opinion, he did make numerous remarks over the course of his career suggesting how one ought to read sacred texts in the light of scientific evidence. These remarks are important as indicating the direction from which Henslow approached the subject of the historicity of the flood. These remarks are also important as suggesting what point of view Darwin would have heard expressed at Cambridge from the teaching officer of the university with whom he had the greatest contact and with whom he had considered reading divinity.[54] In his *Autobiography* Darwin emphasized, alongside Henslow's sheer goodness, his orthodoxy: "He was deeply religious, and so orthodox, that he told me one day, he should be grieved if a single word of the Thirty-nine Articles were altered."[55] If examined more closely, however, Henslow's views as expressed at the time were not as set as Darwin's anecdote suggests and indeed were in flux on points regarding biblical interpretation.

Henslow's interest in scriptural interpretation was intense in the late 1820s. In the preface to the published version of a sermon on the "First and Second Resurrection" preached in 1829 he argued for the study of prophecy:

> In critical and philological enquiries the Bible must be studied like any other book, but that we may comprehend what is spiritual, we should remember that the Prophets, among whom are the Apostles, had all of them the same long vista of futurity before their eyes, and in looking down it, each was suffered to catch certain hasty and partial glimpses of events to come, to be seen only through the distorting medium of types and visions, as the Holy Ghost thought fit to represent them.[56]

This quotation illustrates both the seriousness of Henslow's attention to scripture, including prophecy, and his provision for differing modes of interpretation. The next relevant text, scientific rather than religious in character, is Henslow's *Descriptive and Physiological Botany* of 1836. After speculating on the botanical history of the earth, Henslow closed his book with the following statement:

> The commentator who wishes us to pay attention to his interpretations of the sacred text, must not proceed upon the supposition that there has been any thing written in the Bible for our learning, which can possibly be at variance with the clear and undeniable conclusions deducible from other and independent sources. If the letter does not announce a particular fact *revealed* in the works of the creation, a true believer will immediately infer that the letter (though it have the authority of inspiration) was not intended to teach that fact. When the philologist has ably interpreted the letter, the aid of the natural historian may still be needed before the divine

can safely pronounce upon the exact scope and meaning of the instruction which it was intended to convey.[57]

Despite some obscurity (the question of what would count as a revealed fact), Henslow's statement suggests a criterion by which to judge the propriety of interpretations of scripture; where the literal meaning of a text contradicts a known scientific fact, one may presume that the text was not intended to be read for that meaning. Gauging the intent of the author of the text thus becomes paramount, and one may at least speculate that Henslow's elaboration of this view at a prominent point in this book reflected, among other things, recent rethinking of diluvial theory within his Cambridge circle.

What one finds in Henslow, then, is a willingness to take the Bible very far at points with regard to its literal meaning but an insistence that truth is one, and that therefore literal readings yield where scientific findings call them into question. Such a view would accommodate either an integration of geological history with the Noachian flood or a disengagement of the two. Thus, with characteristic caution, Henslow could have altered his position on Buckland's diluvial theory without altering his views on scriptural interpretation. Presumably something of his approach would have been known to Darwin, who, in the latter half of his time at Cambridge, "took long walks with him on most days."[58] In his autobiographical recollections of his thoughts on religion while a student and during the voyage, Darwin cast himself as seeking to be convinced of the simple truth or falsity of the scriptures, but one may posit that at the time Henslow's more nuanced view was available to him as well.[59] When Henslow advised Darwin to get and study a copy of the recently published first volume of Lyell's *Principles*, but "on no account to accept the views therein advocated," he was warning Darwin away from Lyell's uniformitarianism, rather than from his critique of diluvial theory.[60]

Once Darwin had left the hands of Sedgwick and Henslow, he passed into the domain of Robert FitzRoy, commander and from July 1835 captain of HMS *Beagle*, with whom he lived on intimate terms for much of the five years from December 1831 to October 1836. What is known of FitzRoy's views is primarily from his published account. In his account FitzRoy figures in three capacities: as a representative of the Crown who on occasion might negotiate government business; as a surveying officer responsible for work set out by the hydrographic office of the Navy; and, more privately, as a man committed to promoting Christian missions. FitzRoy's activities to promote Christianity among the Fuegian Indians are well known. In addition, FitzRoy interested himself throughout the voyage in missions – commenting, for example, on denominational differences among missionaries – and in efforts made to translate the Bible into foreign languages. Protestant in sentiment, and passionately anti-Roman, FitzRoy approached scripture from the point of view of individual interpretation. It was from this position that he addressed the questions that concern us in the chapter of his book entitled "A very few remarks with reference to the deluge."

As with others discussed in this essay, FitzRoy's views were in transition. However, whereas the others were moving away from linking human history and geological history according to the terms of Genesis, FitzRoy was moving to reassert the bond. As he described his change of views,

> Much of my own uneasiness was caused by reading works written by men of Voltaire's school; and by those of geologists who contradict, by implication, if not in plain terms, the authenticity of the Scriptures. . . .
> While led away by sceptical ideas, and knowing extremely little of the Bible, one of my remarks to a friend [possibly Darwin], on crossing vast plains composed of rolled stones bedded in diluvial detritus some hundred feet in depth, was "this could never have been effected by a forty days' flood,". . . . I was quite willing to disbelieve what I thought to be the Mosaic account . . . though knowing next to nothing of the record I doubted: – and I mention this particularly, because I have conversed with persons fond of geology, yet knowing no more of the Bible than I knew at that time.[61]

In his remarks on the deluge, FitzRoy then proceeded to read Genesis literally, even taking the "days" of creation to refer to 24-hour days. Oddly, though, he combined biblical quotation with elements drawn from contemporary science, including that of Lyell and Darwin. This mixture of sources gives FitzRoy's intended synthesis an imbalance: on the one side a fixed-point notion of human history drawn from a sincere but untutored reading of Genesis, and, on the geological side, observations made honestly but with only very passing connection to the work of those operating within established traditions of geology. On some points FitzRoy's arguments are utterly unconvincing, as in his explaining away of the fossil record. On other points, where his own direct observations came more into play, he is at least plausible. Thus, for example, FitzRoy argued that the compressed appearance of the shelly deposits at Port St Julian in Patagonia indicated that they had once been subjected to a great weight, which he interpreted as having been the biblical flood.[62]

How could FitzRoy have come to the conclusions he did? Even without knowing the circumstances of his turn toward biblical literalism, one can point to two possible factors; his education was at the Royal Naval College, not at university, and, while in a general sense a man of science, his knowledge was in geography and meteorology rather than in geology. These circumstances help to explain the sharp differences between his views and those of the other British authors we have discussed. Unlike them, he did not have at hand the university-inculcated Baconian canon of a "two books" tradition of interpretation. While, as James R. Moore has argued, the Baconian tradition was a political compromise, it was also a productive compromise, for it enabled adjudication of claims regarding knowledge, without eliminating either biblical studies or natural philosophy.[63] These rules of jurisdiction FitzRoy did not learn, or, if he learned them, did not observe. On the geological side, FitzRoy appears to have been ignorant, possibly willfully so, of the vast progress in stratigraphy and paleontology. It is thus ironic that it was FitzRoy who presented Darwin with a copy of the first volume of Lyell's *Principles*. Later, after the voyage, FitzRoy would not have been made easy by the relaxed agreement between his former shipmate and Lyell on the subject of the flood. In 1839, as she was about to read the just-published narrative from the voyage, Darwin wrote to his sister: "You will be amused with FitzRoy's Deluge Chapter – Lyell, who was here to-day, has just read it, & says it beats all the other nonsense he has ever read on the subject."[64]

Sources for considering Darwin's own views on diluvial geology are plentiful, but must be read for what is not there, as well as for what is there. For his student years one has at hand the views of his teachers; for his years aboard the *Beagle* there exists a full run of geological notes, organized chronologically; and for the years after 1836 there are his publications.[65] In addition there are his correspondence and autobiography.

The most noticeable feature of Darwin's writing on the issue is that he used the term "diluvium" throughout his notes from the *Beagle* voyage of 1831–6, but not, except with qualification, in his publications upon returning home. His use of the term reflected what he heard when he was in residence at Cambridge, where both Sedgwick and Henslow had adopted Buckland's vocabulary. (There were those, like Scrope, who never used that vocabulary.) By the time Darwin had returned from the voyage, Buckland's diluvial geology was sufficiently discredited that even its vocabulary was no longer in vogue among the best-informed geologists in Britain. The second striking feature of Darwin's notes from the voyage is that he used the term "diluvium" only with reference to the formation of superficial gravels and boulders. There is frequent reference in his notes to the possible agencies of deposition for these gravels, but there is no mention of a biblical flood, or, indeed, of any event described in an ancient text. This absence of reference is consistent with Sedgwick's warning, issued in 1831, against conflating the imperfectly understood phenomena of superficial gravels with the biblical flood:

> It was indeed a most unwarranted conclusion, when we assumed the contemporaneity of all the superficial gravel on the earth. We saw the clearest traces of diluvial action, and we had, in our sacred histories, the record of a general deluge. On this double testimony it was that we gave a unity to a vast succession of phaenomena, not one of which we perfectly comprehended, and under the name diluvium, classed them all together.[66]

Finally, the third feature of interest in Darwin's notes is that he shifted his explanation of the causes for diluvium during the course of the voyage. Initially, like his teachers, he traced superficial gravels to debacles rushing overland. By the end of the voyage he traced most superficial gravels to submarine deposition. In this he was following Lyell's lead.[67]

Following the voyage Darwin did continue to work with those geological phenomena that had been classified as the diluvium. In particular, he explained the deposition of many superficial boulders present in the south of the South American continent, and elsewhere on the globe, by the mechanism of floating icebergs. Ironically, between the time when the text for Darwin's narrative was set in print and the date of publication of the book, Louis Agassiz had suggested the mechanism of glacial deposition for erratic boulders. In an addendum to his text Darwin countered Agassiz's alternative explanation, with brio if not ultimate success.[68] Darwin, like other geologists, later admitted the glacial explanation for most instances of superficial gravel deposits and erratic boulders previously classed as diluvium.

After returning to England, Darwin also contributed to the other side of what I have termed the Cuvierian synthesis. He did not do so in the manner of Cuvier and Buckland, by interpolating his reading of ancient texts with knowledge derived from geological evidence. Indeed, by this period his autobiography suggests that he no longer accepted the historical claims of the Genesis narrative.[69] (Darwin's change of views on religious matters was facilitated by his own complex religious heritage – part Anglican, part Unitarian, and all touched by the legacy of his grandfather Erasmus.)[70] But he did take up the subject of human origins in a series of private notebooks, opened following his adoption of the transmutationist hypothesis in 1837.[71] This exploration of human origins was thoroughly integrated with his geological views.

In sum, for Darwin, by 1839, the date of publication of the narrative of the *Beagle* voyage, the task of integrating human and geological history was very much in process, even without the unifying event of the biblical flood. In this light the Cuvierian synthesis, signified in Britain by the term "diluvium," seems not so much erroneous as premature. To supply all of the elements for a stable synthesis would require the efforts of many scholars – Darwin among them – over the course of succeeding decades. In the meantime, the presence of unstable, if recurring, solutions, such as FitzRoy's, served in part to underline the absence of consensus.

In reviewing the diluvial debate one is struck by Gillispie's characterization of it as "one of religion . . . *in* science rather than one of religion *versus* science."[72] A complicating feature for the debate was that the religion that was *in* science included the ancient history of human society as presented in sacred texts. Thus much of the debate focused on questions of interpretation, that is, whether the ancient narratives ought to be read comparatively, or literally, or with consideration of the intent of the author. With the flood out of the way, however, geologists wished to step away from the texts and interpretations that had figured in the debate. They wished to separate Genesis from geology. This wish on the part of geologists entailed what Gillian Beer has described as "the desire for autonomy which has, from time to time, involved repudiating and suppressing links between the fields."[73] Thus certain combinations would have seemed in poor taste to geologists in the 1840s, such as that suggested by the title Buckland planned to give the second volume of his book on the flood: *Reliquiae Diluviales et Glaciales* – Diluvial and Glacial Remains.[74] Although Buckland had repudiated the biblical connection of the last flood, and had integrated Agassiz's glacial key into his work, his use of diluvial language, recalling the scriptures, would have seemed as atavistic to his fellow geologists as his Latin.

NOTES

1 E. E. Evans-Pritchard, "Nuer time-reckoning," *Africa*, 12 (1939), pp. 215-16.
2 Francis C. Haber, *The Age of the World: Moses to Darwin* (Baltimore, Md., 1959), p. 109.
3 Ursula B. Marvin, "Meteorites, the moon and the history of geology," *Journal of Geological Education*, 34 (1986), p. 141.
4 Rhoda Rappaport, "Geology and orthodoxy: the case of Noah's flood in eighteenth-century thought," *British Journal for the History of Science*, 11 (1978), p. 15.
5 Charles Coulston Gillispie, *Genesis and Geology: A Study in the Relations of Scientific Thought, Natural Theology, and Social Opinion in Great Britain, 1790-1850* (Cambridge, Mass., 1951; paperback, New York, 1959).
6 Sandra Herbert, "Darwin as a geologist," *Scientific American*, 254 (May 1986), pp. 116-23.
7 Haber, *Age of the World*, p. 206. Although she does not use the phrase "Cuvierian synthesis," my interpretation follows Dorinda Outram, *Georges Cuvier: Vocation, Science and Authority in Post-Revolutionary France* (Manchester, 1984), ch. 7.
8 Georges Cuvier, *Recherches sur les ossemens fossiles de quadrupèdes*, 4 vols (Paris, 1812). The "Discours préliminaire" was published separately in English as *Essay on the Theory of the Earth*, trans. Robert Kerr, with mineralogical notes by Robert Jameson (Edinburgh, 1813). The "Discours" appeared separately in French as *Discours sur les révolutions de la surface du globe, et sur les changements qu'elles ont produit dans le règne animal* (Paris, 1825). While the *Discours* went through many editions in the nineteenth century, published alone or as part of the *Recherches*, the only four new versions were those of 1812, 1821, 1825, and 1830. This information is on the authority of Jean Chandler Smith who is presently preparing a Cuvier bibliography. For comparison of the different editions of the *Discours*, see Outram, *Georges Cuvier*, pp. 239-40, n. 1.
9 Cuvier, *Essay on the Theory of the Earth* (1813), p. 147.
10 Ibid., pp. 147-8.
11 Ibid., pp. 147, 181.
12 Ibid., pp. 148, 171.
13 For explanations of Cuvier's paleontology, see M. J. S. Rudwick, *The Meaning of Fossils: Episodes in the History of Palaeontology* (London and New York, 1972), ch. 3; and William Coleman, *Georges Cuvier, Zoologist: A Study in the History of Evolution Theory* (Cambridge, 1964), ch. 5.
14 For a summary of the contents of Cuvier's work on fossil quadrupeds and for outlines of geological and paleontological successions and catastrophes as understood by Cuvier, see Coleman, *Cuvier*, pp. 126, 128, 133.
15 Cuvier, *Essay on the Theory of the Earth* (1813), pp. 16, 15.
16 Ibid., p. 1. On Cuvier's enlarged sense of his role as a paleontologist, see Outram, *Georges Cuvier*, p. 150.
17 Cuvier, *Essay on the Theory of the Earth* (1813), sections 6, 32, 30.
18 Toby A. Appel, *The Cuvier-Geoffroy Debate: French Biology in the Decades before Darwin* (Oxford, 1987), pp. 56-7. For a differing view see Outram, *Cuvier*, pp. 143-7.
19 Cuvier, *Discours sur les révolutions*, pp. 288-9; Georges Cuvier, *Essay on the Theory of the Earth*, with geological illustrations by Robert Jameson (5th edn, Edinburgh and London, 1827), pp. 243-4.

20 Charles Lyell, *Principles of Geology*, 3 vols (London, 1830, 1832, 1833).
21 Robert FitzRoy (ed.), *Narrative of the Surveying Voyages of His Majesty's Ships "Adventure" and "Beagle" between the Years 1826 and 1836, Describing their Examination of the Southern Shores of South America, and the "Beagle's" Circumnavigation of the Globe*, 3 vols and appendix, Vol. 1: *Proceedings of the First Expedition, 1826-1830 under the Command of Captain P. Parker King, RN, FRS*; Vol. 2: *Proceedings of the Second Expedition, 1831-1836, under the Command of Captain Robert FitzRoy, RN* (and appendix); Vol. 3: *Journal and Remarks, 1832-1836*, by Charles Darwin (London, 1839).
22 Robert Jameson, "Preface," in Cuvier, *Essay on the Theory of the Earth* (1813), p. v.
23 As an example of an author respectful toward Cuvier without engaging his historical method in regard to texts, see (W. H. Fitton), "Geology of the deluge," *Edinburgh Review*, 34 (1824), pp. 206, 229-30. Identification of Fitton is from *The Wellesley Index to Victorian Periodicals, 1824-1900*.
24 Joan Eyles, s.v. "Robert Jameson," *Dictionary of Scientific Biography* (New York, 1981); Leroy Page, "The rise of diluvial theory in British geological thought" (Ph.D, University of Oklahoma, 1963), pp. 148-9; and James Secord, "Edinburgh Lamarckians: Robert Jameson and Robert E. Grant," *Journal of the History of Biology*, 24 (1991), pp. 1-18.
25 William Buckland, *Reliquiae Diluvianae; or, Observations on the Organic Remains contained in Caves, Fissures, and Diluvial Gravel, and on Other Geological Phenomena Attesting the Action of an Universal Deluge* (London, 1823).
26 W. F. (S. F.) Cannon, s.v. "William Buckland," *Dictionary of Scientific Biography*; also, Page, "Rise of diluvial theory," pp. 75-7.
27 Nicholaas A. Rupke, *The Great Chain of History: William Buckland and the English School of Geology, 1814-1849* (Oxford, 1983), ch. 4. Rupke's emphasis on university politics and disciplinary hierarchies is surely correct. However, he does bring in the reaction against the French Revolution rather later (pp. 224-5) than one might wish in his accounting for the spirit of the times. Better in this aspect is Adrian Desmond, *The Politics of Evolution: Morphology, Medicine, and Reform in Radical London* (Chicago, 1989). On the bearing of disciplinary hierarchies on the interpretation of texts, see Robert S. Westman, "The Copernicans and the churches," in David C. Lindberg and Ronald L. Numbers (eds), *God and Nature: Historical Essays on the Encounter between Christianity and Science* (Berkeley, Calif., 1986), pp. 76-113.
28 William Buckland, *Vindiciae Geologicae; or the Connexion of Geology with Religion* (Oxford, 1820), pp. 35-8.
29 Buckland, *Reliquiae Diluvianae*, p. 146.
30 Buckland, *Vindiciae Geologicae*, pp. 28-9.
31 On the geological usage of the term, see *The Oxford English Dictionary*; also William Buckland, "Description of the quartz rock of the Lickey Hill . . .," *Transactions of the Geological Society of London*, 5 (1821), p. 533.
32 See Buckland's remarks of 1819 quoted in Rupke, *Great Chain of History*, p. 91; also Buckland, *Reliquiae Diluvianae*, p. 170. The issue of human remains in the diluvium was of greater concern for Buckland than for Cuvier since Buckland believed the land and sea held their same relative relation during the deluge as at present, which Cuvier did not. Buckland did find flints contemporaneous with fossil mammal remains at Paviland Cave, but did not recognize them as such. See F. J. North, "Paviland Cave, the 'Red Lady', the deluge, and William Buckland," *Annals of Science* 5, 2 (1942), pp. 113-14.
33 Rupke, *Great Chain of History*, pp. 203, 95.
34 A student in 1832 recorded Buckland's remarks on the cause of diluvial gravel: "whether is Mosaic inundation or not, will not say." Quoted in Rupke, *Great Chain of*

History, p. 95. Buckland's printed retraction of his former views came in his *Geology and Mineralogy Considered with Reference to Natural Theology*, 2 vols (London, 1836), Vol. 1, p. 95.

35 J. H. Ashworth, "Charles Darwin as a student in Edinburgh, 1825–1827," *Proceedings Royal Society of Edinburgh*, 55, pt 2 (1934–5), pp. 97–113; James Secord, "The discovery of a vocation: Darwin's early geology," *British Journal for the History of Science*, 24 (1991), pp. 133–57; and Sandra Herbert, "Charles Darwin as a prospective geological author," *British Journal for the History of Science*, 24 (1991), pp. 159–92.

36 Ashworth, "Charles Darwin as a student," p. 98.

37 Robert Jameson, "On the universal deluge," in Cuvier, *Theory of the Earth* (1827), pp. 436–7.

38 Secord, "Edinburgh Lamarckians," pp. 9–11.

39 Ashworth, "Charles Darwin as a student," p. 102.

40 The exchange between Fleming and Buckland is contained in the following series: John Fleming, "Remarks illustrative of the influence of society on the distribution of British animals," *Edinburgh Philosophical Journal*, 11 (1824), pp. 287–305; William Buckland, "Professor Buckland's reply to Dr Fleming," *Edinburgh Philosophical Journal*, 12 (1825), pp. 304–19; John Fleming, "The geological deluge, as interpreted by Baron Cuvier and Professor Buckland, inconsistent with the testimony of Moses and the phenomena of nature," *Edinburgh Philosophical Journal*, 14 (1826), pp. 205–39. On Fleming, see Gillispie, *Genesis and Geology*, pp. 123–4; Page, "Rise of diluvial theory," pp. 146–50; Page, "Diluvialism and its critics in Great Britain in the early nineteenth century," in Cecil J. Schneer (ed.), *Toward a History of Geology* (Cambridge, Mass., 1969), pp. 267–71; Page, s.v. "John Fleming," *Dictionary of Scientific Biography*. In the *DSB* entry, but not elsewhere, Page considered the consequences of Fleming's literalism.

41 Fleming, "Remarks illustrative," p. 305.

42 Fleming, "Geological deluge," p. 213 (also see pp. 209–10 against Cuvier's approach to biblical history); Lyell, *Principles*, Vol. 3, pp. 271–3.

43 Fleming, "Remarks illustrative," p. 290.

44 George Poulett Scrope, *Memoir on the Geology of Central France* (London, 1827), p. 165.

45 Charles Lyell, "Analogy of geology and history [1828]," in Leonard G. Wilson, *Charles Lyell: The Years to 1841* (New Haven, Conn., 1972), p. 216. Also see M. J. S. Rudwick, "Historical analogies in the geological work of Charles Lyell," *Janus*, 64 (1977), pp. 89–107.

46 Gillispie, *Genesis and Geology*, p. 140.

47 K. M. Lyell (ed.), *Life, Letters and Journals of Sir Charles Lyell, Bart.*, 2 vols (London, 1881), Vol. 1, p. 139.

48 Michael Bartholomew, "Lyell and evolution: an account of Lyell's response to the prospect of an evolutionary ancestry for man,' *British Journal for the History of Science*, 6 (1973), pp. 261–303.

49 Obituary, Sir Charles Lyell, Bart., *Unitarian Herald* (Manchester), 5 Mar. 1875. Also see R. K. Webb, "The Unitarian background," and Jean Raymond and John V. Pickstone, "The natural sciences and the learning of the English Unitarians," in Barbara Smith (ed.), *Truth, Liberty, Religion: Essays Celebrating Two Hundred Years of Manchester College* (Oxford, 1986), pp. 3–30, 129–64.

50 Dendy Agate in the *Christian Life* (London), 5 Oct. 1912. I am indebted to R. K. Webb for the references to Unitarian newspapers. Leonard G. Wilson kindly supplied me with information regarding Lyell's religious upbringing as well as the reference containing the following reminiscence from Frances Power Cobbe: "The Lyells

regularly attended Mr Martineau's chapel in Little Portland Street, as we did; and ere long it became a habit for us to adjourn after the service to Harley Street [Lyell's home] and spend some of the afternoon with our friends, discussing the large supply of mental food which our pastor never failed to lay before us. Those were never-to-be-forgotten Sundays." F. P. Cobbe, *Life*, 2 vols (Boston and New York, 1984), 2: 404.

51 Leonard Jenyns, *Memoir of the Rev. John Stevens Henslow* (London, 1862),.pp. 261–2.
52 Gillispie, *Genesis and Geology*, pp. 112–13, 142–8; Sandra Herbert, "Darwin as a prospective geological author," *British Journal for the History of Science*, 24 (1991), pp. 170–4.
53 John Stevens Henslow, "On the deluge," *Annals of Philosophy*, 6 (1823), pp. 344–8.
54 Frederick Burkhardt and Sydney Smith (eds), *The Correspondence of Charles Darwin* (Cambridge, 1985), Vol. 1, p. 104.
55 Nora Barlow (ed.), *The Autobiography of Charles Darwin, 1809-1882* (London, 1958), pp. 64–5.
56 John Stevens Henslow, *A Sermon on the First and Second Resurrection Preached at Great St Mary's Church on Feb. 15, 1829* (Cambridge, 1829), p. viii.
57 John Stevens Henslow, *Descriptive and Physiological Botany* (London, 1836), pp. 313–14.
58 Barlow, *Autobiography of Charles Darwin*, p. 64.
59 Ibid., pp. 56–7, 85–7.
60 Ibid., p. 101.
61 FitzRoy, *Narrative of the Surveying Voyages*, Vol. 2, p. 658.
62 Ibid., Vol. 2, p. 666.
63 James R. Moore, "Geologists and interpreters of Genesis in the nineteenth century," in Lindberg and Numbers, *God and Nature*, pp. 322–50.
64 Charles Darwin to Caroline Wedgwood, 27 Oct. 1839, in Burkhardt and Smith, *Correspondence of Charles Darwin*, Vol. 2, p. 236.
65 Darwin's geological notes are in the Cambridge University Library.
66 Adam Sedgwick, Presidential Address (18 Feb. 1831), *Proceedings of the Geological Society of London*, 1 (1826-33), p. 313.
67 Herbert, "Darwin as a prospective geological author," pp. 173–4
68 FitzRoy, *Narrative of the Surveying Voyage*, Vol. 3, pp. 615–25.
69 Barlow, *Autobiography of Charles Darwin*, p. 85.
70 Ibid., p. 22.
71 Paul H. Barrett, Peter J. Gautrey, Sandra Herbert, David Kohn, and Sydney Smith (eds), *Charles Darwin's Notebooks, 1836-1844: Geology, Transmutation of Species, Metaphysical Enquiries* (London and Ithaca, NY, 1987).
72 Gillispie, *Genesis and Geology*, p. ix.
73 Gillian Beer, "Darwin and the growth of language theory," in John Christie and Sally Shuttleworth (eds), *Nature Transfigured: Science and Literature, 1700-1900* (Manchester, 1989), p. 152.
74 Rupke, *Great Chain of History*, pp. 106–7.

Chapter 5

Cultural pluralism and the Board of Deputies of British Jews

David C. Itzkowitz

This essay examines certain developments in the experience of the Anglo-Jewish community during the first forty-five years of the Victorian period, from the 1830s, which saw both the accession of Queen Victoria and the emergence of the Board of Deputies of British Jews[1] as an active body representing the Jewish community, to the late 1870s, when the nature of the Anglo-Jewish community was dramatically changed by the beginning of a massive influx of eastern European Jewish immigrants.[2]

Beginning in the late eighteenth century, the Jewish communities of Europe, which held the vast majority of the world's Jews, underwent the greatest transformation of their existence. In country after country the ghetto walls that had enclosed the communities, both physically and metaphorically, began to crumble. For the first time, Jews were faced with the opportunity of living in a non-Jewish environment, but simultaneously they were faced with the new problem of what it meant to be Jewish in a world where the differences between Jews and non-Jews were no longer defined by law. The way that Jews reacted to this opportunity and to this challenge has been rightly called "one of the central problems of Jewish historiography."[3] In recent years it has become increasingly clear that there were great national variations in the experience of the European Jewish communities and that the German model, which had once been thought to apply to European Jewry as a whole, does not accurately describe the experience of other Jewish communities.

The Jewish experience in England was strikingly different. In England, Jews had not been bound by restrictive laws, and native-born Jews were full English subjects even before the ghetto walls began to crumble elsewhere in Europe. As a result, the English pattern did not conform to that of other European countries.[4] It is my contention that during the Victorian period the leaders of the Anglo-Jewish community, and particularly the members of the Board of Deputies of British Jews, the quasi-official body that represented the Jewish community to the larger community around it, worked toward enunciating a vision of the relationship of Jews and non-Jews that was unique in the European experience, a vision that contained within it elements of cultural pluralism.[5] Nowhere else in European society was the majority community expected to accommodate itself to the cultural peculiarities of minority populations in its midst. Indeed, it has been a major theme of recent historiography to stress the accommodations that Jews had to make in order to fit into European society rather than the reverse.

It has long been recognized that the leaders of Anglo-Jewry were determined, above all, to Anglicize the Jewish community.[6] Anglicization, however, was not an effort to lessen Jewishness. Although the leaders of Anglo-Jewry were determined to purge the community of its foreignness, an impulse rooted in part in the fact that the community continued throughout the nineteenth century to draw immigrants from the Continent, it would be a mistake to view this process of acculturation as an attempt to strip the community of its Jewish character. In fact, the opposite was the case. Throughout the nineteenth century the Board of Deputies sought to create a climate in which it was possible for Jews fully to assimilate into almost all walks of English life without having to move away from the practice of orthodox religion. Indeed, the board sought to maintain the spiritual authority within England of the orthodox authorities, primarily the Chief Rabbi. Thus, the board maintained, as tenaciously as possible, the near-monopoly granted it by the government to regulate the certification of Jewish marriage registrars, in order to prevent the reform movement of the mid-nineteenth century from establishing itself as a religious alternative for British Jews.

The board, therefore, often with the prodding of more activist members of the community, worked hard to create legal avenues through which Jews could continue to practice their religion without suffering undue social or financial hardship. If Jews were truly to become integrated into English life it was necessary for them not to be unnecessarily restricted by law, whether that law was English law or Jewish law. The first stage of the board's activity was aimed at creating a situation in which English law did not restrict Jews. This was a comparatively easy principle to have accepted by a country that prided itself on its religious tolerance, even if that tolerance was often more apparent than real. To be sure, the right of Jews to sit in Parliament, perhaps the most symbolic example of the way that English legal restrictions adversely affected Jews, was achieved only with difficulty, but the right to sit in Parliament was a special case and, in any event, affected only a tiny minority of English Jews.[7] In fact, other than the right to sit in Parliament, most of the legal restrictions against the Jews had long since disappeared from English life by the nineteenth century.

The second set of prohibitions against the full integration of Jews into English life, those raised by Jewish law, were more difficult to overcome. There were, after all, two distinct ways of attacking these difficulties. The first was to weaken the force of Jewish law. This was the most common way that Jews in other European countries, faced with similar dilemmas, reacted. Some Jews, like the adherents of the religious reform movement in Germany, attempted to create a set of Jewish religious practices that were less restrictive and less likely to stand in the way of the "modern" Jew. Other Jews fell away from participation in Jewish religious life. While some continued to maintain a formal connection with Judaism, making a number of personal compromises to overcome the uncompromising tenets of Jewish Law, particularly in the areas of dietary restrictions and sabbath observance, other Jews simply abandoned any sort of religious practice.

What is most striking is the fact that the Board of Deputies rejected this approach. Instead it sought remedies within the laws of England that would allow Jews exemptions from regulations that applied to the bulk of the English population, in order that Jews might integrate into English life without having to violate Jewish law. This approach is unique in nineteenth-century European history and demonstrates that, long before the term was in use, the vision that the Board of Deputies had for England was one that embodied cultural pluralism.

To be sure, even those who held this view were in the process of developing it during the period covered by this essay, and even then held to it only tentatively. Still, however tentatively this position was held, the very fact of it being held at all was unique in the European Jewish experience of the nineteenth century and further extends our understanding of just how "English" the experience of Anglo-Jewry really was.

Although the Board of Deputies was founded in 1760, it remained relatively inactive during the first seventy-five years of its existence.[8] It was only in 1835 that the board drew up its first constitution, which stated that the purpose of the organization was to represent the Jews of Britain "in all matters touching their political welfare." The constitution authorized the board to "adopt such measures as they may deem proper" to "protect and promote the welfare of the Jews." While the constitution makes it clear that the board represented only four London synagogues, it did allow for future growth, providing that other congregations, both in and out of London, could at some future date also send deputies and assume their share of the costs.[9] Over the course of the nineteenth century the size of the board was to grow, though never quickly enough to satisfy those critics within the community who argued, correctly, that it continued to be an oligarchic body composed, for the most part, of members of the London Jewish establishment.

In the following year, 1836, two acts of Parliament gave the board the authority to represent the Jewish community to the state for certain purposes. The Marriage Act and the Registration Act,[10] which were designed to regularize and regulate marriages, provided the forms by which Jewish marriages were recognized by the state. Although Jewish marriages were to be solemnized according to Jewish usages, they were only held to be valid if they were performed in synagogues having an officially recognized secretary who was authorized to keep a marriage register. Authorization was to be granted by the government only to synagogues that were certified by the president of the Board of Deputies. This, of course, gave to the board a great deal of power, because without its certification a synagogue could not be empowered to solemnize marriages.[11] The board, throughout the long period of ascendancy of Sir Moses Montefiore, was to exercise this power, in conjunction with the Chief Rabbi, to protect what it saw as the prerogatives of religious orthodoxy in England.

The new official recognition conferred by the Marriage and Registration Acts led the board, in a letter to the Chancellor of the Exchequer, to claim that it was the only official channel of communication between the Jewish community and the government on all issues touching the secular and political interests of the Jews.[12] Though this claim was not, in fact, recognized as valid by many Jews, including some of the most influential members of the community like Isaac Lyon Goldsmid and David Salomons, it was, generally speaking, recognized as such by most of the non-Jews in England.[13]

From the late 1830s the board became increasingly active on a number of fronts. It never passed up the opportunity to send a loyal address to members of the royal family on their birthdays, on the births of their children, or on any major event in their lives; it increasingly looked out for the interests of persecuted Jews abroad, communicating on their behalf with the Foreign Office, and sending Sir Moses Montefiore, its long-serving president, on a series of overseas missions to intercede on their behalf; and until the admission of Jews to Parliament, it agitated in favor of Jewish political emancipation.

Throughout the 1840s, however, the board's attention was largely taken up either with foreign issues or with continuing to struggle to attract the support of the provincial congregations.[14] Indeed, in its half-yearly report of February 1839, the board observed that "nothing of a Public Nature has transpired affecting the interests of the Jewish Community in the United Kingdom."[15] Much of the energy of the Anglo-Jewish community through the 1840s and early 1850s was sapped by the struggle between the forces of orthodoxy and the adherents of the first reform movement within Anglo-Jewry. By the standards of German reform, the West London Synagogue of British Jews, whose name reflected the attitude of its founders that its members were neither Sephardic nor Ashkenazic but British, was barely distinguishable from orthodoxy. In England, however, the West London Synagogue was regarded with horror by the ecclesiastical authorities and by most of the leadership of lay Anglo-Jewry. Despite attempts made by some within the community to effect reconciliation between the reformers and the orthodox, the West London Synagogue remained ostracized by orthodox Jews and by their supporters, chief among them the leadership of the Board of Deputies. In 1842 the congregation applied to the board for certification of its marriage secretary; but after consulting with the Chief Rabbi, the president of the board, Moses Montefiore, refused to certify the secretary.[16] When, in 1853, several provincial congregations elected prominent reformers as their delegates to the Board of Deputies (the reformed congregation was barred from sending its own representatives) the refusal of the board to allow them to sit led to such uproar at one meeting that it had to be abandoned and the police called to restore order.[17] The controversy surrounding the admittance of the reformers was particularly heated because 1853 also marked the expansion of the Board of Deputies to include many more provincial representatives and the beginning of greater pressure within the Jewish community to expand the political activities of the board. It is no coincidence that in the following year, 1854, the board created its first standing committee, the Law and Parliamentary Committee, "to observe and report legislative measures affecting the Jewish community."[18]

It was not until around midcentury, therefore, that the board was able to devote its full attention to lobbying for legislation designed to place the Jewish community on a footing of equality with other religious groups. Even then, some of its attention was taken up with small matters such as the ratability of synagogue property and the protection of Jewish burial grounds.[19] But attention was increasingly paid to more important issues such as the validity of those Jewish marriages that appeared to be in variance with English law. Questions of marriage were to be a constant feature of the board's work over the years. This was, in part, the result of the official position of the board as the certifier of marriage secretaries. It was also a result of the anomalous position Jews held with regard to the marriage laws, which allowed Jews to solemnize marriages in accordance with their own rites. The validity of marriage was, of course, an important issue because questions of property and inheritance as well as the legitimacy of children all depended upon legal recognition of the validity of Jewish marriage.

Generally speaking, the state, in the person of the Registrar-General, was sensitive to Jewish interests and often took the initiative of contacting the board to be certain that any prospective changes in the law met the needs of the Jewish community. The relationship between the Board of Deputies and the Registrar-General's office exemplified the vision of the place of Jews in British society that had become accepted by the first half of the nineteenth century. This vision held that, though Jews had their own particular religious rites and beliefs that had to be respected, they were, in other respects, fellow subjects with all other British people. Where Jewish laws and customs did not conflict with the laws of the larger community, special efforts could and should be made to allow the Jews to continue their own practices. On those occasions where Jewish custom did conflict with English law, on the other hand, Jews were expected to conform to English law. One example of a possible conflict was the law governing the legality of certain marriages. English law prohibited marriages between people who were related in degrees that would be no bar to marriage according to Jewish law. In those cases, the state made it clear that it could not recognize Jewish marriages that came within the prohibited degrees, and the Jewish authorities, notably the Chief Rabbi and the board, acquiesced even though they felt it to be a hardship and periodically raised the possibility of applying to the government to change the law.[20]

This accommodation between the Jewish community and the state was rarely challenged before the late 1850s. The first major challenge, the controversy over the Divorce Act of 1857, represented an area of conflict between competing views of the place of Jews in English life.[21] Although a legal marriage in England could only be dissolved by act of Parliament before 1857, Jewish law had always recognized the validity of divorce. It was unclear whether English law recognized the validity of Jewish divorce before 1857, although the Chief Rabbi, Nathan Marcus Adler, believed that it did. The Divorce Act of 1857 created a new divorce court and thus raised the question of whether the new act affected the legality of Jewish divorce. To clarify the law and to protect the privilege of the Jewish ecclesiastical authorities, Chief Rabbi Adler and the Board of Deputies had pressed for an amendment to the bill that would exempt the Jews from the provisions of the act, thus implicitly recognizing the validity of Jewish divorce if both parties to the marriage were Jews. Although the Lord Chancellor, Lord Cranworth, agreed to this and a clause was drafted by the solicitor to the Board of Deputies and accepted by the government, the clause was dropped by the government before the third reading of the bill. The decision to drop the clause was the result of private pressure by David Salomons and Lionel de Rothschild, who apparently feared that any legal recognition of the special position of the Jews would harm the campaign for the admission of Jews to Parliament, a campaign being waged on the grounds that there were no essential differences between Jews and other British subjects. It is unclear to what extent the opposition of Rothschild and Salomons was based on purely pragmatic considerations and to what extent their position was based on the strongly held belief that Jewish Emancipation demanded a disappearance of the distinctions between Jews and non-Jews. Whatever the personal beliefs of these two powerful people, however, their influence was enough to ensure the failure of the amendment, and the Board of Deputies was forced to acquiesce.

The admission of Jews into Parliament after 1858 changed the situation. With the granting of what was referred to as emancipation, the attentions of the Jewish community and its leaders could turn to other issues. Emancipation made it possible for them to do so in two ways. First, by leading to the election over the next several years of a number of Jewish Members of Parliament, the measure gave the Jewish community several sympathetic voices inside the House of Commons. The Board of Deputies often approached the Jewish MPs with prospective legislation, and the suggestion was made to grant Jewish MPs ex officio membership on the Board of Deputies. The suggestion was never carried out, however. The leaders of the board, as well as the organs of the Jewish press, carefully took the public position that Jewish MPs represented their constituencies and not the Jewish community.[22] This public position was, of course, a necessary one, for the campaign for Jewish Emancipation was based directly on the argument that Jews were not a separate people but full members of the British polity. Nevertheless, there can be no doubt that, within limits, the Jewish MPs could be expected to remain sensitive to Jewish issues.[23] More importantly, the passage of Jewish Emancipation cleared the Jewish agenda of the last legal bar to full membership of Jews in British life. Or at least it seemed to. If Jews were now legally able to do anything, those things that stood in the way of Jews actually being full participants became all the more glaring. It also became increasingly clear to Jews in England, as it was to Jews elsewhere in Europe, that it was not only legal restrictions that prevented them from this full participation. Jewish rules and customs, among other things, blocked that assimilation into European life that so many of the adherents of emancipation had envisioned.[24]

There were a number of different ways to react to this situation. What was unique to the Anglo-Jewish response was the recognition that, if Jews were to be full members of English society, it was necessary for that society to make special concessions to them. This was different from expecting the larger society to change itself in ways that made it "neutral" to all religious groups, as for example in the abolition of religious tests for taking degrees at Oxford and Cambridge. Increasingly after the late 1850s the Board of Deputies was willing to argue that Jews deserved special exemption from laws that continued to apply to non-Jews. This willingness was not the result of a belief in Jewish separatism, but rather the result of a growing belief that it is legitimate for a polity to recognize the cultural differences among its constituent parts.

In examining the activities of the Board of Deputies from the late 1850s to the late 1870s, it might be useful to divide the domestic activities into several categories for purposes of analysis. I would list these categories in ascending order on a scale of cultural pluralism. At one end are those activities designed to change the climate or the law in England so as to allow Jews to compete and participate in all areas of English life without any real reference to their position as Jews. This position is best exemplified by the campaign to repeal the University Tests, which stood in the way of any other than a member of the established church first from taking degrees at Oxford and Cambridge, and then from obtaining a fellowship. By removing the religious tests, the aim was to make university education and fellowships religiously "neutral," to allow members of all religions to compete for university places and fellowships without any regard to the religion of the candidates.[25] Other such activities included the attempt to legalize marriages that were permitted by Jewish law but prohibited by English law. The energies of the Jewish community were devoted to amending the law so as to legalize these marriages for everyone, rather than working for a Jewish exemption.[26]

The next steps along the continuum were attempts to allow Jews to be excused from taking part in Christian activities. This effort included the attempt to insert conscience clauses in school rules so as to allow Jewish pupils to absent themselves from required worship services.[27] Generally speaking, it was relatively easy to achieve these ends because, by the middle of the nineteenth century, the ideal of religious tolerance had become firmly enough established in English society that few could argue with the principle of not forcing people to take part in the religious worship of a faith not their own, even if they could also agree that compelling people to take part in some kind of religious worship was perfectly acceptable.[28] Thus, when the board opened communication with the government in 1851 over the possibility of allowing Jewish schools to receive the same sort of parliamentary grants that had been made available to the schools of other denominations, the government first had to satisfy itself that there were to be daily readings from the scriptures in the schools. The fact that these readings were entirely drawn from the Old Testament, so as to satisfy the religious scruples of the Jews, was perfectly acceptable to the authorities.[29]

A slightly more problematic case was when Jews began to demand the right, on religious grounds, to be excused from obligations that were imposed on non-Jews where those activities were not themselves of a religious nature. Thus, Jews asked to be excused from performing duties on the sabbath that were forbidden to Jews even though those duties were not specifically religious activities. This is somewhat more extreme than the demand to be excused from taking part in Christian worship because the case could be made that full participation in English life demanded that Jews cast off certain religious scruples. Even in England that was not an unknown position. Henry L. Keeling, a prominent member of the Board of Deputies, for example, was proud of the fact that the government was able to carry a vote on the Reform Bill in 1866 only because the Jewish members of the House of Commons voted on the sabbath. "Patriotism," he wrote, "was rendered paramount to every other feeling, and forms one of the peculiar results arising from Jewish emancipation."[30]

The board exerted its influence to obtain sabbath exemptions in a number of areas. In 1869 the board lobbied, unsuccessfully, to insert a clause in the Endowed Schools Bill to allow Jewish pupils at endowed schools to be excused from school activities on the sabbath and festival days.[31] Similarly, the board was in regular communication with the authorities at Oxford and Cambridge attempting to convince them to schedule examinations so that they did not fall on the sabbath when Jewish candidates could not take them, or barring that, to arrange special examinations on other days to allow Jewish candidates to take them.[32] At the other end of the social scale, the board regularly communicated with both the central government and various local authorities to allow Jewish inmates of prisons and workhouses to be excused from required labor on the sabbath and festivals, a request that was generally granted.[33] The introduction of the ballot in 1872 provided yet another area where Jews could ask for special exemptions. On a number of occasions the board requested local returning officers to schedule polling days so that they did not take place on Jewish sabbath or festival days, and on several occasions the board was willing to assume the expense of rescheduling polling days.[34] It also secured the right of Jews to have their ballot paper marked for them by an elections officer if the election took place on the sabbath, a right they shared with the illiterate.[35]

The most extreme example of political activity undertaken by the Jewish leadership of Victorian England in the service of cultural pluralism was the campaign to secure for Jewish factory and workshop owners an exemption from those provisions of the Factory Acts that forbade work on Sunday. This campaign is an interesting one because it represented the furthest that the leaders of Anglo-Jewry were willing to go, asking not that Jews be allowed to refrain from doing what offended their own religious scruples, but rather that they be allowed to do what offended the religious scruples of others. To be sure, this attempt is somewhat less extreme than it might appear at first glance. The Factory Acts, which prevented the employment of women, children, and young persons on Sunday, had been justified on the grounds of protecting the weak rather than the enforcement of sabbatarianism. As a result, Jews were able to argue that the exemptions they sought could be justified purely on the grounds of fairness, since they limited the number of hours in Jewish workshops to the same number allowed in other workshops. Nevertheless, the request was unprecedented in the history of European Jewry and was extreme enough to divide the members of the board, some of whom were fearful that any such attempt would lead to resentment against the Jewish community.

Even before the coming of political emancipation, the board had found itself involved in attempts to impose sabbatarianism on the English nation. In 1855, following a public protest meeting organized by London Jews, a deputation from the board met with Lord Robert Grosvenor, who had introduced a bill into the House of Commons prohibiting certain kinds of Sunday trading. As a result of the meeting, Grosvenor agreed to introduce a clause exempting the Jews from the operation of the bill. In fact, the bill was dropped, but similar bills continued to be introduced over the course of the century, and the board continued to press either for the defeat of the bills or for the introduction of exemptions in favor of Jews.[36]

It was not until 1867, however, that the board was forced to begin to exert itself in more serious ways. By and large, Sunday trading legislation was the work of a few enthusiasts, and did not have the weight of the government behind it. Thus, although Sunday trading bills were brought in with regularity, they rarely had a chance of passing. Legislation regulating the hours of labor in factories and workshops, on the other hand, was a more serious matter because these laws were, in fact, government measures. The Factory Bill of 1867, which limited the hours that could be worked by women and children in workshops and factories, also prohibited their labor on Sunday and after 2:00 PM on Saturday. This was, obviously, felt to be a hardship by observant Jews who closed their workshops and factories on Saturday, and who made up the hours they lost by employing labor at other times. Several Jewish manufacturers, therefore, pressed the board to intervene in the interests of the Jewish community. The issue first came before the board at its meeting of 30 April 1867, and the deputies were split. Those who favored intervening in the matter argued that this was precisely the sort of issue that the board had been created to deal with. Those on the other side argued that

> it was undesirable to seek special legislation for the Jews, now that they had been emancipated and were on a par with their fellow citizens; that this would be the means of raising prejudice against them; and precedent showed as for instance the Act prohibiting marriage with a deceased wife's sister, that it was contrary to the practice of the Board to seek exemption for the Jewish body from the operation of the Acts which religiously affected it.[37]

In the end, however, the interventionist side won the argument and the board voted, 4–2, to write to the Home Office and to attempt to modify the bill so as to benefit the Jews.[38]

After long negotiations, the government agreed to modify the bill; and as passed, the Factory Act of 1867 contained a provision allowing Jewish manufacturers who closed their factory or workshop on the Jewish sabbath to employ women and children on Saturdays between the hours of sundown, when the sabbath ended, and 9:00 PM.[39]

In fact, however, the exemption granted to the Jews was not of much use. For several months in the year, sunset takes place after nine o'clock, and for the rest of the year, it was difficult to obtain efficient work on Saturday night. Many Jewish workshop owners, particularly in the tailoring and cigar-making trades, in which a significant number of working-class Jews were employed, simply ignored the law and employed Jewish labor on Sunday.[40]

As a result, there followed a number of prosecutions, which were reported prominently in the Jewish press and which were instrumental in arousing a desire within the Jewish community to modify the law. The sense of urgency over the Factory Act was heightened because, although the act was not justified on the basis of Christian sabbatarian principles, the steady introduction of a series of Sunday trading laws throughout the 1860s and 1870s led to a sense that it was becoming more difficult to live a Jewish life in England.[41] This was felt all the more strongly by the growing population of poor, often immigrant Jews who, on the one hand, were likely to be more observant of the sabbath and, on the other, were increasingly crowding into the tailoring and cigar-making trades in London and other English cities.

In the aftermath of the prosecutions, some of its members began to pressure the Board of Deputies into working to secure exemptions. M. S. Oppenheim, who was to take the lead within the board on this issue, proposed an amendment to the Factory Acts, providing that any Jewish factory or workshop occupier who closed his premises on Saturday be allowed to employ women, children, and young people until 2:00 PM on Sunday, this being the hour that the Act mandated the closing of factories on Saturday. Oppenheim's proposal, therefore, provided that the total number of hours worked in the week was the same in the Jewish and non-Jewish factories, the sole difference being that Sunday labor was to be substituted for Saturday labor in the Jewish factories and workshops.[42] Members of the board were split on whether to press the issue. Although Oppenheim carefully made a distinction between the Sunday Trading Acts, which he presented as religiously inspired sabbatarian legislation, and the Factory Acts, in which the Sunday closing provisions were simply aimed at limiting the hours of labor of women and children, there were those on the board who feared the results of pressing for an amendment to favor the Jews. As one member, H. Harris put it: "we should be acting unwisely, considering that our religious disabilities had only of late years been removed and all rights of citizenship and freedom been granted us, were we now to attempt to become an aggressive body."[43] Despite these misgivings, however, the board agreed to refer the matter to the Law and Parliamentary Committee, which decided that, while Oppenheim's suggested changes in the law were "desirable in the interests of the Jewish working classes," nothing ought to be done for the time being other than monitoring the course of possible future legislation.[44]

In fact, however, it was difficult for the board to exercise its usual caution in this matter. The prosecutions, which were prominently reported in the Jewish press, built up pressure within the Jewish community to attempt to do something about the Factory Act.[45] The *Jewish Chronicle*, which had proudly trumpeted Jewish successes at integration into English society, nevertheless took up the cause of those who wished to secure Jewish exemption from the law. "Disposed as we are at all times to uphold the authority of the law," it declared,

> we do not hesitate to say that in the instance of this particular statute, the Jews are subjected to most oppressive and unjust legislation. Such a grievance would not, we believe, be so patiently borne by any other religious section of the community. . . . The facts of the case are that *Jewish* manufacturers are indicted even for employing *Jewish* women and children on a day which they do not consider to be their Sabbath. We admit that so long as the majority of our fellow-countrymen choose to take Sunday as their Sabbath, Jewish masters should be debarred from employing young Christian children on that day. But we fail to see on what principle of common justice, or with regard to freedom of the subject, a delegate of the bureaucracy which is gradually creeping over us can be permitted to enter a Jew's manufactory and ascertain what is going on there; nor why persons who are Jews should be punishable for employing persons who are also Jews.[46]

The real threat of the legislation, the editor of the *Chronicle* pointed out, was not to the Jewish factory owners, who could simply employ Christian labor and keep their shops open on Saturday, but to the Jewish workers, who would thereby be forced out of employment.

Although, on the whole, the authorities expressed some sympathy with the

Jewish position and imposed the minimum penalties on those prosecuted under the act,[47] the Factory Act was perceived by many within the community as an attack on the essence of Judaism. Further, the Board of Deputies, which had already come under attack in some communal circles for being too quietist,[48] was blamed for the situation, since the concessions contained in the act were seen as laughingly ineffectual, a position recognized as accurate by the Inspector of Factories.[49] A mass meeting organized by the City of London Jewish Tailors' Benefit Society called on the board to get involved; and in the face of such mounting criticism, the board became more active in the affair.[50] In February 1870 a deputation from the board, led by Oppenheim, met with the Home Secretary, Henry Austin Bruce, who expressed sympathy with the Jewish position but advised against any action, saying that the government intended to amend the act in the near future.[51] In fact, the government introduced legislation amending the act later in that year. Although a clause allowing Jews to employ women and children on Sunday was prepared by the board and introduced into the bill, it was dropped by the Select Committee to which it had been referred.[52]

This failure gave new urgency to the campaign to exempt Jewish factories and workshops from the operations of the act, especially since, in early 1871, the magistrates in Manchester began enforcing it against Jewish tailors who worked in their own homes on Sunday.[53] In 1871 Sir David Salomons MP entered the lists. At first glance, Salomons seems an unlikely figure to have taken up this particular issue. As we have already seen with regard to the laws on marriage, Salomons seemed committed to the position that emancipated Jews ought to be subject to precisely the same laws as the other members of the community. That he now was willing to work for the exemption of the Jews from the Factory Act is a sign of how seriously the Jewish community took the issue and how central the whole question of sabbath observance was to the community. Typically, Salomons, whose relations with the board were always cool and distant, operated on his own, introducing in 1871 a bill that did, in fact, offer Jews the exemptions they wanted. Unfortunately, Salomons's bill applied only to tobacco workshops. Although the board requested him to extend it to all factories and workshops, Salomons refused, on the grounds that a less narrow bill was less likely to pass.[54] Salomons's bill did become law in 1871, and provided that women and children could work on Sunday in a tobacco workshop, provided that they were Jewish, that the owner of the factory was Jewish, that the factory was closed on Saturday, and that it was not "open for traffic" on Sunday.[55]

From the beginning, of course, it was clear that Salomons's act only offered partial relief; and in the aftermath of its passage, the board, stung by the fact that it was its old nemesis Salomons and not the board who was successful, took up the cause with new vigor.

Appearing before the Royal Commission of 1876, which investigated the workings of the Factory Acts, M. S. Oppenheim, speaking for the board, outlined the objections of the Jewish community to the Factory Acts as they then existed, and requested several modifications, including the extension of Salomons's act to all factories employing Jewish labor, the extension of Saturday-night labor from nine to eleven o'clock, and, most radically, that Jewish factory owners employing non-Jewish labor be allowed to operate their factories longer hours during the week if they were closed on Saturday as well as on Sunday.[56] It is clear from the questioning of the commissioners that this last request was the most controversial. Parliament had already shown itself willing to allow Jewish workers exemptions from the Factory Acts because fairness seemed to demand such exemptions, because they affected only a small number of people, and because by insisting, as it had in earlier legislation, that those workshops that were to remain open on Sunday had to appear to be closed to the casual passerby, the legislation had been carefully designed to avoid offending the sensibilities of Christians. The request to allow Jewish factory owners to employ Christian labor longer hours, on the other hand, even though it did not pose a challenge to sabbatarianism, might appear to some to give Jews too much of an advantage over Christians. Remarkably, the commission was, in fact, willing to accept the request. Although they stressed that they were unwilling to allow Jews to employ Christians on Sunday, a privilege that the representatives of the Jewish community had not requested, the commissioners did state that, since

> it appears that the Saturday evening work is rarely to be obtained, and that many holidays over and above the legal number are given in the course of a year, we think that a special over-time relaxation to the extent of one hour daily may fairly be conceded, subject to the condition that no work be done on Saturday either before or after sunset.[57]

Further, the commissioners recommended that the provisions of Salomons's act be extended to other trades. These recommendations were, in fact, incorporated in the Factory Act of 1878.[58]

The Factory Act applied only to the employment of women and young people. There remained restrictions on other kinds of Sunday labor by adults. When some Jewish workmen appealed to the board after being arrested for working on Sunday, the board refused to intervene. "No doubt a hardship is occasioned in most cases in which the Lord's Day Act is enforced against persons professing the Jewish religion who observe the seventh day Sabbath," explained the board,

> but such instances are rare, and the magistrate usually takes a lenient view of the case. He did so in the present instance, for he imposed no fine, but simply ordered the defendant to pay the costs; the Board, however, should watch any legislation relative to Sunday observance, or Sunday trading, and will avail themselves of any opportunity that may be found of endeavouring to secure relief for such cases as the present.[59]

By the late 1870s, however, the social context in which the board was to act was changed dramatically by the beginning of the great influx of eastern European Jews that was to transform the character of the Anglo-Jewish community. Their later activities are outside the scope of this essay.

The struggle for Jewish Emancipation in England created an atmosphere in which it was necessary for the leaders of the Jewish community to stress the ways English Jews were no different from their Christian neighbors. This was the tack taken by leaders such as Lionel de Rothschild and David Salomons. No doubt they were correct in doing so and their efforts were ultimately crowned with success. In the years following political emancipation, however, the leaders of the Jewish community, faced with many of the same problems that bedeviled the Jewish communities of the rest of western Europe, were driven by necessity to realize that if Jews were to be successfully integrated into the larger society it was sometimes necessary to stress the way Jews were different from their neighbors and to work for legislation that took account of this difference. In doing so they were not arguing for Jewish separateness, as David Salomons and Lionel de Rothschild had feared during the debate over the Divorce Act. They were, on the contrary, arguing for Jewish inclusion in British society and were, by implication, enunciating a new vision of British society based on pluralism.

NOTES

The research for this essay was supported by grants from the Lucius N. Littauer Foundation and by the DeWitt Wallace Fund of Macalester College. I would like to acknowledge the cooperation of the Board of Deputies of British Jews in giving me access to their Minute Books, which are kept at the office of the board. These books are cited in the notes as BD Minute Books. The published reports of the board, which were issued half-yearly until 1874 and yearly thereafter, are cited as BD *Reports*.

1 For the entire period covered by this essay, the formal title of the deputies was the London Committee of Deputies of British Jews. Like most contemporaries, however, I will use the more familiar name, Board of Deputies.

2 Not entirely coincidentally, these years are also the ones that are not discussed by the two books on Anglo-Jewish history that most closely touch on the themes dealt with in this essay. The two are Todd M. Endelman, *The Jews of Georgian England 1714-1830: Tradition and Change in a Liberal Society* (Philadelphia, Pa, 1979); and Eugene Black, *The Social Politics of Anglo-Jewry 1880-1920* (Oxford and New York, 1988).

3 Jacob Katz (ed.), *Toward Modernity: The European Jewish Model* (New Brunswick, NJ, and Oxford, 1987), p. vii. For the classic examination of this problem, see Jacob Katz, *Out of the Ghetto: The Social Background of Jewish Emancipation 1770-1870* (New York, 1978).

4 Our knowledge of the particular situation of English Jews owes a great deal to the work of Todd M. Endelman. In particular see his *The Jews of Georgian England*; and "The Englishness of Jewish Modernity in England," in Katz, *Toward Modernity*, pp. 225–46.

5 The concept of cultural pluralism is derived from the American, rather than the European, experience. See Bernard Wasserstein, " 'As individuals everything . . . as

a group nothing': the flawed emancipation of the Jews in Europe," *European Studies Review*, 12 (1982), p. 201, for criticism of Paula Hyman for using this American model in a European context. I am, of course, arguing that it is applicable to the English experience.

6 See, for example, Bill Williams, "The anti-Semitism of tolerance: middle-class Manchester and the Jews, 1870–1900," in Alan J. Kidd and K. W. Roberts (eds), *City, Class and Culture: Studies of Social Policy and Cultural Production in Victorian Manchester* (Manchester, c. 1985), pp. 76–7.

7 For two accounts of the campaign for Jewish admission to Parliament, see M. C. N. Salbstein, *The Emancipation of the Jews in Britain: The Question of the Admission of the Jews to Parliament, 1828–1860* (Rutherford, NJ, 1982); and Abraham Gilam, *The Emancipation of the Jews in England 1830–1860* (New York, 1982).

8 Charles H. L. Emanuel, *A Century and a Half of Jewish History Extracted from the Minute Books of the London Committee of Deputies of the British Jews* (London, 1910), pp. 14–23.

9 Emanuel, *Century and a Half*, pp. 23–5.

10 6, 7 Will. IV, c. 85, 86.

11 Emanuel, *Century and a Half*, p. 26.

12 Ibid., p. 26.

13 In 1838 the prominent financier I. L. Goldsmid sent the board a long angry letter disputing its claims of exclusivity. The board could not afford to alienate so influential, politically active, and wealthy a man as Goldsmid, especially during the initial stages of the campaign to secure political emancipation, and it was forced to pass a resolution declaring that the board could not stand in the way of any individual Jew from pressing his political desires with the government: BD Minute Book 3, p. 47.

14 BD Minute Books 4, 5.

15 BD Minute Book 3, p. 54.

16 Emanuel, *Century and a Half*, p. 44.

17 From Aug. 1853 to early 1854 this issue dominated the pages of the *Jewish Chronicle*. For a full discussion of the episode, see Israel Finestein, "The Anglo-Jewish revolt of 1853," *Jewish Quarterly*, 26, 3–4 (autumn–winter 1978–9), pp. 102–13. Also see Israel Finestein, "The uneasy Victorian: Montefiore as communal leader," in Sonia Lipman and V. D. Lipman (eds), *The Century of Moses Montefiore* (Oxford, 1985), p. 46.

18 Finestein, "Anglo-Jewish revolt," p. 109. See, too, the editorial, "The expiring Board of Deputies," *Jewish Chronicle*, 25 Apr. 1856, p. 564.

19 BD Minute Book 5, p. 109; Emanuel, *Century and a Half*, pp. 43–4, 47.

20 For a full discussion of this issue, see Israel Finestein, "An aspect of the Jews and English marriage law during the emancipation: the prohibited degrees," *Jewish Journal of Sociology*, 7, 1 (June 1965), pp. 3–21.

21 For a discussion of this controversy, see Israel Finestein, "Anglo-Jewry and the law of divorce," *Jewish Chronicle*, 19 Apr. 1957, p. 11.

22 See, for example, the editorial in the *Jewish Chronicle* of 17 Sept. 1869, which labeled as "monstrous" the suggestion that a Jewish MP represented anyone other than his constituency and the interests "of all England." Similar sentiments were expressed by S. Moses, a member of the Board of Deputies, during a discussion in the board over the question of whether the Jewish MPs were sufficiently active in promoting Jewish causes: *Jewish Record*, 2 July 1869, pp. 4–5.

23 See Todd Endelman, "Communal solidarity among the Jewish elite of Victorian London," *Victorian Studies* (spring 1985), pp. 491–526.

24 Katz, *Out of the Ghetto*. Cf. Wasserstein, " 'As individuals everything . . .'," pp. 199–206.

25 BD *Report*, Aug. 1869, p. 14; Mar. 1871, pp. 16–17; BD Minute Book 10, p. 348.

26 *Jewish Chronicle*, 18 May 1855, p. 172; BD *Report*, Aug. 1869, p. 15; Mar. 1871, p. 16.

27 BD Minute Book 10, p. 352.

28 See BD *Report*, Aug. 1869, pp. 10–11, for the conscience clauses in the Endowed Schools Bill.

29 R. R. W. Lingen to Sir Moses Montefiore, 17 Dec. 1851, in London Committee of Deputies of the British Jews, *Report of the Committee Appointed on the Subject of Parliamentary Grants for Education to Jewish Schools* (London, 1852), p. 11. As was often the case, this relatively simple request was to lead to controversy within the community over the extent to which the Board of Deputies had the right to oversee the religious content of the curriculum of Jewish schools. For details of the successful attempt to secure government education grants to Jewish schools, see ibid., as well as BD Minute Book 7.

30 *Jewish Chronicle*, 4 May 1866, p. 5.

31 BD *Report*, Aug. 1869, p. 12. The government position was that the schools commissioners could achieve the same end without the need for special legislation: BD *Report*, Mar. 1870, p. 13.

32 The first communication between the board and the Oxford University Local Examination Board took place in 1859, and was successful in making arrangements for Jewish candidates: Emanuel, *Century and a Half*, pp. 73–4.

33 BD Minute Book 11, pp. 249–50, 282–4; BD *Report*, Mar. 1873, pp. 15–17; Apr. 1876, pp. 20–2; Mar. 1877, p. 12.

34 BD *Report*, Apr. 1880, pp. 26–7; Emanuel, *Century and a Half*, p. 111.

35 BD *Report*, Sept. 1871, p. 23; Sept. 1872, pp. 9–11; Apr. 1881, pp. 19–20.

36 Grosvenor's bill, which would have prohibited the sale of most articles in London with the exception of certain foodstuffs (and those only during certain hours, particularly those that would not interfere with church services), was regarded by some segments of the Jewish community as a hardship because it required them to abstain from business two days out of seven if they also observed the Jewish sabbath: *Jewish Chronicle*, 11 May 1855, pp. 164, 166; 13 July 1855, p. 236; BD Minute Book 8, pp. 44–5; Emanuel, *Century and a Half*, pp. 68–9. For some later attempts, see *Jewish Chronicle*, 12 Mar. 1869, p. 5.

37 *Jewish Chronicle*, 3 May 1867, p. 5.

38 BD Minute Book 10, pp. 148–9; *Jewish Chronicle*, 3 May 1867, p. 5.

39 Two acts were passed in 1867, the Factory Acts Extension Act (30, 31 Vict., c. 103), and the Workshop Regulation Act (30, 31 Vict., c. 146). The latter act extended certain of the protections of the Factory Act to persons employed in workshops that were too small to be covered by the Factory Act.

40 *Jewish Chronicle*, 26 Feb. 1869, p. 5; 15 Oct. 1869, p. 2; 3 Mar. 1871, p. 8; *Jewish Record*, 15 Oct. 1869, pp. 2, 6; 22 Oct. 1869, p. 5.

41 For the linkage of the Factory Acts and the Sunday trading bills, see BD *Report*, Sept. 1867, p. 9.

42 BD Minute Book 10, pp. 274–5; *Jewish Chronicle*, 26 Mar. 1869, p. 7.

43 *Jewish Chronicle*, 26 Mar. 1869, p. 7.

44 BD Minute Book 10, p. 281.

45 *Jewish Chronicle*, 15 Oct. 1869, pp. 2, 7.

46 *Jewish Chronicle*, 15 Oct. 1869, p. 7.

47 *Jewish Chronicle*, 15 Oct. 1869, p. 2; 4 Feb. 1870, p. 11; BD Minute Book 10, pp. 188–9.

48 See *Jewish Chronicle*, 1 June 1854, p. 301,   for a letter from "Shalom" (written in Hebrew characters), which claimed that "the Board of Protestant Dissenters are striving for *their* civil and religious rights, whilst *our* Board of Deputies of British Jews made not the least move in behalf of the bill lately before the House of Commons for the alteration of the oaths of allegiance, supremacy and abjuration." See, too, *Jewish Chronicle*, 16 July 1858, p. 245, for the letter from "An Ex-Deputy."

49 BD Minute Book 10, pp. 288–9. For scathing criticism of the board, see the letter from M. De Haas, the owner of one of the factories, *Jewish Record*, 15 Oct. 1859, p. 2.

50 *Jewish Record*, 7 Jan. 1870, p. 4; BD Minute Book 10, pp. 333–7, 347.

51 *Jewish Chronicle*, 11 Mar. 1870, p. 8.

52 *Jewish Chronicle*, 29 July 1870, p. 5.

53 *Jewish Chronicle*, 3 Mar. 1871, p. 8.

54 BD *Report*, Apr. 1876, p. 14.

55 34 Vict., c. 19.

56 *Report of the Commissioners Appointed to Inquire into the Working of the Factory and Workshops Acts*, in *Parliamentary Papers*, 1876, Vol. 30, pp. 193–4.

57 Ibid., Vol. 29, p. 51.

58 41 Vict., c. 16.

59 BD *Report*, Apr. 1880, p. 17.

Chapter 6

The manliness of Christ

Peter Gay

In 1879 Thomas Hughes published an arresting little book, *The Manliness of Christ*. It is an arresting text not only for its title, not only for its incursion into popular biblical exegesis in which Hughes had hitherto shown little competence, but also, and above all, for its readiness to draw delicate discriminations between different types of manliness. The ideal of manliness was, as is well known, highly prized and much discussed in the Victorian century, and not in Britain alone. Hughes had been a preeminent participant in developing the English version of the ideal and in shaping it for the public mind. With his famous *Tom Brown's Schooldays* and his far less known *Tom Brown at Oxford*, he had dramatized the argument in highly palatable terms. Now, with *The Manliness of Christ*, he sought at once to confirm and to revise that ideal. To be sure, "manliness" had been the special province of English divines for some decades, but Hughes now outdid them; he was attempting nothing less than to elevate this all-too-human ideal to the level of divinity.

This preoccupation, it is hardly necessary to document for a knowledgeable audience, was anything but eccentric. In 1867 the Religious Tract Society published a "popular and representative religious work," titled *Christian Manliness*, compiled by the Reverend S. S. Pugh.[1] More, it has been suggested that " 'Christian manliness' was a common Victorian preacher's catchphrase."[2] Of course, religious faith – and for some, religious doubt – was a pivotal emotional as well as social experience for most Victorians. Publishers feeling the pulse of their reading public knew this; especially in the first half of the nineteenth century, they threw on the market books with a religious theme in impressive numbers, even outnumbering the increasingly popular novel. As R. K. Webb has reminded us: "of the roughly 45,000 books published in England between 1816 and 1851, well over 10,000 were religious works, far outdistancing the next largest category – history and geography – with 4,900, and fiction with 3,500."[3] Hughes's particular concern in this published course of lectures, then, fits into Victorian culture without a seam. Yet *The Manliness of Christ* remains a fascinating and instructive instance of religious sentiment in nineteenth-century Britain, instructive all the more because it is relatively little known.[4] Hence it invites, virtually demands, summary.

In an introductory chapter, Hughes outlines his reason for bringing Jesus into the discussion. To be sure, in the hands of its best-known advocate, Charles Kingsley, the emphasis of "muscular Christianity" had been as much on Christianity as on muscularity.[5] But Hughes was confronting a particular problem. He had been wondering "what method it would be best to adopt in Sunday-afternoon readings in the Working Men's College" in London, an institution he had helped to found in the early 1850s. The issue had been raised for him by a letter he had received from "persons living in our northern town," who were proposing to establish a "new association" to be called the Christian Guild. The promoters of this plan for Christian activism had grown alarmed at the "bad reputation" for "savage assaults and crimes of violence" that the burgeoning cities of the North had acquired – and acquired with justice. They had asked themselves, reasonably enough, what they could do to reverse the deteriorating situation (and, with that, the deteriorating reputation) of their cities.

This anguished worry was the grain of sand around which Hughes cultivated his pearl. The "Young Men's Christian Association," he noted, "had increased of late, indeed, in numbers," but it was failing "to reach the class which most needed Christian influences."[6] To that extent, he could second his correspondents' apprehension, and agree with their desire to enhance the influence of domestic missions. Hughes, like them, was facing a dilemma that had faced religious reformers for centuries; those who needed the healing message of Christianity the most were heeding it least.

In their letter to him, Hughes's correspondents thought they were supplying at least part of the solution. "There was a widespread feeling, they said," Hughes reported, "that these associations – valuable as they allowed them to be in many ways – did not cultivate individual manliness in their members, and that this defect was closely connected with their open profession of Christianity." For one thing, these Christian associations were too remote from the deprived, often desperate, lives of the poverty-stricken folk they were determined to reach; these associations were after all – or appeared to be – on principle committed to withdrawal from the world. For another thing, the ideas for which they were reputed to stand did not appeal to the working-class youth, notorious as they were for their impiety, intemperance, and sheer pleasure in fighting. Hence, Hughes reported, the promoters aimed "at something like a revival of the muscular Christianity of twenty-five years ago, organized for missionary work in the great northern towns." What they had in mind for each branch of the proposed association was to make "the most vigorous and athletic young men of its district," youths noted for wrestling, running, or rowing, eligible for membership. In this way, "the sports and occupations which absorb the spare time and energies of young Englishmen" would be endowed with "a higher tone."[7] And with the bait of sports, the promoters hoped to capture new recruits for the divine pacific message that Christianity had to offer.

Even though – perhaps just because – Hughes had been prominently associated with muscular Christianity, even though he was a good friend of

Charles Kingsley, by all means the most emphatic spokesman for that movement, he had no confidence in these plans. In fact, he was fairly certain that the proposed associations must fail. Still, he found the correspondence of use to him: "The proposal set me thinking on the state of things amongst us which the Christian Guild was intended to meet." He could, after all, draw on long experience with working-class youngsters, and he acknowledged that in London, as in the North, the Christian associations were "said to lack manliness" in their "tone and influence." Concretely, this meant that those the YMCA wished to enlist perceived its kind of Christianity as cowardice, even effeminacy. It seemed to "appeal habitually and mainly to men's fears," to "that in them which is timid and shrinking, rather than to that which is courageous and outspoken." Now, Hughes strongly demurred from these perceptions; they struck him as a "strange delusion." But he was experienced enough in the world to recognize that a delusion is a reality for those who are possessed by it. And that once understood, Hughes decided that he must do nothing less than counter this dangerous misperception by redescribing Christ. To show Christ as the embodiment of courage – indeed, of manliness – mattered greatly; for, Hughes concluded, "the conscience of every man recognizes courage as the foundation of manliness, and manliness as the perfection of human character." And if Christianity "runs counter to conscience," even if it should be merely seen to run counter, then "Christianity will go to the wall."[8] Hughes would do his pious utmost to prevent that from happening.

What he set out to do, then, with a touching simplicity, was to paint Christ's character and life as the incarnation of pefect manliness. Just as modern men faced evil every day of their lives, so had Christ faced it. But, unlike most men then and now, he had triumphed over it. In his striving against the forces of darkness, the "first requisite" had been "courage or manfulness," gained precisely not by avoidance but through "conflict with evil."[9] In Hughes's revisionist life of Christ, the Savior bestrides the scene as a warrior wrestling with an assortment of wicked adversaries – with priestly arrogance, with devilish temptations to desert his calling, with distrust and mean derision, with sordid betrayal and cruel death.

Ever the teacher, Hughes gave himself some 166 pages for his tendentious biography. He begins with sketching in the scene, the Holy Land around 30 AD, which is the "battle field of the great captain." In a rapid survey of Roman history in Christ's lifetime, he discusses the Roman annexation of Judea, the peculiar position of the Jews in the occupied territory, and the unfortunate role played by the "high priest and scribe and pharisee," which rested like a heavy "yoke" on "the necks of their own people," heavier even "than that of the Romans." As for Galilee, where Herod Antipas, "the weakest of that tyrant family," ruled, the yoke of Jewish officialdom was more relaxed and the populace more diverse. But the historical phenomenon to which Hughes called particular attention was the widespread "expectation of a coming Messiah – a King who should break every yoke from off the necks of his people, and should rule over the nations, sitting on the throne of David." It was this fervent eschatological hope of the enslaved Jewish people that made the time "propitious" for Christ's ministry.[10]

That much for the external circumstances of Christ's life. But before turning to that life itself to demonstrate its essential manliness, Hughes inserted a crucial chapter in which he defined that manliness, and provided tests for its recognition. His correspondents from northern England – plainly they were much on his mind – seemed to believe that "manliness" and "manfulness" were synonymous with "courage." But in clinging to that misconception, they were blurring the very distinction on which Hughes rested much of his case. Plainly, Hughes set great store by this distinction, and a glance at his definitions will show why. Those difficult terms, "manliness" and "manfulness," have a wider meaning than "courage," for they include "tenderness, and thoughtfulness for others." To be sure, courage "lies at the root of all manliness," but it constitutes merely "its lowest or rudest form." After all, animals like the weasel or the bulldog display courage, often exceeding humans in that quality. Hence it cannot define the kind of pure humanity that Hughes was attempting to propagate.

Hughes did not want his reservations to be read as a disposition to make light of courage. On the contrary, he described it as a quality much to be praised, including as it does "persistency, or the determination to have one's own way, coupled with contempt for safety and ease, and readiness to risk pain or death in getting one's own way." No doubt, this is "a valuable, even a noble quality," but it is – as the behavior of the weasel and the bulldog makes abundantly clear – an "animal quality." Hence the promoters of the Christian Guild cannot have been in search of this virtue for their potential recruits. After all, courage "is by no means incompatible with those savage or brutal habits of violence which the Guild was specially designed to put down and root out amongst our people." What they plainly wanted was "not animal, but manly, courage."[11] In a word, Hughes's northern friends were on the wrong scent.

How wrong they were – and here Hughes approaches the heart of his argument – emerges from the fact that, as we have seen, the promoters thought "proficiency in athletic games" a sign of the quality they were looking for. But had they thought this matter through, they would have discovered that such proficiency cannot be a test of manly courage; it cannot even be a reliable test of animal courage. All it attests to is "muscular power and physical training." In short, athleticism was a most unsatisfactory criterion for discovering manliness. In the light of what Hughes had written earlier, especially in *Tom Brown's Schooldays*, this recognition was something of a departure for him. He was complicating his image of the good life. Indeed, Hughes now insisted, "athleticism is a good thing if kept in its place, but it has come to be very much over-praised and over-valued amongst us."[12] He protested that he had no intention of depreciating athleticism, but was merely pointing to its most striking limitations.

But these limitations were severe. Hughes was now prepared to defend the proposition, bluntly, that "true manliness is as likely to be found in a weak as in a strong body." True, it was likely that, other things being equal, a physically strong person would be more courageous than a weak one. "But we must take this caution with us, that a great athlete may be a brute or a coward, while a truly manly man can be neither."[13] The strategic value of these discriminations for a polemicist seeking the quality of manliness in so meek a creature as Christ should be obvious. After all, he who preached turning the other cheek, he who washed his disciples' feet, was a hard case. Hughes made it a little easier for himself by illustrating the distinction he was working to enforce with some choice vignettes from Sir William Francis Patrick Napier's *Peninsular War*. True manliness was, he tried to show, a matter of motive, a desire not just to be obstinate and to show contempt for death, but to serve others. Manliness incorporated nothing less than the desire for self-sacrifice.

However chary Hughes might have become of pugnacity, it should be evident by now that martial metaphors did yeoman service in his exposition. There are, it seems, many kinds of conflict. "We are born into a state of war; with falsehood and disease and wrong and misery, in a thousand forms, lying all around us, and the voice within calling on us to take our stand as men in the eternal battle against these." And "in this life-long fight, to be waged by every one of us single-handed against a host of foes, the last requisite for a good fight, the last proof and test of our courage and manfulness, must be loyalty to truth – the most rare and difficult of all human perfections."[14] Hughes will spend the rest of the book showing that Christ passed these military tests in the most splendid fashion. He, too, was a soldier with a manly code of ethics all his own.

As a brave soldier in his – and all mankind's – cause, Christ, Hughes insists, displayed manliness through all of his life. In a sequence of chapters dealing with Jesus' boyhood, his call, his several ministries, and his death, Hughes persists in discovering that quality in word after word, act after act. But in the very first chapter, "Christ's Boyhood," he admits that at times he has found his apologetic work veritable Sisyphean labor.

It was hard going right from the beginning. For one thing, we know virtually nothing about Jesus' youth, and can therefore gather only sparse clues to his boyish manliness. But for another thing – and this, Hughes thought, was far more troublesome – virtually the only episode in Jesus' early life recorded in the Gospels must strike the common reader as "baffling, even discouraging." Hughes is, of course, referring to the visit of the 12-year-old Jesus to the Temple where he confounds the doctors with his wisdom. The scene, Hughes acknowledges, is far from agreeable; the boy is being willful, almost rude. He shows himself exceedingly ungracious to, even impatient with, his parents as they anxiously hover around him. Hence the incident in the Temple seemed to Hughes's exacting standards to display anything but the "perfect manly life" that he was seeking to document. In his perplexity, Hughes turned to Holman

Hunt's "great picture" depicting this scene, and found the solution there; Hunt shows the boy's expression as that of one just becoming aware of the "terrible majesty and suffering and grandeur" of his mission. It is a moment of awakening, of recognizing that "he was not altogether like those around Him." This dawning awareness fully explains his curt response to his mother's reminder, "thy father and I have sought thee sorrowing." When he tells her, and Joseph, "How is it that ye sought me? Wist ye not that I must be about my Father's business," he is in deadly earnest. "To the young spirit before whose inward eye such a vision is opening," Hughes comments in evident relief, "all human ties would shrink back, and be for the moment forgotten." His call "was haunting Him." And that once understood, Jesus' reply "loses all its apparent willfulness and abruptness."[15] One might add, though Hughes does not, that since the "Father" Jesus is invoking here is not his mother's husband but a heavenly visitation, one might find his abruptness perfectly comprehensible. It was a symptom of a growing boy's confusion over who his parents are – and with that, who he himself is. In any event, to Hughes's satisfaction, once sympathetically studied, the boy Christ's performance in the Temple in no way diminishes his manliness.

His baffling silence during the next years yields to a similar interpretation. Once again, Hughes's dialectical virtuosity shows itself to good advantage. A critic might object to Christ's remaining at home, "idling," when there is a great work to be done in the world. But in truth Christ was being active in his own way; his passivity is only on the surface. For he is, in those quiet years, making sure of his duty in the terrible time ahead, "patiently preparing Himself for whatever his work might be." To sit silently and to reflect, Hughes insists, is the most manly thing Christ could have done in his circumstances. To enforce his point, Hughes addresses his listeners and, later, his readers quite directly:

> I hope I may have been able to indicate to you, however imperfectly, the line of thought which will enable each of you for yourselves to follow out and realize, more or less, the power and manliness of the character of Christ implied in this patient waiting in obscurity and doubt through the years when most men are at full stretch.[16]

He is waiting for the Call.

In the remainder of his pious polemic, Hughes pursues this line of reasoning with commendable consistency. Faithful to the truth that is in him, Christ does battle with sin and wickedness; as in Hughes's earlier writings, especially in *Tom Brown's Schooldays*, so now, too, good and evil confront one another in unrelieved contrast; psychological nuances were never Thomas Hughes's strong suit. The iniquity Christ must wrestle with is powerful and well entrenched, and he confronts it manfully. There are moments in his life, though, even after his boyhood, when his conduct invites a certain skepticism about his manliness. It is, of course, at these points that Hughes must deploy all of his skills. Just as the conduct of the 12-year-old Christ in the Temple required interpretation before its essential manliness emerged, so the Christ who collapses in the garden of Gethsemane, or who preaches meekness before the enemy, is, as Hughes again ruefully observes, hardly an ideal figure that the roughnecks of London, or Birmingham, would want to look up to, let alone identify with.

But Hughes proves himself equal to the task. Is not Christ manly, he asks rhetorically, when he takes the burden of the general contempt, and fearful isolation, upon his shoulders?

> To stand by what our conscience witnesses for as truth, through evil and good report, even against all opposition of those we love, and of those whose judgment we look up to and should ordinarily prefer to follow; to cut ourselves deliberately off from their love and sympathy and respect, is surely, I repeat, one of the most severe trials to which we can be put.[17]

Christ's apparent flaws fade before his superb valor in face of the injuries the world lavishes on him. Far from being disappointing, his fortitude in the face of foreknowledge that his most faithful disciples will disown him and that he must suffer on the Cross, and the resolute determination with which he will undergo his last hours, are nothing less than inspiring.

What can we do, Hughes demands, but adore the sufferer who sturdily rises above the viciousness of his enemies? "In all the world's annals, there is nothing which approaches, in the sublimity of its courage, that last conversation between the peasant prisoner, by this time a mass of filth and blood" – filth and blood, a clever touch that, to snare tough working-class listeners – "and the Roman procurator, before Pilate led Him forth for the last time and pleaded scornfully with his nation for the life of their King." It must be said that Hughes does not make his plea easy for himself: "There must be no flaw or spot on Christ's courage," he insists, "any more than on his wisdom and tenderness and sympathy." Yet Christ (and this pugilistic vocabulary comes to Hughes quite naturally; he invites his audience to judge his battles with evil as they might judge a boxing contest), however beaten and bruised, comes through the rounds with flying colors. To repeat – and Hughes, a practiced rhetorician, often repeats himself – all of Jesus' apparent failures, all of his superficial docility, turn out to be the qualities reserved for the most sublime – the most manly – figure ever to walk this earth. "The more we canvass and sift and weigh and balance the materials," Hughes concludes his overgrown tract, "the more clearly and grandly does his figure rise before us, as the true Head of humanity, the perfect Ideal" – and Hughes takes care to capitalize both "Head" and "Ideal" – "not only of wisdom and tenderness and love, but of courage also, because He was and is the simple Truth of God."[18] To put it briefly for once, Christ's manliness was, literally, incomparable.

One is bound to read this extraordinary text with some wonderment. It is not just the author's daring to make his God into the manliest of men that makes for astonishment. The Hughes who wrote *The Manliness of Christ* is preaching muscular Christianity with a difference. He seems to be advocating a doctrine rather different from the one that Charles Kingsley had articulated, giving unexpected scope to the positive value of what is usually called the "feminine" element in a manly man's character. Beyond that *The Manliness of Christ* reads like a radical departure from the classic we remember, *Tom Brown's Schooldays* – or, better, the classic we *think* we remember. For in fact, as a closer look at that midcentury bestseller will confirm, it harbored germs of Hughes's plea for Christ's manliness, germs that become rather more visible in retrospect.

With *Tom Brown's Schooldays*, published in 1857, Hughes made his mark with a broadly sentimentalized portrait of Dr Arnold's Rugby, a public school he had attended and obviously never quite outgrew. The book made him a national, in fact an international, celebrity in rapid order. True, he had done little publishing before (though he would do much after) but all his early life had been a preparation for it. Living at Uffington, near the Dover chalk downs, squire Hughes, his sober and civilized father whom he worshiped, had shown "true popular sympathies." He had played "cricket and football all his life with the villagers" – just like the Browns with their villagers. And so had young Thomas Hughes. What is more, Dr Thomas Arnold, that almost proverbial educational administrator and innovator, had been his father's close friend since Oxford. And so, when he entered Rugby in 1833, at 10, he had his father and his father's friend to look up to; what more likely than to have him blend them into one paternal figure, at once admonishing and encouraging the bright boy? Rugby was surely the shaping experience that *Tom Brown's Schooldays* hints it was. "You may well believe," Hughes recalled much later, "what a power Rugby has been in my life." He added: "I passed all those years under the spell of this place and Arnold, and for half a century have never ceased to thank God for it."[19]

He had other experiences to pour into his bestseller. Growing into adulthood with an outsized social conscience and soon happily married – again like Tom Brown – lawyer, Christian Socialist, Radical Member of Parliament, broad-church Anglican, and Christian propagandist, Hughes seems almost to have been gathering material for the book that made him a household word. *Tom Brown's Schooldays* offers a jolly, benign, middle-class version of the manly prototype. At first, Hughes hesitated to publish it, but, encouraged by a friend's enthusiasm, he submitted it to the house of Macmillan, which set his doubts at rest. Quickly converted to optimism, he advertised the manuscript as a sure winner: "My chief reason for writing is, that," he told Alexander Macmillan, "as I always told you, I'm going to make your fortune."[20] Macmillan quickly recognized that Hughes was scarcely exaggerating, and it must say something about Macmillan's and Hughes's culture that the book roused the reading public to the most unmeasured response; almost everyone, not merely nostalgic public-school graduates, found entertainment and reassurance in Hughes's good-tempered and easily digestible pages.

"The huge success of *Tom Brown's Schooldays*," Hughes's biographers suggest, "was owing in large part to its genuine literary merits." Perhaps. What is more plausible is their observation that the book was an innovation, "literally the first work of fiction to present a real world of boys in the setting of a real English public school."[21] No wonder that the publishing history of *Tom Brown's Schooldays* should be one continuous success story. The book outran the publisher's expectations time and again; in ten months it ran through some six printings, and it kept on selling, enjoying numerous editions in Britain and the United States. Translations into the major European languages rapidly followed.[22] Even so, the "literary merits" of the book were scarcely formidable. What mattered more was that it gave the public what it wanted, an optimistic, breezy, "realistic" tale with moral attached. It was a tale that, moreover, showed manliness in the most attractive light.

Tom Brown's manliness, Hughes alerts his readers on the opening pages, is a worthy inherited trait. "The Browns are a fighting family. One may question their wisdom, or wit, or beauty. But about their fight there can be no question." Thus the author sets the tone firmly; clearly he loves his Browns, all of them. And one reason he loves them is because he permits no nonsense about effeminate intellect or pale refinement to sully their character. On the contrary, they display far worthier qualities. The Browns are, to begin with, fiercely loyal to each other, determined in their views, admirably outspoken, firm in adversity. Snobbery has simply no place in their lives. Young Tom, a good Brown in this as in all else, is a "robust and combative urchin," an acclaimed sportsman from his earliest youth on. He wrestles, goes fishing, and plays football; he excels in the rural sport of back-swording, an English version of the German student duel fought with sticks, which draws blood and leaves painful welts. This, too, is an autobiographical touch; like Tom Brown, Thomas Hughes had enjoyed back-swording.[23] Not surprisingly, *Tom Brown's Schooldays* is filled with fighting, and Hughes's defense of fighting. It is instructive for the pugilistic atmosphere in which Thomas Hughes revels that he devotes the chapter where Tom is first introduced to Rugby to a lovingly detailed melee, a strenuously contested football match.[24]

Tom Brown's world is a world of decency, independence, informality, self-sacrifice, and authentic inward religious faith, of games hard fought and honestly won. It is a world without women, except, of course, for "dear mamma." Dear mamma is always in Tom's heart, even when – especially when – he is far from home. There is one particularly tense moment in the book when Tom is set upon and brutally tortured by some of his vicious schoolmates. He faints, and when he regains consciousness, his first word is "Mother!"[25] But she is the exception that is no exception; Tom's love for his mother, the one woman in his life until, much later, he falls in love with a young lady his own age, only guarantees the purity of his manliness. And in any event, that adult love appears not in *Tom Brown's Schooldays* but in a sequel.

Predictably, manhood is steadily on Tom Brown's – and Thomas Hughes's – mind. The village boys who were Tom's companions before he goes to school, and with whom he played his rough games as though they were his social equal, were "manly and honest." And at Rugby, manliness rules as the overt ideal and is discussed, or exemplified, with obtrusive regularity. In a grand oration to his schoolmates, one of the most admired among the older boys, Old Brooke, warns them that, whatever they may hear, "drinking isn't fine or manly." Hughes's regular authorial interventions, or the speeches he lends his favorite characters, little homilies all of them, are exercises in selling manly convictions and conduct. Thus, "play your games and do your work manfully," Hughes exhorts his readers, and "quit yourselves like men, then; speak up, and strike out if necessary for whatsoever is true and manly, and lovely, and of good report." The word "lovely" in this short catalogue should pull one up short, but it is not a slip of the pen or an unmotivated intrusion. It belongs, as we shall see, in Hughes's very definition of manliness.

For Hughes, as he leaves no doubt in *Tom Brown's Schooldays*, the unsurpassed exemplar of human excellence was, of course, Dr Arnold, Rugby's famous headmaster. Arnold was a very model to his pupils and the world. His "manly piety," we read, had transformed the school, and his weekly sermons admirably incarnated the Christian masculinity Hughes was now seeking to inculcate in others. In his sermons, the headmaster had told his boys to strive "against whatever was mean and unmanly and unrighteous," and had made a moral difference even to those among his boyish listeners too callow and too inexperienced to grasp the full extent of his message. Tom Brown would walk away from these inspiring occasions filled with good intentions.[26] In his collective portrait of Rugby, Hughes assigns places to the bully, the snob, and the intellectual – but only as foils. The virtue of manliness rises above all these excrescences.

As early as 1858, though, the year after he published *Tom Brown's Schooldays*, Hughes publicly observed that his own message had become somewhat worrisome to him. In a preface he added that year to a new printing of the book, he reprinted a long letter from a friendly reader who had criticized the author for not censuring bullying more sternly than he had. Hughes's response did not quite satisfactorily dispose of his friend's objection, but it suggests a certain uneasiness. "Boyishness in the highest sense," he notes, sounding more tentative than usual, "is not incompatible with seriousness, – or earnestness, if you like the word better."[27] He was becoming aware of a problem with "manliness" without, at this point, seeing his way clear to the solution.

But in 1861, when he published *Tom Brown at Oxford*, a sequel to the story of Tom Brown at Rugby, Hughes engaged in a strategic, if still partial, retreat from athletic religiosity, or religious athleticism. He still applauded "the brotherhood of muscular Christians" that, from the early 1850s on, had formed "an actual and lusty portion of general British life." But he was pleased to observe that these chivalrous Christian men had been a decisive improvement over what Hughes now chose to call, a little surprisingly, the "musclemen." The mindless athlete, he argued, lacks all

> belief whatever as to the purposes for which his body has been given him, except some hazy idea that it is to go up and down the world with him, belabouring men and captivating women for his benefit or pleasure, at once the servant and fermenter of those fierce and brutal passions which he seems to think it a necessity, and rather a fine thing than otherwise, to indulge and obey.

It may be that young men "will have fits of fighting, or desiring to fight with their poorer brethren, just as children have the measles. But," he sternly concluded, "the shorter the fit the better for the patient."[28] If the fighting Browns had read these lines, they might have been a little disconcerted by all these qualifications. They had remained fixated on their early adolescence all their lives, but their inventor now seemed to be asking them to grow up.

In his sequel, in fact, Thomas Hughes has Tom Brown grow up, and not just chronologically. Tom of Rugby has gone on to the university and out into the world, and has married the young woman he loves. And Mary Brown is a worthy companion to her manly man; Hughes concludes *Tom Brown at Oxford* with an earnest discussion between the couple, a discussion that raises questions, if largely implicitly, about man's monopoly on the manly virtues. In this sequel, quite as much as in *Tom Brown's Schooldays*, Hughes makes villainy, like goodness, easy to recognize; the heroism of his heroes is strictly predictable, thoroughly domesticated, and attainable by sincere, far from extraordinary men. But now he intimates that it is also attainable by far from extraordinary women as well. This proposition must strike most historians of the nineteenth century, who have been told very different things about the Victorians, as rather astonishing. But like many other really gentle spirits, Hughes had come to recognize, once he confronted his Tom Brown with an adult love, that life is a matter of shadings rather than of absolutes.

This is what happens. The couple are very happy together. But, as an imprudent and impecunious social idealist, Tom Brown finds his financial prospects dim. Anticipating a horseless and servantless future, and married to a woman who has always enjoyed both her riding and her domestic help, he feels humiliated at subjecting his Mary to these sacrifices. His first response to his predicament is manly silence; he will carry the burden himself. But she is too perceptive to overlook, and too loving to tolerate, a shadow between them. Prompted, he tells her all, but Mary's stalwart resolution upon hearing the news does not reassure him at first. She will do without her accustomed amenities, she tells him, and gladly. He is grateful but, then, is she not stepping out of her fated role? She is, he informs her, "a brave, generous pitying angel" who really ought to be protected from the deprivations he is imposing on her. "It is a man's business," he tells her. After all, he asks her rhetorically, "why is a woman's life to be made wretched?" His responsibility as a husband makes it imperative upon him to keep her from wretchedness: "Life should be all bright and beautiful to a woman. It is every man's duty to shield her from all that can vex, or pain, or soil."[29] The name Tom bestows on his wife – angel – is a reminiscence of another complex Victorian ideal, as open to question by the 1860s as manliness itself.

His is a heartfelt appeal; even if he is repeating well-worn clichés, he is speaking from a genuine magnanimity as he understands it. The thought that he is failing his wife by not providing her with the comforts to which she has been used, and to which she has a perfect right, depresses him. But Mary Brown will have none of it. Women's souls, she tells him earnestly, are the same as men's, and women are strong enough to go out into the wicked world and to labor, in their husband's company, toward its reformation. "Why not put me on your own level?" she pleads:

Why not let me pick my way by your side? Cannot a woman feel the wrongs that are going on in the world? Cannot she long to see them set right and pray that they may be set right? We are not meant to sit in fine silks, and look pretty, and spend money, any more than you are meant to make it, and cry peace where there is no peace.

It is a noble, stirring speech. She is realistic enough to recognize that in her time women are not likely to be as active as men. They do not have the opportunities. But, she concludes, "if a woman cannot do much herself, she can honour and love a man who can." And her husband recognizes the justice of her argument and accepts her as a worthy partner in the marital enterprise.

To be sure, Mary Brown's peroration is a rather lame anticlimax to her brave effort at self-assertion. Still, there can be little doubt that Hughes's last chapter in *Tom Brown at Oxford* raises some serious questions about the absolute distinctions that we have long thought differentiated the sexes in Victorian ideology. The Victorian era, presumably so familiar to us, still requires more research, a new look at familiar facts.[30] I offer one tentative hypothesis here: the ideology of manliness was by no means so clear-cut, even among the most arduous defenders of the ideal, as has usually been suggested. Certainly *Tom Brown at Oxford*, read in conjunction with *The Manliness of Christ*, suggests that the more complex definition of manliness that Thomas Hughes was reaching toward in the 1860s and 1870s includes loveliness, generosity of spirit, manly tears, and a stab, even, at recognizing the manliness of women.

Psychoanalysts have a humorous methodological aphorism: don't generalize from one case, generalize from two cases. The second witness I want to call to the stand is that arch-muscular Christian, Charles Kingsley. He was the strenuously hiking, boldly mountain-climbing, indefatigably vigorous outdoorsman who served his Protestant God by denouncing faint-away Anglicans and ascetic Roman Catholics, and who regularly assailed their teachings, their distrust of the body, and their denigration of its highest realization in marital sexual intercourse. Their effeminate teachings, he said over and over, were damnable assaults on nature and on nature's God. He, in militant contrast, stood for a "healthful and manly Christianity, one which does not exalt the feminine virtues to the exclusion of the masculine."[31] Outwardly he was implacable.

Most of his admirers and most of his critics saw him precisely that way. In 1857 the *Saturday Review*, appreciatively noticing Kingsley's *Two Years Ago*, flatly identified him as "spreading the knowledge and fostering the love of muscular Christianity." He was, the anonymous reviewer said,

> a man who fears God and can walk a thousand miles in a thousand hours – who, in the language which Mr Kingsley has made popular, breathes God's free air on God's rich earth, and at the same time can hit a woodcock, doctor a horse, and twist a poker round his fingers,

thus endeavoring "to show that the good may be bold, and the bold good."[32] Three years later, in 1860, W. R. Greg, that liberal and prolific commentator on current English culture, described Kingsley as "fearfully pugnacious," with Carlyle one of the two "most combative writers" of the age. "Nature sent them into the world full of aggressive propensities." Greg charged that Kingsley's professed virile ideals simply legitimized the pleasure he took in combativeness; he saw those ideals, with some justice, as alibis for virtually unsublimated aggression.

> It must be delightful to array all the energies of the old Adam against the foes of the new. What unspeakable relief and joy for a Christian like Mr Kingsley, whom God has made boiling over with animal eagerness and fierce aggressive instincts, to feel that he is not called upon to control those instincts, but only to direct them.

Kingsley, by characterizing his enemy to be "God's enemy," permitted himself to hate "with a perfect hatred," to act as "a war-horse panting for the battle." Greg, then, saw Kingsley, as did many others, as a "gladiator by nature."[33]

Yet if Kingsley was a pugilist, he was a deeply troubled one. Greg astutely noted, though he failed to pursue, an element of "tenderness" in Kingsley, one that was, if not profound, "manly, prompt, and genuine."[34] The observation is revealing in itself, not just for its psychological penetration, but also for its willingness to identify tenderness with manliness. This was precisely the point that Hughes was attempting to clarify for himself. It is in any event true that Kingsley, who saw himself engaged in unceasing strife with personal temptations, public degeneracy, and religious error, did not disdain manly tears. While, as we have seen, he inveighed against what he derided as the effeminacy of High Anglican and Roman Catholic clerics, he was obscurely worried over possible symptoms of effeminacy within himself. John Martineau, Kingsley's loyal disciple and close friend, whose "tender recollections" Kingsley's widow later allowed into print, discovered in his master "with all his man's strength," a "deep vein of *woman*," a "nervous sensitiveness, and intensity of sympathy," and, what was more, a "tender, delicate, soothing touch."[35] It was this "feminine" side in him that allowed Kingsley to complicate his definition of heroism by adding to muscular qualities, justice, restraint, modesty, and the readiness for self-sacrifice.[36]

It is interesting in this connection that Elizabeth Barrett Browning should have been taken with Kingsley for displaying precisely that touch. She was too intelligent to take all of his bluster literally. "He is original and earnest and full of a genial and almost tender kindliness," she wrote in 1852 upon meeting him for the first time, "which is delightful to me." His ideas might be "wild and theoretical in many ways," but as a man she found him "good and noble." A year later, she confided to her close friend Mary Russell Mitford, poet and playwright, that she really liked and admired Kingsley. " 'Manly,' do you say? But I am not very fond of praising men by calling them *manly*. I hate and detest a manly man." If she found Kingsley neither hateful nor detestable, that must be because she saw in him qualities the world did not see. "*Humanly* brave, true, direct, Mr Kingsley is – a moral cordiality and an original intellect uniting in him."[37] We may conjecture that Kingsley was more appealing, more polished, more pacific, talking in the drawing room than writing pamphlets at his desk or exhorting his audience from a lectern. No doubt, manliness was a quality far richer than we have long thought.

NOTES

1 See Norman Vance, *The Sinews of the Spirit: The Ideal of Christian Manliness in Victorian Literature and Religious Thought* (New York, 1985), p. 1.

2 Ibid.

3 R. K. Webb, 'The Victorian reading public,' in Boris Ford (ed.), *The New Pelican Guide to English Literature*, Vol. 6: *From Dickens to Hardy* (Harmondsworth, 1958; rev. edn, London, 1982), p. 199. Webb is drawing on a monograph by Charles Knight, *The Old Printer and the Modern Press* (1854), pp. 262-3.

4 The book was reprinted in the following year and several times after, and an edition of 1894 was enlarged with three further addresses that Hughes had given at Rugby. See Edward C. Mack and W. H. G. Armytage, *Thomas Hughes: The Life of the Author of "Tom Brown's Schooldays"* (London, 1952), pp. 292, 218–19. But Mack and Armytage, Hughes's conscientious biographers, mention *The Manliness of Christ* only three times in passing, while Vance, in his fine monograph, *Sinews of the Spirit*, also refers to the book only three times, just as casually.

5 Vance suggests a somewhat different emphasis when he writes: "The trouble with the phrase 'muscular Christianity' is that it draws attention more to muscularity than to Christianity": *Sinews of the Spirit*, p. 2. One sees what he means, but certainly neither Kingsley nor Hughes, nor for that matter their readers, ever wholly elided the religious dimension as they brooded on this idea.

6 Thomas Hughes, *The Manliness of Christ* (1879; unaltered edn, 1896), pp. 7–8.

7 Ibid., pp. 8–9.
8 Ibid., pp. 9–11.
9 Ibid., p. 12.
10 Ibid., pp. 13, 15–16, 19.
11 Ibid., pp. 23–5.
12 Ibid., pp. 25–6.
13 Ibid., pp. 27, 28.
14 Ibid., pp. 34, 34–5.
15 Ibid., pp. 43, 44, 45, 48, 47.
16 Ibid., pp. 56, 57, 56.
17 Ibid., p. 98.
18 Ibid., pp. 136, 137–8.
19 Ibid., pp. 10, 25.
20 Ibid., p. 87.
21 Ibid., pp. 90–1.
22 Ibid., p. 90. Mack and Armytage list the English and American editions: *Thomas Hughes*, pp. 294–5. It is an impressive catalogue.
23 See ibid., p. 98.
24 Thomas Hughes, *Tom Brown's Schooldays* (1857; 1913 edn), pp. 5, 20 (pt I, chs 1, 2); for the match see pt I, ch. 5.
25 Ibid., pp. 55, 158 (pt I, chs 3, 8).
26 Ibid., pp. 121, 195, 123, 144 (pt I, ch. 7; pt 2, ch. 1; pt I, chs 7, 8).
27 "Preface to the edition of 1858," *Tom Brown's Schooldays*, p. xlvii.
28 Thomas Hughes, *Tom Brown at Oxford* (1861; 1914 edn), pp. 99–100.
29 Ibid., p. 478.
30 I have been doing some of that research, much encouraged by Bob Webb's beautifully informed and refreshingly open mind. I refer to the opening two volumes of my *Bourgeois Experience: Victoria to Freud*, Vol. 1: *Education of the Senses* (New York, 1984), and Vol. 2: *The Tender Passion* (New York, 1986); I plan to include a chapter on the subject in the forthcoming third volume, *The Cultivation of Hatred*.
31 Charles Kingsley, *His Letters and Memories of His Life*, ed. by his wife, 2 vols (1877), Vol. 1, p. 180.
32 *Saturday Review*, III (21 Feb. 1857), p. 176.
33 W. R. Greg, "Kingsley and Carlyle" (1860), in *Literary and Social Judgments* (1873), pp. 116–17.
34 Ibid., p. 119.
35 Kingsley, *Letters and Memories*, Vol. 1, p. 240.
36 See Charles Kingsley, "Heroism," in *Sanitary and Social Lectures and Essays* (1880), pp. 225–6.
37 Elizabeth Barrett Browning to Mrs Martin, 2 Sept. 1852, in Frederic G. Kenyon (ed.), *The Letters of Elizabeth Barrett Browning*, 2 vols (1897), Vol. 2, p. 83; the same to Mary Russell Mitford, 20–1 Aug. 1855, ibid., p. 134.

Chapter 7

"More sweet and liquid than any other": Victorian images of Mary Magdalene

Patricia S. Kruppa

Saint Mary Magdalene was among the most popular saints in Britain from early medieval times to the Reformation. Taverns and ships were named for her; both Oxford and Cambridge had collegiate foundations bearing her name; several cycles of mystery plays celebrated her story. There were 187 ancient dedications of churches to her, and the city of Exeter boasted of her finger, housed in a tenth-century shrine, the first dedicated to the saint in the West. Eleanor of Aquitaine walked barefoot to Westminster Abbey to place a lock of the Magdalen's hair upon the tomb of Edward the Confessor. Her feast day, 22 July, was one of the most important in the ecclesiastical calendar, and continued to be observed into Victorian times, when it was often the occasion for a high churchman to deliver a sermon to the inmates of one of the many penitential associations that bore her name. Mary Magdalene would remain popular through the centuries because she represented one of the most powerful of all Christian images: the sinner redeemed by love.[1]

The image of Mary Magdalene as a penitent sinner, weeping at the feet of Jesus, the fallen woman who will be raised to a purposeful life, is the most familiar of all the images that surround her name, although it is one based upon tradition rather than scripture. There are six women named "Mary" mentioned in the Gospels: the Virgin Mary; Mary Magdalene; Mary the wife of Cleophas; Mary the mother of James the Less and Joseph; Mary the mother of John; and Mary the sister of Lazarus and Martha. In addition, there are three Gospel accounts in which Jesus encounters unnamed women who have been guilty of sexual sins: the woman of Samaria (John 4: 7–43); the woman taken in adultery (John 8: 3–11); and the "woman of the city which was a sinner," who visited Jesus in the house of Simon the Pharisee, "and stood at his feet behind him weeping, and began to wash his feet with tears, and to wipe them with the hairs of her head, and kissed his feet and anointed them with the ointment" (Luke 7: 27). Mary Magdalene's name appears in the Gospels fourteen times: five times in John, four in Mark, two in Luke, and three in Matthew. Mark 16:9 identifies her as the woman whom Jesus delivers from seven demons. John's account of Mary Magdalene is the fullest and most intimate – he puts her at the foot of the Cross and in the garden alone at the

Resurrection.[2] There is nothing in any of the Gospels that links Mary Magdalene to the women who have sinned, but nearly all medieval writers combined all the women named Mary together with the anonymous sinner under the name of Mary Magdalene. In the sixth century Pope Gregory the Great declared Mary Magdalene, Mary the sister of Martha, and the sinner of Luke 7 to be the same person. From this time on, whatever scholars might argue, Mary Magdalene became "the model of female penitence and contemplation."[3] She became both weeping penitent and female icon, a woman who had sinned much, but one who had loved much, and who would be the first person to see the risen Lord.

The shrines and miracles associated with the Magdalen vanished with the Reformation, but her name and example remained to provide inspiration to poets, artists, novelists, and preachers. Interestingly, it was in the seventeenth century that the distinctive English pronunciation of "Magdalen" as "maudlin" emerged, an association that linked her name to one of her most distinctive attributes, her tears.[4] In the eighteenth century her name became formally associated with a refuge for penitent prostitutes with the establishment of the Magdalen Hospital in 1758. Although there had been Magdalen communities scattered throughout western Europe from at least the fourteenth century, these had usually been operated by nuns, frequently of the order that bore her name. The Magdalen Hospital for the Reception of Penitent Prostitutes was founded by a layman, Robert Dingley, and supervised by a board of lay governors.

In the nineteenth century there was a strong revival of interest in the legendary figure of St Mary Magdalene. The Victorian fascination with the Magdalen took many forms: fiction, the visual arts, religious prescription, and, inevitably, in analogies to "fallen women." The interest was inspired by a variety of social and intellectual currents. The hectic pace of nineteenth-century life led romantics to look backward to simpler times. Many, like Wordsworth, regretted the passing of

> Angels and saints in every hamlet mourned!
> Oh! if the old idolatry be spurned
> Let not your radiant shapes desert the land!
> . . . weeping Magdalene,
> Who in the penitential desert met
> Gales sweet as those that over Eden blew!

Mary Magdalene's story was one of extremes and appealed to romantics inclined to see life in terms of fateful choices. Because the historical Magdalen was so ambiguous, the symbolic Magdalen was more potent. As the Victorian writer Anna Jameson declared:

> Of all the personages who figure in history, in poetry, in art, Mary Magdalene is at once the most unreal and the most real – the most *unreal*, if we attempt to fix her identity, which has been the subject of dispute for

ages; and the most *real*, if we consider her as having been for ages, recognized and accepted in every Christian heart as the impersonation of the penitent sinner absolved through faith and love.[5]

As a Christian symbol, Mary Magdalene was a recurrent theme in religious discourse that ranged across the entire Victorian spectrum from ritualism to rationalism. The Tracterian movement, the Catholic revival, "the second evangelical awakening" of midcentury, and the rationalist attempts to explain the Gospels in human terms all were contributing factors in the Victorian debate over the character of Mary Magdalene. Finally, Mary Magdalene had symbolic significance in the continuing debate over the nature of woman. There was no Victorian consensus on Mary Magdalene. There was disagreement over her history, her character, and her personal qualities. An examination of the various Victorian interpretations of Mary Magdalene offers a small but interesting window into nineteenth-century attitudes toward gender, sexuality, and social class.

The task of reconciling the traditional image of the penitent Magdalen with the limited scriptural evidence proved a challenge some Victorian clergymen could not resist. "Mary Magdalene: who was she?" was a question that yielded a number of answers. What is striking about an otherwise rather sterile clerical debate is the assumption that whoever Mary Magdalene might have been, she was surely a woman of the upper class. The scriptural Magdalen may or may not have been a harlot; but to her Victorian interpreters, her poise, grace, and presence were proof of her upper-class origins. For the Reverend George Wray, prebendary of York, the very fact that she was an associate of Jesus was proof of her high social standing. "The company in which Mary Magdalene is found repudiates the idea of her incontinency," he wrote. Mary Magdalene was not one of the anonymous sinners, he argued, but a woman mentioned – along with Susana and Joanna – as a recipient of the special mark of Jesus' healing power. "But Mary Magdalene is mentioned first. . . . All of these women seem to have been persons of superior condition of life, for they ministered unto Jesus of *their substance*."[6] Catholic writers often cited St Jerome, who denied that the woman who visited Jesus in the home of Simon and anointed his head with oil from an alabaster box could have been a harlot; for "indeed a harlot could not have at once been made worthy of our Lord's head."[7]

Fictional accounts of the life of Mary Magdalene drew freely from *The Golden Legend*, a much reprinted collection of lives of the saints compiled in the thirteenth century by Jacobus de Varagine, to support the idea that she was a prostitute, but one of the highest social class. The heroine of Edgar Saltus's *Mary Magdalene: A Chronicle* (1891) is an heiress who lives in a castle at Magdala. She moves to Rome, where she becomes "the toast of the tetrarchy." In a dramatic encounter with John the Baptist she tells him that she will "sleep on the down that the Teutons bring. I shall drink pearls . . . I shall sup on peacock's tongues."[8] The Magdalen of Maurice Maeterlinck's symbolist play,

Mary Magdalene (1910), is "no vulgar courtesan," but a favorite of powerful Romans, a woman who dismisses Jesus as a "rude brigand."[9] Middle-class writers often had trouble with working-class characters, and it was a stock device in nineteenth-century fiction for the working-class hero or heroine to be revealed in the end as the long-lost heir or illegitimate offspring of the aristocracy. In Wilkie Collins's *The New Magdalen* (1873), the heroine, Mercy Merrick, a former prostitute, is revealed to be the illegitimate daughter of a gentlewoman fallen upon hard times and a man "of the highest rank." Blood will tell, and the new Magdalen, in common with the old, is "one of the noblest of God's creatures."[10] The trend continued well into the twentieth century. Edith Olivier's *Mary Magdalen* (1934) is "fastidious, luxurious, and sensual, a child of Cyrus of the race of kings."[11] The assumption that Mary Magdalene was a woman of aristocratic origins makes the circumstances of her fall more poignant and her redemption more satisfying. It is ironic, however, that this image prevailed precisely at a time when the evidence compiled by reformers, journalists, and sociologists was pointing to the conclusion that the overwhelming number of women who became prostitutes came from the working-class urban poor. They were not the pampered daughters of the powerful, but domestics, shopgirls, seamstresses, and slop-workers.

Those revisionists who sought to correct the popular image of Mary Magdalene as a fallen woman had a difficult task. Most Victorians would probably have agreed with the Puritan divine, Stephen Charnock, that "seven devils would make her sooty to some purpose and so many did Christ cast out of her." One of the more interesting defenders of Mary Magdalene's reputation was the peripatetic American, Moncure Conway. Conway's religious progression took him from a Methodist ministry in Virginia to the Unitarian South Place Chapel in London and finally into the freethinking ranks of the Secular Union. Such a pilgrimage, as he conceded in his *Autobiography*, implied "a career of contradictions."[12] Perhaps a man whose career had been marked by contradictions was drawn to a figure whose life was one of dramatic change. Or it may have been his feminist sympathies that drew him to the Magdalen. He admired strong-minded women; in 1883 he lent his pulpit to Elizabeth Cady Stanton, who preached on the topic, "What has Christianity done for women?"[13]

Conway's circle of friends included the artist Dante Gabriel Rossetti, who, in 1867, gave Conway a photograph of his original drawing for *Mary Magdalene at the Door of Simon the Pharisee.* Conway eventually purchased several of Rossetti's works, including an etching of *Mary Magdalene*, and *The Gate of Memory*, a painting of a fallen woman based upon W. B. Scott's poem, "Mary Anne." Conway described Rossetti's painting of *Mary Magdalene at the Door of Simon* in these words:

A large company of merry-makers is passing along the narrow street with music, all in rich costumes and garlands, led by the fairest of them, Mary

Magdalene. But as they pass, Mary sees at the open window a face that makes her pause: the eyes of Jesus have met hers. She is seen ascending the few steps that lead to the door, not heeding the youths trying to restrain her, tearing off her garlands; her long wavy hair floats back, and the pathetically beautiful face is stretched forward, forever turned away from her gay companions.[14]

The painting started Conway "on a quest concerning the Magdalene with the result of my discovery that the story of immorality and her penitence were not only unauthorized by the New Testament, but inconsistent with it."[15] His search for the real Mary Magdalene continued into the twentieth century. In "A new view of Mary Magdalene" (1903), he wrote that "there is not another instance in history of woman's name having become proverbial through thirteen centuries as representative of a certain type of character without the slightest historical foundation for it."[16] When the Bishop of London preached a sermon in St Paul's in which he referred to Mary Magdalene as "the penitent," Conway wrote to the *Westminster Gazette* challenging the bishop to provide the scriptural basis for his characterization. According to Conway, the bishop answered him with "a candid note" conceding there were no scriptural grounds, but "it is an ancient Church tradition."[17] Conway finally had to admit that it was not Mary Magdalene's detractors who perpetuated the view of her as a fallen woman, but her admirers, for most people were unwilling to part with "the romance which poets and artists have found so fascinating."[18]

The Victorian Magdalen was always lovely; she came, as John Henry Newman said in 1841, "young and beautiful, and rejoicing in her youth."[19] The Baptist preacher Charles Spurgeon, preaching to a packed congregation at the New Park Street Chapel in 1855, evoked the saint in vivid terms:

When the grand orchestra shall send out its music, when the organs of the skies shall peal forth their deep-toned sounds, we shall ask, "what was that sweet note heard there, mingling with the rest?" . . . Ah! Mary Magdalene's voice in heaven, I imagine, sounds more sweet and liquid than any other.[20]

In sermons, in fiction, and in the visual arts of the Victorian age, Mary Magdalene is young and possessed of a beauty "so invincible that she had been unaware of its existence."[21] Her long, flowing hair – her most distinctive physical attribute – is golden or red; dark hair, as Anna Jameson wrote, was reserved for Magdalens of "the Spanish school."[22] In English fiction, "the heavy masses of her yellow hair fell almost to her feet." "The wonders of her eyes, which looked the haunts of hope fulfilled, the wonder of her mouth, which seemed to promise more than any mortal mouth could give, were forgotten in her hair, which was not orange or flame, but a blending of both."[23]

The youth and beauty of Mary Magdalene made her transformation from prostitute to penitent more emotionally satisfying to the Victorians. The combination of youth and beauty, especially in a sinner, can be very appealing.

Josephine Butler observed that she had been told by prostitutes that the prettier ones were less likely to be detained by the police than were their less well favored sisters.[24] The image of a young and beautiful Magdalen was at odds with what many Victorians felt were the consequences of a life of sin, or even of a solitary fall. Must the Magdalen always be beautiful, when so many fallen women were not? John Ruskin pondered this question and came to an interesting conclusion. In Volume 2 of *Modern Painters* he was sharply critical of the *Mary Magdalene* by Titian that hangs in the Pitti Palace. He found her "disgusting," "ignoble," and "shallow," "a stout, red-faced woman, dull and coarse of feature, with much of the animal in even her expression of repentance." But in a subsequent volume he remembered another of Titian's Magdalens in the National Gallery, "where she is just as refined as in the Pitti Palace she is gross." This led Ruskin to conclude that there was a purpose in Titian's portrayal of the Magdalen as unlovely:

> He was the first to doubt the romantic fable and reject the narrowness of sentimental faith. He saw that it was possible for plain women to love no less than beautiful ones, and for stout persons to repent as well as those more delicately made. . . . the Magdalen would have received her pardon not the less quickly because her wit was none of the readiest, and would not have been regarded with less compassion by her Master because her eyes were swollen and her dress disordered.[25]

Ruskin's point was a good one, but it remains true that most viewers, and certainly most buyers, prefer paintings of lovely women to homely ones. Indeed, in this, Ruskin was no exception. When he saw Rossetti's pen-and-ink drawing of *Mary Magdalene at the Door of Simon the Pharisee* (1853), he tried to persuade the artist to exchange it for a *St Catherine* he had purchased earlier. "That 'Magdalen' is magnificent to my mind, in every possible way: it 'stays by me' " (meaning "stays in my eyes and head").[26] Rossetti refused the trade; he already had a customer in the prominent nonconformist, Thomas Plint of Leeds.[27]

Mary Magdalene was a favorite subject of Victorian painters. G. F. Watts, Edward Burne-Jones, Frederick Sandys, Holman Hunt, and Rossetti were among the Victorian artists who executed versions of the life of Mary Magdalene. In Victorian art, the subject of the fallen woman was prominent almost to the point of obsession.[28] The subject reflected contemporary social concerns, offered an opportunity for art to serve a moral purpose, and provided one of the few ways for artists to treat human sexuality in a socially acceptable form. Of course, not all artists were motivated by religious or social concerns, nor were the results always successful, even when these were the motives. Mary Magdalene, in nineteenth-century art, seems as often seductress as penitent, and as frequently *femme fatale* as fallen woman.

She was understandably attractive to the Pre-Raphaelites and their followers, for whom "loose, luxuriant hair was an emblem of female sexuality."[29]

Rossetti portrayed the Magdalen in a variety of forms: drawings, watercolors, oils, and photographs. His Mary Magdalene is a blonde beauty of the distinctly Pre-Raphaelite type, a sensuous woman of generous mouth, half-lidded eyes, with flowers in her long, curling hair. Rossetti described her in a poem, as she prepared to leave her companions and enter the house of Simon:

Oh loose me! Seest thou not my bridgegroom's face
That draws me to him? For his feet my kiss,
My hair, my tears He craves today;
– and oh!
What words can tell what other day and place
Shall see me clasp those blood-stained feet of His?
He needs me, calls me, loves me: let me go![30]

Rossetti had no trouble finding buyers for his paintings of Mary Magdalene. His unfinished oil replica (1865), based upon *Mary Magdalene at the Door of Simon the Pharisee* of 1858, was purchased by a Norwich manufacturer, W. H. Clabburn, whom Rossetti had candidly admitted he intended to "nail" with "a pot-boiler."[31] His cynicism about his customers and his own work, according to Linda Nochlin, helps explain his obsession with prostitutes; he came to regard his own pandering to collectors as a form of artistic prostitution. His attitude toward fallen women reflected his view of himself. "The painting of the fallen woman can almost be seen as a synecdoche of Rossetti's disillusion with painting and with himself as a painter."[32]

Rossetti, unlike his friend William Holman Hunt, did not believe that art served a moral purpose. Hunt declared his desire "to use my powers to make more tangible Jesus Christ's history and teaching." According to F. G. Stephens, Rossetti was "thoroughly indisposed toward attempts to ameliorate anybody's condition by means of pictures."[33] Conway wrote that the artist was drawn to "whatever was poetic and picturesque, in ancient legends and visions, Madonnas, Magdalens, damozel, angel, they all became lovable and familiar phantoms to him, forms of feeling."[34] Certainly Rossetti's Magdalens were often complex works, and they had strong commercial appeal. Recognizing this, Rossetti was not pleased when his associate, the painter Frederick Sandys, did a version of *Mary Magdalene* (c. 1858–60), which Rossetti believed was too similar to his own work of 1857. He accused Sandys of plagiarism.[35] Sandys's lovely, sloe-eyed Magdalen is identified by her twin emblems, her hair and her alabaster ointment pot. Her red-gold hair cascades almost to her waist; her bright red mouth is slightly, tantalizingly open, a woman who is clearly on the edge.

Sandys painted a second Magdalen in 1862, which was purchased by the same Mr Clabburn of Norwich who bought the Rossetti Magdalen of 1865. Collectors purchased works of art, as they do now, from a variety of motives. For some Victorian collectors of religious art, the motive was conventional piety, made more sentimentally satisfying if the subject was a pretty young woman. Many collectors undoubtedly had mixed motives, and were drawn to works that aroused instincts they were unwilling to admit. Consciously or not, some painters offered Magdalens in which the sexual charms of the subject were more apparent than her spiritual qualities – "Magdalenes *à la pompadour*," in Anna Jameson's pungent phrase.[36] Nude Magdalens were uncommon but not unknown. More sophisticated collectors were less likely to be interested in the religious overtones of a work than with its aesthetic appeal. This is certainly the case with Oscar Wilde, who had a version of Burne-Jones's *Christ and the Magdalen* hanging in his rooms at Magdalen College, Oxford.[37] It may be the case as well with Clabburn, for, in addition to Sandys's *Magdalen*, he owned the artist's *Morgan le Fay*, a classic example of the *femme fatale*.

Most Victorians did not own paintings or visit the galleries or exhibitions where paintings of Mary Magdalene were displayed. The average devout Victorian was far more likely to encounter an image of the Magdalen in church than in a museum or gallery. Stained-glass windows were an important form of visual communication from medieval times on. One wonders how many Victorians there were like E. F. Benson's character Reggie in *The Babe*, who allowed their attention to wander from the sermon to the glowing figures of the windows:

> Reggie's seat was just east of the choir opposite to the window representing Christ standing in the garden after the resurrection. To the right kneels Mary Magdalene, gaudily dressed, just having turned and seeing that he was not, as she supposed, only the gardener. To the left rises a green hill, on the top of which, below a row of brown, ragged rocks, stands the empty tomb, with the women found round it. By a quaint but curiously felicitous idea of the artist, the figure of Christ is holding a spade in his hand, as if to give color to Mary's mistake. His face is Divine, but graciously human, and he waits for their recognition.[38]

Benson's character is looking at the glorious sixteenth-century "great window" at King's College, Cambridge. Those who attended newer churches were likely to find a Victorian Magdalen, often the work of Morris and Company. Magdalens by Burne-Jones were to be found at churches at Rochdale, Arington, Brighton, Torquay, East Hamstead, and Peterhouse College, Cambridge.[39]

Not all Victorian clergymen found Mary Magdalene – at least in her Pre-Raphaelite guise – to be an edifying subject, however. When Rossetti died in 1882 at Birchington-on-Sea, his mother and sister, Christina, commissioned his associate, Frederick Shields, to design a memorial window for the church at Birchington where he was buried. Shields chose to design a window based upon Rossetti's *Mary Magdalene at the Door of Simon the Pharisee*. The vicar, Mr Alcock, rejected the design, declaring that a Magdalen tearing at her tresses and garments was unlikely "to inspire devotional thoughts, and I fear in some cases it might rather do the reverse." Shields was forced to substitute a design of the holy family.[40]

In her Victorian incarnation, Mary Magdalene's attributes are essentially feminine ones. In her role as penitent, she is remembered for her physical beauty, her touching remorse, her tears, and her emotional nature. She wept, she trembled, she was abject, she feared to raise her head. Her tears, wrote Henry Ward Beecher, were copious, her locks disheveled, her heart trembling.[41] Charles Kingsley described her as faithful and humble, and more sensitive than a man:

> We, men, are made of coarser stuff; we do not feel pain as keenly as women; and if we do feel, we are rightly ashamed to shew it. But a tender woman, who feels pain and sorrow infinitely more than we do, who need not be afraid of being frightened, and who perhaps is terrified of every mouse and spider – to see her bearing patiently pain, and sorrow, and shame . . . that is Christ's likeness.[42]

John Henry Newman stressed her ardent, passionate, and impetuous nature, though by the company in which he numbered her, he makes these qualities androgynous ones. Newman defined two types of saints: saints of purity, and saints of love – the calm and innocent, and the penitent and ardent. In this second class of saints he names "three great ones" – Peter, Paul, and "an illustrious third . . . the loving Magdalen":

> That poor, many-coloured child of guilt . . . she, who but now was vain of her attractions – how withered is that comliness, of which the praises ran through the mouths of her admirers! . . . Those wanton hands, those polluted lips, have touched, have kissed the feet of the Eternal, and He shrank not from the homage. . . . Henceforth, love was to her, as to St Augustine and St Ignatius Loyola . . . as a wound in the soul, so full of desire as to become anguish.[43]

Her metamorphosis from harlot to saint was an inspiration to the many earnest Victorian men and women of all creeds who were engaged in rescue work. If the Magdalen could experience such a radical transformation in her life, then why not her lost sisters? She had been a "bruised reed," said Spurgeon, but Christ had taken the bruised reed, mended it, and fitted it into the pipes of heaven. He told his congregation that one of his sermons on Mary Magdalene had been a turning point for one of London's outcasts:

> A poor harlot determined she would go and take her life on the Blackfriars Bridge. Passing by these doors on Sunday night, she thought she would step in, and for the last time hear something that would prepare her to stand before her Maker. She forced herself into the aisle, and she could not escape until I rose from the pulpit. The text was "seest thou this woman?" I dwelt upon Mary Magdalene and her sins; her crushing the Saviour's feet with her tears, and wiping them with the hairs of her head. There stood the woman, melted away with the thought that she should thus hear herself described, and her own life painted. Oh! to think of saving a poor harlot from death, to

deliver such a one from going down to her grave, and then, as God pleased, to save her soul from going down to hell![44]

The story is melodramatic, but very like an episode in Collins's *The New Magdalen*, when Mercy Merrick is transformed when she hears Julian Gray preaching in the Refuge, as "he touched my heart as no man has touched it before or since." Bernard Shaw wrote that Mercy Merrick as a character was unlike any typical prostitute, "except in point of the susceptibility to sentimental sermons."[45]

If more fallen women were not reformed, it was certainly not for lack of sermons. From the 1840s on, efforts to rescue prostitutes proliferated. Female Aid Missions, Moonlight Missions, Penitentiary Associations, Refuge Unions, Magdalen Associations, Houses of Mercy, and Women's Missions actively sought out the fallen. It is worth noting that most Victorian efforts to wipe out prostitution focused solely on the woman. There was no male counterpart to the fallen woman. Indeed, as Nochlin points out, the very word "fallen" applied in a different way according to gender; women "fell" from virtue into vice, while men "fell" in battle.[46] Mary Magdalene was celebrated as a reformed harlot, but there was no male saint remembered for turning away from a life of seduction. Archdeacon Henry Manning, preaching on behalf of the Magdalen Hospital at St George-in-the-Fields in 1844, was one of the few early Victorians to challenge the sexual double standard. "What is so utterly destroyed as a fallen woman: so outcast, spurned, degraded?" His answer: her seducer. "Even the most abandoned were once purer than the possessed being by whom they were betrayed."[47] It would be another thirty years before Josephine Butler challenged the conspiracy of silence that surrounded the role played by men in fostering and encouraging sexual license for men while denouncing prostitutes as "foul sewers." Butler raised not only the issue of gender, but that of class as well: "They regard as frailty in high life what is called prostitution among the humbler classes."[48]

The emergence of feminism in the mid-nineteenth century added another dimension to the symbolic significance of Mary Magdalene. Her role as a penitent might be debated, but her place at the foot of the Cross and in the garden was clearly scriptural. Christ revealed himself first to a woman. The first word spoken by the angel at the tomb was, "woman." Mary Magdalene witnessed the miracle of the Resurrection that the male disciples did not see. If male artists, preachers, and writers found the penitent Magdalen an appealing and edifying subject, female writers and artists found the contemplative companion of Christ an inspiring example for their sex.

Anna Brownell Jameson, who has been quoted earlier, was a mid-Victorian writer whose popular art histories introduced a large audience to the work of the old masters. She was born in Dublin in 1794, the daughter of Brownell Murphy, an Irish miniature painter who became court painter to the Princess Charlotte. In 1825 she married a barrister, Robert Jameson, but the marriage proved unhappy and they eventually separated. Mrs Jameson supported herself, her mother, and a sister with her writings. Her personal experience made her very sensitive to the wrongs of her sex; too much so, according to her friend, Harriet Martineau, who believed that her "incessant recurrence to considerations of sex" weakened her writing.[49] Anna Jameson was certainly quick to defend her sex, and she had many friends among the creative women of her time. When Elizabeth Gaskell's novel, *Ruth*, was published in 1853, Mrs Jameson wrote to encourage the author. Mrs Gaskell's subject was the controversial one of a young unwed mother. The frontispiece of *Ruth* is a poem by Phineas Fletcher on Mary Magdalene:

> Drop, drop slow tears!
>> And bathe those beauteous feet,
> Which brought from heaven
>> The news and Prince of Peace.
> Cease not, wet eyes,
>> For mercy to entreat:
> To cry for vengeance
>> Sin doth never cease.
> In your deep floods
>> Drown all my faults and fears;
> Nor let His eye
>> See sin, but through my tears.

Mrs Gaskell was surprised by the adverse reaction her novel provoked, and compared herself to St Sebastian, "tied to a tree and shot at with arrows."[50] She was all the more grateful to Jameson for her support, and for understanding what she aimed to do in the novel.[51]

Anna Jameson was a deeply religious woman – her last years were devoted to the work of the Sisters of Charity – and she found in Mary Magdalene a powerful example of womanhood. She was "majestic," "a noble creature, with strong sympathies, and a strong will, with powerful faculties of every kind."[52] Jameson was critical of those artists who had portrayed the Magdalen as "attenuated by vigils and exposed in haggard unseemliness," or who stressed her sensual side, turning her into a "coarse . . . disappointed virago."[53] In Jameson's writing, the devout Christian and the feminist meet. Describing Mary Magdalene's encounter with Christ in the garden, she wrote:

> Few incidents in Scripture offer such materials as this. On the one side, dignity and beneficence, on the other, grace and beauty, and sorrow merging into sudden joy. . . . His first revelation of Himself after His Resurrection to mortal visitation, and told in those two resounding and ineffable words, Mary! Master! . . . In those blue eyes, suddenly dried, opened, and illuminated, Christ is visible in His own benign Person; come

not only to show that "because I live ye shall live also," but that in "this flesh we shall see God."[54]

The photographer Julia Margaret Cameron was, like Anna Jameson, a devout Anglo-Catholic. She was deeply influenced by John Keble, whose calendar, *The Christian Year*, observed Easter Day with the lines:

Oh! Joy to Mary first allow'd
When roused from weeping o'er his shroud
By his own calm, soul-soothing time,
Breathing her name, as still his own![55]

She believed with Keble that art could produce moral and religious associations.[56] The photograph, for Cameron, was "almost the embodiment of a prayer," and when she approached her subject, "my whole soul has endeavored to do its duty."[57] Photography offered the nineteenth-century artist a new form that combined artistic imagination with scientific realism. Biblical tableaux were a natural choice for Victorian photographers. In 1855 Ruskin's friend Mrs Jemima Blackburn published a volume of photographs illustrating scriptures, and Rossetti did several photographic versions of Mary Magdalene; in 1870 he offered one of his Magdalens to the feminist Barbara Bodichon.[58] No Victorian photographer, however, was as absorbed with the meaning of Mary Magdalene as Julia Cameron. The Cameron scholar Mike Weaver has noted that both Jameson and Cameron were theological feminists for whom "the subjects of the Women at the Sepulchre, the Angel at the Tomb, Mary Magdalene in the Garden, and the Three Marys put women in the position of witnesses charged with the task of bringing men to the faith."[59] Both saw Mary Magdalene as symbolizing female redemption. She was "the last at the Cross, the first at the Tomb," in a position at the sepulchre that morally reversed the one she had assumed in the Garden of Eden.[60]

For Cameron, women were "uniquely capable of understanding the emotions attendant upon nativity and crucifixion, death and resurrection."[61] Weaver dates the beginning of her Magdalen series with a photograph of her niece, Julia Jackson (1860), and with a study of a young girl, done about the same time, named Magdalene Brookfield. Cameron's most frequent model was her maid, Mary Hillier. Weaver notes that the fact that her models were actually named Mary and Magdalene "shows how transparently photography can close the gap between the literal and the metaphysical: the stamp of divinity is to be found, indeed, in real life."[62] From her earlier Magdalen "types" – Julia Jackson, Ophelia, Maud, the woman receiving the apple – Cameron developed her Magdalen series in her studies of *The Three Maries* (1865), *Mary Hillier as La Santa Maria* (1868), and her most glorious photograph of the Magdalen, *The Angel at the Tomb* (1870).[63] In this photograph, the angel has changed sex, and "Mary Magdalene's major attribute, her hair, is dazzlingly presented. At this earthquake in her soul her elaborate tresses are tousled and tangled as never before in the history of art."[64]

Finally, the image of Mary Magdalene has been transformed by Cameron's art and lens into a living woman, with a woman's special attributes of wonder, fidelity, and love.

Not all Victorian feminists were as deeply religious as Cameron, Jameson, and Butler. For those with more skeptical minds, the scene in the garden and Mary Magdalene's actions were open to another interpretation. "She appears to have been a very enthusiastic temperament," wrote Ernest Renan, possessed of a "strong imagination." "Divine power of love! Sacred moments in which the passion of one possessed gave to the world a resuscitated God!"[65] Oscar Wilde drew upon these lines in a poem on Mary Magdalene:

> And was the Rising only dreamed by Her
> Whose love of Thee for all her sin atones?[66]

The freethinking Elizabeth Cady Stanton argued in *The Woman's Bible* (1896) that "The whole foundation of this Christian religion rests upon [woman's] temptation and man's fall, hence the necessity of a Redeemer and a plan of salvation. As the chief cause of this dire calamity, women's degradation and subordination was made a necessity."[67] The commentary upon John: 20 makes it clear the author considered the Magdalen to be a very gullible woman. "Though disciples in visiting the tomb saw nothing but cast-off clothes, yet Mary sees and talks with angels and with Jesus. As usual, the woman is always most ready to believe miracles and fables, however extravagant and beyond all human comprehension."[68]

In November 1895 Wilkie Collins's play, *The New Magdalen*, was revived after twenty years. Bernard Shaw, who reviewed the play, observed the changes that had taken place in the public perception of "fallen women" in that twenty-year period. Shaw found Collins's work dated. Mercy Merrick is "the old-fashioned, man-made angel woman," and Julian Gray was more a cliché than a pioneer: "You will find hundreds of such parsons now: in fact, the Guild of St. Matthew is a Guild of St. Julian Gray." The whole world had moved in twenty years, and "the stage has moved as well." Once, fallen women "as victims were pitied. What has happened since is that we have changed sides to a great extent; and though we may not all care to say so, it is the rebel against society who interests us; and we want to see the rebel triumphant."[69] Fittingly, in the revival of *The New Magdalen*, the title role was played by Janet Achurch, who had become famous in the role of Nora in *A Doll's House*.

By the 1890s mid-Victorian definitions of womanhood and womanliness had undergone significant revision, and a new generation of women – many university-educated and seeking to break down political and professional barriers based upon gender – were no longer content with the same female role models that had inspired their mothers. Neither the submissive and penitent Magdalen nor the passive and contemplative companion of Jesus was a satisfactory example of female accomplishment to the women who would begin the Edwardian years with the militant suffrage campaign. The women who might have earlier engaged in rescue work were now moving into social work, as the problem of prostitution increasingly was considered in sociological and economic terms rather than as a matter of moral frailty. Shaw was correct; the world and the stage had moved by the end of the century, and politics had become an extension of the theater. The young women who challenged the conventions of their society were inspired by rebels and militants. It would be a woman dressed as the warrior-saint Joan of Arc who would lead their parades as they marched, shoulder to shoulder, into a new world.

NOTES

1 David Hugh Farmer, *The Oxford Dictionary of Saints* (Oxford, 1978), p. 270; Marjorie Malvern, *Venus in Sackcloth: The Magdalen's Origins and Metamorphoses* (Carbondale, Illinois, 1975), pp. 3, 79; Helen Garth, *Saint Mary Magdalene in Medieval Literature*, (Baltimore, Md., 1950), p. 12.
2 Garth, *Saint Mary Magdalene*, p. 18; Malvern, *Venus in Sackcloth*, pp. 14, 19.
3 Garth, *Saint Mary Magdalene*, p. 19.
4 Malvern, *Venus in Sackcloth*, p. 9.
5 Anna Jameson, *Sacred and Legendary Art* (Boston, Mass., 1895), Vol. 1, p. 363.
6 Rev. George Wray, *A Vindication of the Character of Mary Magdalene: With Notes on the Resurrection, or the Women who Attended our Blessed Lord, and on the Twelve Apostles* (London, 1870), pp. 4–5. I am grateful to Dr Gail Savage for locating this reference for me.
7 See, for instance, Hugh Pope, OP, "Who was Saint Mary Magdalene?" *American Catholic Quarterly Review*, XXVIII (1903).
8 Edgar Saltus, *Mary Magdalen: A Chronicle* (New York, 1919), pp. 65, 37.
9 Maurice Maeterlinck, *Mary Magdalene: A Play* (New York, 1910), p. 276.
10 Wilkie Collins, *The New Magdalen* (New York, 1908), p. 276.
11 Edith Olivier, *Mary Magdalen* (London, 1934), p. 8.
12 Moncure Conway, *The Autobiography of Moncure Conway* (Boston, Mass., 1904), Vol. 1, p. vi.
13 Ibid., Vol. 2, p. 284.
14 Ibid., p. 125.
15 Ibid., p. 126.
16 Moncure D. Conway, "A new view of Mary Magdalene," *The Critic*, XLII, 3 (Mar. 1903), p. 212.
17 Ibid., p. 215.
18 Ibid., p. 212.
19 John Henry Newman, "Purity and love," in *Discourses to Mixed Congregations* (New York, 1897), p. 75.
20 C. H. Spurgeon, "Sweet comfort for feeble saints," in *The New Park Street Pulpit* (Grand Rapids, Michigan, 1963), p. 45.
21 Olivier, *Mary Magdalene*, p. 15.
22 Jameson, *Sacred and Legendary*, p. 373.
23 Olivier, *Mary Magdalene*, p. 17; Saltus, *Mary Magdalene*, p. 27.
24 Josephine Butler, *The Constitution Violated* (Edinburgh, 1871), p. 105, fn.
25 John Ruskin, *Modern Painters* (New York, 1873), Vol. 2, pp. 317, 322; Vol. 5, p. 248.
26 Cited in Virginia Surtees, *The Paintings and Drawings of Dante Gabriel Rossetti: A*

Catalogue Raisonné (Oxford, 1971), p. 62.
27 Ibid.
28 Linda Nochlin, "Lost and found: once more the fallen woman," *Art Bulletin*, 60 (1978), p. 139.
29 Jan Marsh, *Pre-Raphaelite Women* (London, 1987), p. 23.
30 "Mary Magdalene at the door of Simon the Pharisee (for a drawing)," in Oswald Doughty (ed.), *Dante Gabriel Rossetti: Poems* (London, 1957), p. 141.
31 Letter to Ford Madox Brown, 5 Feb. 1864, in Oswald Doughty and John Robert Wahl (eds), *Letters of Dante Gabriel Rossetti* (Oxford, 1965), Vol. 2, p. 498.
32 Nochlin, "Lost and found," p. 153.
33 Cited in Surtees, *Paintings and Drawings*, Vol. I, p. 27.
34 Conway, *Autobiography*, Vol. 2, p. 130.
35 Betty O'Looney, *Frederick Sandys, 1829-1904* (Brighton, 1974), p. 25.
36 Jameson, *Sacred and Legendary*, p. 366.
37 Richard Ellmann, *Oscar Wilde* (New York, 1988), p. 69.
38 E. F. Benson, *The Babe, BA: Being the Uneventful History of a Young Gentleman at Cambridge* (New York, 1896), p. 177.
39 Malcolm Bell, *Edward Burne-Jones: A Record and Review* (London, 1892).
40 Ernestine Mills (ed.), *The Life and Letters of Frederick Shields* (London, 1912), p. 281.
41 Henry Ward Beecher, *The Life of Jesus the Christ* (New York, 1871), p. 278.
42 Charles Kingsley, *Twenty-Five Village Sermons* (London, 1849), pp. 181, 260.
43 Newman, "Purity and love," pp. 75-6, 78.
44 Spurgeon, "Conversion," in *The New Park Street Pulpit*, p. 344.
45 George Bernard Shaw, "The new Magdalen and the old," *Saturday Review*, LXXX (2 Nov. 1895), p. 576.
46 Nochlin, "Lost and found," p. 139.
47 Henry Edward Manning, *Penitents and Saints: A Sermon Preached in Behalf of the Magdalen Hospital at Saint George-in-the-Fields, May 8, 1844* (London, 1844), pp. 17, 19.
48 Butler, *Constitution*, p. 92 fn.
49 Harriet Martineau, *Biographical Sketches* (New York, 1869), p. 118.
50 J. A. V. Chapple and Arthur Pollard (eds), *The Letters of Mrs Gaskell* (Manchester, 1966), p. 221.
51 Ibid., p. 226.
52 Jameson, *Sacred and Legendary*, p. 402.
53 Ibid., p. 583.
54 Anna Jameson, *The History of Our Lord as Exemplified in Works of Art* (London, 1864), Vol. 2, pp. 278, 283.
55 John Keble, *The Christian Year: Thoughts in Verse for the Sundays and Holidays throughout the Year* (Oxford, 1927), p. 147.
56 *Whisper of the Muse: The Overstreet Album and Other Photographs by Julia Margaret Cameron* (Malibu, 1986), essay by Mike Weaver, p. 24.
57 Helmut Gernsheim, *Julia Margaret Cameron, Her Life and Work*, an Aperture monograph (London, 1975), p. 182.
58 Letter to Barbara Bodichon, 10 May 1870, in Doughty and Wahl, *Letters*, p. 871.
59 Mike Weaver, *Julia Margaret Cameron, 1815-1879* (Boston, Mass., 1984), p. 23.
60 Jameson, *History of Our Lord*, p. 273.
61 *Whisper of the Muse*, p. 30.
62 Mike Weaver, "Julia Margaret Cameron, the stamp of divinity," in Mike Weaver (ed.), *British Photography in the Nineteenth Century* (Cambridge, 1989), p. 159.
63 There are over 200 of Cameron's photographs in the Gernsheim Collection,

Humanities Research Center, the University of Texas at Austin. I am grateful to Andrea Inselmann, Research Assistant of the Photography Collection, for locating the Magdalen images for me.

64 *Whisper of the Muse*, p. 39.
65 Ernest Renan, *The Life of Jesus* (New York, 1863), pp. 27, 296.
66 Ellman, *Oscar Wilde*, p. 82.
67 Elizabeth Cady Stanton, *The Woman's Bible* (New York, 1972), p. 214.
68 Ibid., pp. 142–3.
69 Shaw, "The new Magdalen and the old," p. 577.

Chapter 8

History and religion: J. R. Seeley and the burden of the past

Reba N. Soffer

The natural theology of the eighteenth century, with its solacing revelation of God's order, harmony, and stability, was largely rejected by religious thinkers in the first half of the nineteenth century when the conditions of English life testified instead to disorder, disharmony, and instability. Unprecedented population growth in crowded cities; the failures of public health, housing, and education; unpredictable cycles of boom and bust, creating and exacerbating political and economic discontent; and the deeply pessimistic predictions of Malthusians and evangelicals – all transformed the idea of cataclysm from a biblical admonition to an imminent terror. The attempt of secular historians like Macaulay to extract evidence of moral and spiritual progress from the past and the present contrasted uncomfortably with contemporary events and with evangelical despair about unregenerate individuals living in a society increasingly alienated from God. When Macaulay described Francis Bacon's belief in the "divine authority of Christian revelation" and in "religion as the bond of charity; the curb of evil passions; the consolation of the wretched; the support of the timid; the hope of the dying," he was describing his own faith. But for Macaulay, as he said of Bacon, theology "engaged scarcely any portion of his attention."[1] Macaulay's *History of England* (1848–60) was repudiated by evangelicals and high Anglicans, and especially by Tractarians, who understood that he was interested in the state more as the protector of life and property than as the guarantor of religious values.[2] In common, his religious critics regarded the worst of all possible worlds as an unlikely milieu for the development of public or private good. Anglicans relied on established institutions to remedy individual failings, but they feared that Anglican writ, which controlled education and other formative agencies in national life, would be recast by a Parliament in which Dissenters and even non-Protestants legislated for the church. Extreme evangelicals, who, as Boyd Hilton has argued, established "a moral hegemony over public life" out of proportion to their limited numbers, saw the check to weak and irrational human nature in providential intervention through the rigorous disciplines of election, reprobation, future punishment, and vicarious sacrifice.[3] The evangelical's harshly imagined deity, penalizing a naturally corrupt world marred by historical decay and individual insufficiency, and the Anglican's image of a God whose discipline was exercised through restraining institutions, left little room for love, trust, empathy, and beauty on the side of God or men. A perception of God as a chronically intrusive and vexed patriarch hardly satisfied longings for justice and compassion. If there was a design but its evidences were concealed from men, how could they be held responsible for their own acts? A God who allowed men to make mistakes with tragic consequences diminished not only his omnipotence and omniscience, but his moral responsibility.

Both secular and religious readings of history, in the first half of the nineteenth century, failed to accommodate man and God in a scheme that satisfied intellectual, psychological, emotional, or moral criteria. Secular historians generally thought about religion in terms of its effect upon politics; they tended to look for the origins of disestablishment, or the extension of civil, religious, and educational opportunities to non-Anglicans, or papal aggression, or the relation between religion and the condition of England.[4] But after the 1860s social, economic, and political conflicts yielded to a growing stability, a rise in the standard of living, diffused prosperity, expanding commerce, scientific innovation, and the substitution of genetic models of random process for both religious and mathematical models of static certainty. The excitement of limitless possibilities, expressed in a new aesthetic of process, inspired intellectual turmoil during the last four decades of the nineteenth century. Conventional religious beliefs were challenged in 1859 by two publications that both depended on a sweeping historical sense. In *Essays and Reviews*, the broad-church authors applied historical criticism to religious records; and in *The Origin of Species*, Charles Darwin appeared to question the accuracy of biblical accounts of creation and subsequent human evolution by tracing evidence of natural selection through natural history. Within the next three decades, the study of English history incorporated the new learning to offer a majestic panorama in which dynamic forces begot social, economic, political, and technological benefits. Some intellectuals, such as the positivist Frederick Harrison or the agnostic Leslie Stephen, turned to history as a surrogate for traditional religion.[5] But Harrison and Stephen had little influence on the development of historical study in England.

Instead of threatening religion, the ascendant schools of historical interpretation reconciled human nature and divine purposes by regarding God as a superintending Father who trusted the best and brightest of his children to imagine the world as it ought to be. Both history and religion, influenced by the German higher criticism, combined rational tests for truth with a romantic yearning for personal spiritual meaning. History continued to be written with an eschatological content, and religion, increasingly pluralistic and diverse, turned to history for justification by fact. By the second half of the nineteenth century, intellectuals trained in the universities to find evidence of progress, and to believe in their own abilities to accomplish progressive ends, attributed their success to merit and opportunity. For them, divine authority, like any other authority, warranted deference only when it was rational, humane, predictable, and, above all, consonant with meliorative change. The study of the past confirmed optimistic expectations about a future guided by university graduates who wanted God to be created in their own image.

Among those graduates, an honors BA in history was considered, increasingly, the best training for men, and eventually women, who would lead an expanding nation and empire.[6] From the mid-1870s teaching, curriculum, and examinations in history were set by William Stubbs for Oxford and by John Robert Seeley for Cambridge. Both men impressed their historical visions on their universities. Although the college teachers did most of the teaching, they taught the professor's interpretation of the inner meanings and purposes of history for at least two generations. The two Regius Professors of Modern History were members of the Church of England, with very different views about religion, the church, and history. The Tory Stubbs lived securely in the moderate center and worked painstakingly to affirm the continuities and stabilities responsible for England's constitutional success. His historical work, throughout his professional career, traced the origins and progressive development of institutions, and especially of a national church with roots in Anglo-Saxon England. Stubbs shunned controversy and argued against study of the recent past. If he was a man with religious passions, he concealed them very well. It was fitting that Stubbs should have become a bishop so that he could further the harmonies that he admired in English institutions.

Seeley shared with Stubbs an understanding of history as a schooling in citizenship, but he lived in a different historical and religious world than his Oxford colleague. Enormously energetic, passionate, and controversial, Seeley began his professional life as a religious "enthusiast of humanity," and he concluded it as an untiring advocate of an imperial federation, rooted in religious impulse. Seeley's consuming interest became increasingly the contemporary English state expanding by force, when necessary, for just ends. While the Tory Stubbs venerated the past for creating institutions that perpetuated individual liberty and communal responsibility, the Liberal Seeley saw both the religious and historical past as a burden that had to be discarded so that progress could occur. For Seeley, the present determined the past, and only those aspects of history were worth studying that could solve immediate and future problems. Neutrality was morally impossible because history made clear the right side. Seeley wanted to shape the future by using history, which he defined as political science, to discover and implement practical laws of national development.

Raised within a "severe,"[7] Pentecostal, evangelical family, Seeley became an increasingly latitudinarian Anglican.[8] Eventually, he gave up the church for a natural religion inspired by Old Testament prophecy, poetry, science, and the religious man's burden. His well-known father, Robert Benton Seeley, was a successful publisher and bookseller, and the author of books about social reform, religion, and history. R. B. and J. R. Seeley belonged to very different intellectual generations, each addressing problems made newly imperative by changing times. R. B. Seeley was a contemporary of Karl Marx, Thomas Carlyle, and Charles Dickens, and his rhetoric and social analysis also attacked the ideology of political economy and the idealization of money as an appropriate basis for human and social relations. Although he accepted a class system as God-given, he insisted that God meant the lower classes to have more choices than either "oppression or starvation." What the laboring poor needed, to "restore them to their ancient happiness and good character, is *hope* . . . founded on a reasonable prospect of advancement." No other class in the community, he pointed out, was "denied this privilege." R. B. Seeley relied on individual activism, stimulated by the fear that an "aggravated" God would apply the "scourge that our own hands are twisting, for the purposes of severe chastisement." Unlike Marx, Carlyle, and Dickens, R. B. Seeley welcomed the spur of divine retribution and imminent apocalypse.[9]

His son dismissed such fears as inconsistent with Christ's character and purposes. J. R. Seeley and his generation trusted the good faith of organized groups such as the London Metaphysical and Psychological Society, founded in 1869 to bring together influential men of divergent but generally liberal faiths, so that they could agree and act upon the necessary directions society ought to take.[10] Seeley was also active in the Cambridge Eranus Society, founded in late 1872 by New Testament scholars like Brooke Foss Westcott and Joseph Barber Lightfoot, both subsequently Professors of Divinity at Cambridge and Bishops of Durham, and F. J. A. Hort, the Cambridge theologian influenced by F. D. Maurice. Henry Sidgwick, among the original members, described the group as "representatives of different departments of academic study" who met regularly for the exchange of "ideas somewhat more serious and methodical than is suitable at an ordinary social gathering."[11] Seeley was even more sympathetic to broadly inclusive, nondogmatic groups that attempted to reach wide audiences.[12] He was especially drawn to the Christian Social Union, founded in 1889 and chaired by Bishop Westcott, with a membership of 2,600 members by 1894 and over 6,000 before the First World War. Religious intellectuals were attracted by the union's attempt "To study in common how to apply the moral truths and principles of Christianity to the social and economic difficulties of the present time." Their academic approach, which Seeley shared, was derided by the more radical Guild of St Matthew: "Here is a glaring social evil, let us read a paper on the subject."[13]

Although father and son quarreled about John's increasing attraction to the thought of F. D. Maurice and diverged ultimately in their most basic beliefs,[14] a comparison of the writings of the premillenarian father and of his broad-church son shows a surprising continuity in perceptions of religious experience and its consequences. The assumptions shared by the Seeleys transcend personal eccentricity and suggest that certain religious convictions persisted throughout the nineteenth century. Those aspects of J. R. Seeley's thought that anticipated and touched the thinking and conduct of Balliol men, led by Benjamin Jowett, Arnold Toynbee, and T. H. Green, as well as of Trinity men such as William Cunningham and Henry Sidgwick, can be found in his father's writings of the 1830s. Both Seeleys believed in the necessary connection between religion, ethics, and the paternalistic responsibilities of the state. Both men responded to the God of the Incarnation, who, as R. B. Seeley wrote, "so loved us, we ought also to love one another," and both saw Christ as the model against whom they measured the lives of other men. The elder Seeley called for "a practical studying of the best means by which at once to elevate the national character, and ensure the national stability."[15] His son tried to make history that practical study. Both men regarded moral character and beneficent paternalism as the essential qualities of all great leaders, beginning with Christ. In two books, R. B. Seeley vindicated Edward I as a heroic statesman, wise, strong, sagacious, thoroughly honest, merciful, good, and just, who established a constitutional legislature to enact good laws.[16] J. R. Seeley attributed similar qualities to Karl von Stein, and he condemned Napoleon Bonaparte for not having them. Father and son expected the state, as R. B. Seeley wrote, to make and enforce "good laws" to "protect the defenceless" by preventing misery from occurring. They also agreed that social and moral responsibility followed from God's creation of man under a theocracy governed by helpful rules. To these criteria for good government J. R. Seeley added imperial expansion. R. B. Seeley saw the church as the national agency of education, and he entrusted the clergy with promoting the "temporal comfort and welfare of the poor" in the "name of Him, who went about doing good."[17] His son extended that imperative to include every Christian in every denomination, who bore these responsibilities because of their identity with Christ. But, by the 1880s, he divorced duty from organized religion and made it a necessary attribute of a humanity that worshipped the laws governing men and nature.

J. R. Seeley became a leader in his own generation with the publication of *Ecce Homo* (1865), an examination of Christ's call, the nature of his society, and the content and object of his legislation. *Ecce Homo* was published in a market that, from the 1850s through the 1870s, demanded religious writing and reading. Cultural and social changes in leisure, railway travel, cheap and circulating books, and the observance of a "serious" Sunday, encouraged a variety of writers. But among the new books, the lives of Jesus and the examination of the Gospels became increasingly popular.[18] When *Ecce Homo* appeared, it was acclaimed widely as one of the most important books to affect religious thinking during the second half of the nineteenth century, and a sensation was created when it was discovered that Seeley was the author. Gladstone, who later appointed Seeley to the regius chair but who in 1865 was ignorant of the author of *Ecce Homo*, wrote to Macmillan on Christmas Day: "I know of, or recollect, no production of equal force that recent years can boast of: . . . I hail the entrance into the world of a . . . noble book."[19]

To avoid offending his father, Seeley published *Ecce Homo* anonymously. Seeley may have held fast to many of his father's principles, but the book introduced major themes that were to run consistently through his own subsequent historical and religious writing. *Ecce Homo* was intended for intellectuals who were finding alternative sources of knowledge and ethics more reasonable than Christianity.[20] As early as the 1830s the notion that knowledge itself was progressive meant, for some religious thinkers, that Christian knowledge could not be considered as given and fixed. An Anglican apologist like H. G. Baden Powell, a priest, mathematician, and natural philosopher who became the Savilian Professor of Geometry at Oxford in 1827, felt that the church had to respond to the changing status of knowledge and society or lose ground to the new groups emerging in society, especially since the "alternative culture put forward by dissatisfied Dissenting and radical elites was scientifically oriented."[21]

Seeley appealed to the new critics' respect for facts in 1865 by basing his interpretation on the historical evidence of the Gospels. But his understanding of "evidence," in all his work, was often criticized for its ahistorical nature. Some readers applauded Seeley's presentation of a truly historical Christ. Edward T. Vaughan, an Incarnationist who gave the Hulsean Lectures at Cambridge in 1875, considered *Ecce Homo* a vindication of "our right to believe that the character of our Lord is thoroughly historical, entirely real, not the product of human imagination, and is such as each one of the Gospels presents it to us." Seeley was reliable to Vaughan because, as the Professor of Latin at University College London, Seeley was "familiar with antiquity" and with the historical setting in which Christ belonged.[22] But other reviewers, although sympathetic with Seeley's intentions and effect, pointed out that he had not used historical methods properly. The *Westminster Review* accepted the great and on the whole beneficial influence of *Ecce Homo*, but argued that it was historically faulty because views were attributed to Christ that only developed much later under greatly altered circumstances. Similar criticism appeared in *Fraser's Magazine*. The *Fortnightly Review*, in a favorable essay, suggested that the author of *Ecce Homo* might not be "conversant" with the historical or higher criticism that had already been applied to passages in the Gospel and that his analysis of the historical records substituted what he wanted to see for the evidence that could be derived from "a patient and detailed consideration of the facts."[23]

Seeley was hardly deficient in a historical sense. But he was not interested in testing particular facts either in *Ecce Homo* and his other religious writings or in his historical work. Historical details were useful only for establishing the generalizations or laws of history for a prescriptive science that would make both religion and history applied subjects. When Seeley interpreted collected and organized facts or compared existing states, by their resemblances and differences, his goal was to reach explanatory generalizations.[24] History was a reliable "compass," necessarily "reassuring," because it showed the student that his life was not aimless but rather a voyage "to a definite port." Even if he failed occasionally, he could go on "supported by faith in a law of Good, of which he has traced the workings" in history.[25] In *The Expansion of England*

(1883), Seeley asserted that history "should pursue a practical object" so as to "modify" the reader's "view of the present and his forecast of the future." Concerned far more with the future than with the past, for both religion and the fate of England, Seeley wanted the history of England "to end with something that might be called a moral. Some large conclusion ought to arise out of it; it ought to exhibit the general tendency of English affairs in such a way as to set us thinking about the future and divining the destiny which is reserved for us."[26] Seeley's closest colleague at Cambridge, the historian G. W. Prothero, pointed out that Seeley was interested in using history only for the "solution of some problem; the establishment of some principle, which would arrest the attention of the student, and might be of use to the statesman. History pure and simple, that is narrative without generalisation . . . appeared trivial, unworthy of serious attention."[27]

In Seeley's study of religion, as in his history, he left the determination of what had actually happened to specialized scholars. But he understood historical relativity very well. Other liberal religious thinkers wanted to place the Bible within history without jeopardizing its teachings as a source of ethics beyond the currency of time. But Seeley, two years after *Ecce Homo* was published, while granting that the Bible contained universal principles, argued that each age was a new society requiring a new teaching. What could be read in the Bible was the "philosophy of a society that has long passed away." To make "Christianity a practical power" in our lives, we had to study two books: "the Bible and the Time." What the churches needed to reverse their declining position was a current "philosophy of society," that would make them "perpetual, incorruptible" critics "upon all social proceedings." The church "should bring all the lights of science and learning to bear upon human life; it should probe everything, and try by its own high principles, and perpetually bring institutions and usages before the judgment seat of Christ."[28]

It was not Christ the judge but Christ the teacher whom Seeley loved. Another theme established in *Ecce Homo* was that Christ's personal interest in every individual made them better people. Philosophy helped us to reflect "deeply on human affairs and social laws," but Christ surpassed rational thought by making emotional and psychological demands that were so compelling as to be irresistible. Christ personally influenced our feelings and made us good so that we could choose morally among the competing courses of conduct rationally demonstrated by philosophy. Christ was influential because he was a model of "striking and conspicuous goodness" whom people could worship as an ideal of what they themselves might become.[29] There was no problem of evil for Seeley because Christ had done everything divinely possible to give men not only free will but lessons in how to use their will for good.

Privately, Seeley worried that the compelling person of Christ had been lost in the historical development of Christianity. He believed that Christianity became after the Reformation a divisive rather than unifying influence, repeatedly opposing freedom and truth and retarding social and political progress. The result was that there were so many skeptics and disbelievers that he sometimes wondered whether the church and Christianity would endure for another generation.[30] Seeley acknowledged "the almost hopeless alienation of the leaders of the new generation from Christianity,"[31] by abandoning his father's emphasis on the Bible, to stress instead a "magnanimous" God who would not damn people for heterodoxy or even for atheism, because such people could be "honest and virtuous."[32] If religion were to appeal to these new leaders, it would have to be credible on both intellectual and moral grounds. History gave religion credibility by explaining how different beliefs were produced by different times and places. The effect of Seeley's reasoning was that since religious conceptions and institutions were historically determined, they could be replaced by new conceptions and institutions when the old ones no longer fitted the intellectual and spiritual needs of new times.[33]

By 1878 Seeley talked less about emulating Christ and more about emulating Germany. Just as God demonstrated personal goodness in Christ, so he demonstrated his providential dispensation for nations in leaders like the early nineteenth-century statesman, Stein. German unification and expansion taught a lesson that England had to learn. Seeley's promise in *Ecce Homo* to discuss Christ's divinity in a later volume[34] was fulfilled in his mind by his three-volume *Life and Times of Stein, or Germany and Prussia in the Napoleonic Age* (1878).[35] *Stein* demonstrated how spiritual principles could be applied effectively in the contemporary world when politics and the role of the state were properly understood. Stein was, in great part, Seeley's historical alter ego. When he described Stein's most deeply felt emotions and his practical policies, he was describing his own carefully guarded feelings and his own political ideals. He used the life of the great statesman as a proof of the validity and congruence of his own religious and historical ideas.

Seeley assumed that Stein was "inarticulate" about purely religious issues because he felt them so deeply. But the Prussian statesman surmounted his spiritual reticence by transforming religious inclinations into political and administrative activities. Whether or not Stein ever felt "spiritual disquiet," his mind had "in the large original sense of the word, piety." Practical piety meant to Seeley that, although Stein was a reformer, he never undervalued traditional institutions, including the church. As "a ruler, as a student of the influences which move great masses of people," he "valued religion, and held cheap the philosophies which speak only to the few." The practical imperatives of governing "great masses of people" led Stein to a political religion, an "approbation of Christianity as a good basis for national well-being." Stein was concerned with the public good and not with "the saving of the soul," the part of evangelicalism Seeley discarded with distaste. Seeley attributed to Stein the subordination of a personal religion to a faith supplying "that agreement in elementary principles without which a well-ordered state is not conceivable."

In his letters to his sister, which echo Seeley's own letters to his sisters, Stein emphasized the "mystery of self-sacrifice or duty," which he often conveyed in his habit of using the adjective "religious-moral." Seeley attributed the depth of Stein's sublimated religious feelings to the self-sacrificing example of a pious mother and sister. Seeley's own sisters shared an evangelical sense of piety with their father rather than sympathizing with his own movements toward an increasingly "natural" religion. But the habitual expression of strong religious emotions in the Seeley household may have allowed him to write passionately about religion from the mid-1860s. Stein, unlike Seeley, was so cautious about expressing his religious motivations that critics doubted their existence. Not Seeley, who argued that "no grander lesson of faith in Providence was ever given to any man than Stein." The conquest of Prussia by Napoleon had forced Stein into exile. But when Napoleon was overthrown and Stein could return to his country, property, and family, he learned then that there was "no calamity so dark and universal . . . but that Providence might be trusted speedily and splendidly to restore the daylight."[36] In this demonstration of divine intervention for a greater good, Seeley fulfilled the promise made in *Ecce Homo* to affirm the divinity of Christ.

Although his *Life and Times of Stein* made personal religion relatively less important than a national religion, Seeley held fast to a union of personal and social religion that he had defined in *Ecce Homo* as the "enthusiasm of humanity," a necessarily "inspiring passion" for active morality.[37] But Arnold Toynbee, who read *Ecce Homo* while struggling to understand how best to live a moral life, was troubled by Seeley's "throwing aside" the distinction between personal and social religion. The social side of religion meant to Toynbee "a passionate devotion to our fellowmen, to the higher interests of civilization," while personally he felt "the effect of such devotion, and of other pursuits, and of our general conceptions as to the world we live in, on the inner life."[38] Seeley did diminish the individualistic meaning of religion by subordinating the individual to a higher social good, just as in his historical writing he diminished the role of great men, even Stein, by making them serve the greater nation. His political journey from liberalism to liberal imperialism began with his argument in *Ecce Homo* that a Christian and a citizen both derived their moral and spiritual meaning from membership in a greater community. But Seeley agreed with Toynbee and other liberal religious thinkers that those "painful questions, concerning articles, subscriptions, and clerical texts, which have hampered men especially in Universities for so long," are solving themselves and there was a new way for "Christian devotion which young men may enter without any painful hesitations and perplexities." Repudiating emphases upon theology, form, and religious debate of all kinds, Seeley turned to institutions such as Toynbee Hall to encourage both personal and social regeneration of the spirit.[39]

A fourth and persistent theme in *Ecce Homo* and in *Stein* was the definition of Christianity as the "union of morals and politics." When Christ established his church as an active, beneficent state that obliged its members to "love one's neighbour as oneself," Christianity became an effective force.[40] Stein exemplified Christ living morally in the immediate world by becoming a statesman. Seeley became a teacher.[41] The regius professorship in modern history from 1869 to 1894 was an opportunity to study and teach "scientific" laws that determined not only England's history but its spiritual obligations to the larger world. Seeley never perceived his university chair as a refuge for the quiet pursuit of independent scholarship. Instead he portrayed the historian as he may have thought of himself, as a kind of secular priest, reading the auguries of the times.[42] In 1893 Seeley told the decade-old Japanese Club, formed by students from the ruling families of Japan, "to study" and "cultivate the training and character" of "the English Gentleman," that if they were "to enter into our Western civilization, it will not be enough" to "take institutions from us, you must also seek an ethical and religious ideal."[43] Such ideals were revealed unambiguously to Seeley in modern English history.

In contrast to almost every English historical writer in the second half of the nineteenth century, J. R. Seeley was interested in the Middle Ages and the Tudor and Stuart reigns only as a prelude to the evolution of his major concern, the contemporary national state. In his inaugural address as Professor of Latin at University College London, in 1863, Seeley had called for a new study of history that would go beyond the provision of moral examples to become a generalized science derived from an inductive and comparative study of facts. Imperial Rome interested Seeley more than Greece because it revealed a history that was the "mould in which our European system was shaped" and in which Christianity was "cradled."[44] Rome had expanded in the world to create a unity and a law that still affected the present. Seeley came to see England in the late nineteenth century as the heir to Rome.

Seeley admired, and tried to emulate in Cambridge, the new generation of "public-spirited thinkers" trained in the University of Berlin, where the "higher life" brought politics and culture together as a bulwark "of the State . . . a kind of spiritual weapon."[45] Just as Stein represented the highest achievements in politics, Goethe was Seeley's model for high culture. Although critics suspected Goethe's Christianity, Seeley read in Goethe's writings "grand and large ideas, which will not disappoint those who try to reduce them to practice; precepts which are not merely earnest, but, what is so much rarer, serious."[46] Seeley defended Goethe as a moral, genuinely religious person by arguing that it was a mistake to assume that "conventional Christianity is the one form, and conventional morality the one evidence, of true religion." Goethe worshipped "God in Nature" and believed, as Seeley did by the 1880s, that whoever had science and art had religion, too. Seeley grew convinced that there were only three classes of men who were genuinely religious. They were the poets and other artists of unique genius, the scientists, and those Christians willing to move and change with history. But he suspected those conspicuous individuals who resisted the nationally unifying tendencies in history. A Bonaparte had "vast intelligence" that was "dissociated from virtue," but he exerted "an irresistible attraction upon his fellow-men" and could arouse "in others noble sentiments of which he is incapable himself."[47] This kind of argument, very much like Hegel's cunning of reason, justified God's creation of morality from potential evil. But for Seeley, all great men, whether Steins or Bonapartes, "do not act but are acted on, they are hurried forward by vast forces of which they can but slightly modify the direction." Bonaparte was bound to fail because he was unpatriotic, opportunistic, immoral, and cynical.[48] Stein's Germany was a successful nation because it supported national unification. Bonaparte's France failed because it attempted a unification that ignored the historical integrity of nations.

Seeley discovered the sources of religion and nationalism in the "long epic of the formation, growth, sufferings, death, and resurrection of a nationality which had its roots among the Jews." That spiritual nationality rose again in the Roman Empire when Christianity was "idealized in the form of a world religion which extended Jewish citizenship to the Gentiles."[49] England, the new Rome, was obligated to extend its inherently religious civilization to less fortunate peoples. But the English, oblivious of their own recent history, were handicapped further by provincial ignorance of the history, literature, and culture of other nations. The result was that the English were unaware of their own destiny, unable to learn from other national mistakes; and, even more serious, patriotism had atrophied as a national virtue.[50] Seeley studied France and Germany only as cautionary examples for England. German success was to be imitated and French failure to be avoided. Seeley was entirely correct about the Anglocentric emphasis in the schools and universities and about the limitation of English history to the centuries before 1800. But English history, taught by every educational and religious agency in late Victorian England, including Seeley's own university and largely as a result of his influence, had become an uninterrupted lesson in patriotism and national obligation.[51]

Patriotism depended, he was convinced, on a systematic and dispassionate study of politics. When people understood the objective laws that governed their past and predicted their future, they would feel a selfless duty to further their country's noblest ends. History, and the judicial method of rational inquiry and comparison that it represented, considered "facts without bias." Citizenship within a moral community relied on "trustworthy historical information" as a requisite for political choices.[52] Scientific history, which included political economy, explained politics and the "place of government in human affairs." But, most important, history was "the school of public feeling and patriotism," and more still, the "school of statesmanship,"[53] a political science of normative, empirical principles that would serve as the foundation for the unbiased study of politics. In order to understand those principles within their appropriate historical context, Seeley argued that the focus of history must be the state, studied by inductive, observational methods similar to those of astronomy or the natural sciences.[54] Impartiality toward politics did not imply an absence of strong sentiments. On the contrary, Seeley argued that a disinterested study of historical phenomena was entirely consistent with "the strongest feeling or the most decisive action." But beyond party conflict, or acts of Parliament, or the decision of the ballot box, politics had to rest on "systematic and reasoned truth" enshrined in the principles of a political science taught by great thinkers and writers such as Tocqueville or J. S. Mill. Such truth was not arrived at by voting or by consensus. The object of a science was to "find the truth"; and while a majority "may be a respectable thing," it had "no function in the investigation of the truth." From the new democracy, deficient in religion and history, Seeley turned to the elite leaders within the universities who, he expected, would "give coherence, connexion, and system to the thinking of the nation."[55] Education, whether in the universities or in any other agency, had to mean "a grasp of principles, a sense of distinctions, a power of perceiving something beyond class interests, and desiring something besides material happiness."[56]

The ethical sources of Seeley's patriotism were religious. But the origins and nature of ethics and its relation to political issues were hotly debated from the 1870s to the century's end. Seeley tried to settle the secularist, religious, and political controversies of his time by finding science, religion, history, utilitarian morality, nationalism, and imperial federation compatible within an orderly universe. Seeley suggested that the creator of the universe be worshipped through natural religion, which included art and science, as well as more traditional organizations of faith. And he argued that all religions, developed historically among national groups, were still progressing in new forms and in new institutions. In *Macmillan's Magazine*, between 1875 and 1878, Seeley published a series of essays which he largely rewrote as *Natural Religion* (1882). The least popular of all his books, perhaps because the divergent views in history, religion, science, and morality that he attempted to reconcile had become irreconcilable, *Natural Religion* was his most serious attempt to explain the imperatives of belief. The central figure in the book was not the God of the atonement, but the God of the Old Testament. Such a God, most familiar in the Book of Job, would often neglect "us in our need" and often be "deaf to prayers." But the God of "hebraic awe" was closer to the religion of science, in which "Nature including Humanity would be our God." Seeley rejected the sunny natural religion of such eighteenth-century apologists as William Paley to contend that theology was not "a collection of the evidences of benevolent design in the Universe" but rather a "true," or scientific, "deduction of the laws which govern the Universe." Late nineteenth-century science turned "her smoked eye glass upon God, deliberately diminishing the glory of what she looks at that she may distinguish better. Here too she sees mechanism where will, purpose, and love had been supposed before; she drops the name God, and takes up the less awful name of Nature instead."[57]

If the essence of religion was the "worship" of nature, the recognition of "the Unity in the Universe," then there was no difficulty in abandoning miracles, and all other incomprehensible phenomena in traditional Christianity. Instead, in human and especially moral matters, the "ordinary laws of nature" resulted "on the whole" in rewards for the just and punishment for the evil. To many nineteenth-century intellectuals, history provided more satisfying evidence of divine justice and of God's design than miracles, especially since arguments for the miraculous made God seem insufficiently aware of the uniformity of natural laws that He himself had created. Seeley wanted religion and history to testify together to the greater glory of science. The Old Testament increasingly appealed to Seeley because it had united the worship of natural laws with the worship of God. History "scientifically treated," he wrote, "restores the ancient gift of prophecy" by providing laws of development. The "great founders of the semitic religion" had understood that the laws that govern the universe enable us to understand the present and anticipate the future. They worshipped "the God who habitually maintains his laws" rather "than the God who occasionally suspends them" through supernatural occurrences.[58]

An earlier version of Seeley's "scientific" dispatch of the problem of evil appeared in 1855 in Baden Powell's *Essays*, which argued that the existence of evil in nature proved the insufficiency of the human concept of benevolence and providence.[59] Baden Powell eliminated the individual as the possible victim of evil by assuming that Providence was unconcerned with individuals. Moreover, Baden Powell found that instead of intervening benevolently in the arrangement of natural phenomena, Providence simply preserved "preordained causes for the general good."[60] Seeley, too, reserved providential dispensation for those great issues that guaranteed the progress of civilization, such as the defeat of Napoleon Bonaparte. He came to use the word "God," as the ancient prophets and the poets had, to convey "beauty and greatness and glory" and "whatever more awful forces stir within the human heart, whatever binds men in families, and orders them in states." In passionate rhetoric, Seeley celebrated God as "the Inspirer of Kings, the Revealer of laws, the Reconciler of Nations, the Redeemer of labour, the Queller of tyrants, the Reformer of Churches, the Guide of the human race towards an unknown goal." This God and his "religion of Unity" were far better equipped to build and maintain empires than the loving social worker whom Seeley had depicted as Christ in *Ecce Homo*.[61]

The empire to which Seeley was committed provided England with a providential mission. Modern religion must carry to less civilized nations

> the true view of the universe, the true astronomy, the true chemistry, and the true physiology to polytheists still lapped in mythological dreams; let us carry progress and free will to fatalist nations and to nations cramped by the fetters of primitive custom; let us carry the doctrine of a rational liberty into the heart of Oriental despotism; in doing all this – not indeed suddenly or fanatically, nor yet pharisaically, as if we ourselves had nothing to learn – we shall admit the outlying world into the great civilized community, into the modern city of God.

Seeley cautioned that England must first "rigorously test our own civilization" to determine "how far our contact is life-giving and how far it may be noxious and noisome." In such probing, people will see that it is not institutions, the heart of every other contemporary interpretation of English history, but rather "a personal influence issuing out of every Englishman," which was "neither more nor less than our religion." But religion could hardly be "the basis of societies and of states," the "practical view of life which whole communities live by," when it was disputed and a subject of chronic and debilitating debate. Religion had to be both unimpeachable and absolutely convincing.[62]

To provide certainty for religious skeptics, Seeley turned to history and discovered there that the great "function of religion has been the founding and sustaining of states." When religion decayed, the state was in peril. As a remedy, "using scientific method alone" we can "lay down such a Natural Religion" as "may be a sustaining principle to the civilization of this world." Unlike his colleagues in history who were tracing the continuities that made institutions endure, Seeley wrote that an "institution is healthy in proportion to its independence of its own past, to the confident freedom with which it alters itself to meet new conditions." Seeley rejected the constraint of the past upon the future of the English state and he repudiated the church's "retrospectiveness, that unhealthy inclination for revival and what is called reformation." Both political and religious history could become the worst of ramshackle structures, upheld because those "who cannot see the end fix their eyes, as the next best thing, upon the beginning." In both religion and the state, England had to decide first on national purposes and then "consciously" will "the end and the means." One of the laws that history taught was that it was "more evident with every century that churches like states can live only on the condition of changing freely and perpetually."[63] Seeley was always excited by new habits and ways of thinking that encouraged "perpetual change and unintermitted improvement," and he shrank from the stationary "as from stagnation and death."[64]

But the optimistic Seeley admitted reluctantly in the last decades of the nineteenth century that many recent "changes" were not the "uninterrupted improvements" he was prepared to welcome. He had tried to place Christ, social morality, and national destiny within a historical dynamic that propelled the present into a more spiritually satisfying future. But when the expanding democracy ignored the historical laws that his political science was studying and when Ireland threatened to destroy the national unity he valued, Seeley looked for remedies in the empire of Britain rather than in the empire of Christ. In order to teach a higher, more serious life that would serve the spiritual needs first of the English state and then of a wider humanity, Seeley provided a "scientific" interpretation of English history and a "scientific" interpretation of English religion. Seeley was an aggressive member of an intellectual community that wanted to believe that it would succeed in carrying out its elevated sense of duty. A reconciliation of the progressive lessons of history, understood as laws rather than as fortuitous events, with the spiritual depths of religion and the remarkable record of science's technological and analytical marvels, provided a formidable arsenal to be used against the most apparently intractable problems. For all his optimism, Seeley recognized by the end of his life that God often had a dark face. But Seeley and his contemporaries were not prepared for the more sinister face of science.

NOTES

1 Thomas Babington Macaulay, "Lord Bacon," *Edinburgh Review*, 65 (July, 1837), p. 87.
2 I am grateful to Timothy Lang for his manuscript, "Macaulay's *History of England* and Victorian religious controversy." It is hardly surprising, as Lang demonstrates, that Macaulay was accused of "religious indifference."
3 See Boyd Hilton's marvelous *The Age of Atonement: The Influence of Evangelicalism on Social and Economic Thought, 1795–1865* (Oxford, 1988), p. 219.
4 Atheists, from at least the publication of Charles Southwell's periodical, the *Oracle of Reason*, in 1841, had assailed William Paley's *Natural Theology* (London, 1802), the best-known argument from design. See F. B. Smith, "The atheist mission, 1840–1900," in R. Robson (ed.), *Ideas and Institutions of Victorian Britain* (New York, 1967), p. 208; and Martha Garland, *Cambridge before Darwin: The Ideal of a Liberal Education, 1800–1860* (Cambridge, 1980), p. 55, for a discussion of Paley's benevolent and cheerful image of the human condition.
5 See Frederic Harrison, *Autobiographic Memoirs* (London, 1911); and Leslie Stephen, *History of English Thought in the Eighteenth Century*, 2 vols (London, 1876); also see Martha Vogeler, *Frederic Harrison: The Vocations of a Positivist* (Oxford, 1984); and Noel Annan, *Leslie Stephen: The Godless Victorian* (New York, 1984).
6 The great majority of first- and second-class graduates in history at the major colleges in Oxford and Cambridge entered secular professions serving the public good rather than religious professions. For a discussion of the careers of graduates of Balliol College, Oxford, and King's College, Cambridge, for the years 1873 to 1929, see Reba N. Soffer, *The Modern University and National Values: History and the Making of an Elite, 1850–1930* (forthcoming).
7 This is how one of J. R. Seeley's sisters described their upbringing: *In the Light: Brief Memorials of Elizabeth Phebe Seeley, by Her Sister* (London, 1887), p. 7.
8 See Frank Turner's effective argument that "expansive, intensified religion . . . establishes a faith to be lost" and that "the religious character and role of the evangelical family in and of itself fostered spiritual crisis": "The Victorian crisis of faith and the faith that was lost," in Richard J. Helmstadter and Bernard Lightman (eds), *Victorian Faith in Crisis: Essays on Continuity and Change in Nineteenth-Century Belief* (Stanford, Calif., 1990), pp. 15, 21.
9 R. B. Seeley, *The Perils of the Nation: An Appeal to the Legislature, the Clergy, and the Higher and Middle Classes* (2nd edn, rev., London, 1843), pp. 14, xxvi, 17. Seeley denounced the degradation of the poor, and called for the ministry, Parliament, the church, the professions, and women to play an increased social role in achieving a healthy, moral, and, therefore, religious population.
10 Among the founders were Arthur Penrhyn Stanley, the broad-church Dean of Westminster, the Roman Catholic Archbishop H. E. Manning, the Unitarian leader James Martineau, Richard Holt Hutton, editor of the *Spectator*, W. P. Ward, editor of the *Dublin Review*, Walter Bagehot, editor of the *Economist*, and Sir John

Lubbock, the banker and scientist. On 14 May 1872 a typical meeting heard Archbishop Manning on "Legitimate authority is evidence of truth": announcement in Seeley Papers, Box 3, University of London Library. See A. W. Brown, *The Metaphysical Society: Victorian Minds in Crisis, 1869-1880)* (New York, 1947).

11 Henry Sidgwick in Sir Arthur Hort's biography of his father, *Life and Letters of F. J. A. Hort, sometime Hulsean Professor and Lady Margaret Reader in Divinity in the University of Cambridge* (London, 1896), Vol. 2, p. 184. The other original members included Sidgwick, Clerk Maxwell, and Henry Jackson. Lord Acton, Clifford Allbutt, and George Darwin were among the later members.

12 Seeley was an active university extension lecturer and an officer in both the Ethical Culture Society and the Social and Political Education League; he lectured for the Christian Socialist Working Men's College and sat on the Council of the Church Reform Union.

13 Quoted in David Nicholls, *Deity and Domination: Images of God and Man in the Nineteenth and Twentieth Centuries* (London, 1989), pp. 53, 54.

14 Deborah Wormell cites two letters from John to his father as evidence of the "marked irritability" produced by their theological differences and she points out that John was the only Seeley child who was not a beneficiary under his father's will: *Sir John Seeley and the Uses of History* (Cambridge, 1980), pp. 14, 15, n. 15.

15 Seeley, *Perils of the Nation*, pp. 250, 99-100.

16 R. B. Seeley was taken seriously enough as a historian to be discussed in the Oxford Historical Seminar by Goldwin Smith and Montague Burrows in 1864 and to receive good notices from both Stubbs and his successor, Edward Freeman. See his *Greatest of All the Plantagenets* (London, 1872), a "Historical sketch," incorporated into an extended *Life and Reign of Edward I*, published by Seeley, Jackson, & Halliday (London, 1872), pp. 340-1, 94.

17 Seeley, *Perils of the Nation*, pp. 246, 1-2, 313.

18 Daniel L. Pals, *The Victorian "Lives" of Jesus* (San Antonio, Tex., 1982), p. 68. Seeley's *Ecce Homo* was the most widely read life of Christ until Seeley's friend, F. W. Farrar, a Cambridge Apostle, headmaster of Marlborough School, and chaplain to the Queen and the House of Commons, published his *Life of Christ* in 1874.

19 Gladstone to Macmillan, 25 Dec. 1865, Seeley Papers, Box 1, University of London Library.

20 See Howard R. Murphy, "The ethical revolt against Christian orthodoxy in early Victorian England," *American Historical Review* 60 (July 1955), pp. 800-17; and Ian MacKillop, *The British Ethical Societies* (Cambridge, 1986).

21 Pietro Corsi, *Science and Religion: Baden Powell and the Anglican Debate, 1800-1860* (Cambridge, 1988), p. 172.

22 Edward T. Vaughan, "*Ecce Homo*," *Contemporary Review* (May 1866), p. 57. Vaughan's Hulsean lectures were *Some Reasons of our Christian Hope* (London, 1876).

23 *Westminster Review*, July 1866, pp. 58-88; *Fraser's Magazine*, June 1866, pp. 747-8; Peter Bayne, "*Ecce Homo*," *Fortnightly Review*, 1 June 1866, pp. 137, 138.

24 J. R. Seeley, *An Introduction to Political Science* (London, 1923), p. 386. The lectures on political science were edited and published posthumously by Henry Sidgwick in 1896 and printed seven times before 1923.

25 J. R. Seeley, "The teaching of politics" (1870), in *Lectures and Essays* (London, 1870), pp. 298, 296.

26 J. R. Seeley, *The Expansion of England* (London, 1894), p. 1.

27 G. W. Prothero, "Memoir," in J. R. Seeley, *The Growth of British Policy* (2nd edn, 1897; Frankfurt, 1962) Vol. 1, p. xii. This work, intended as a historical preface to the *Expansion*, was unfinished when Seeley died in 1895 and it was edited and

published by Prothero in 1897. See, too, J. R. Seeley, "The teaching of history," in G. Stanley Hall (ed.), *Methods of Teaching History* (2nd edn, Boston, Mass., 1885), Vol. 1, pp. 196, 199.

28 J. R. Seeley, *A Paper Read before the University College Students' Christian Association*, 29 Oct. 1867 (London, 1867), pp. 6, 7, 9, 6.

29 J. R. Seeley, *Ecce Homo: A Survey of the Life and Work of Jesus Christ* (5th edn, London, 1903), pp. 111, 109, 112. Within one year after publication in 1865, the book went through six editions; there were two more in 1867, and until 1903 it was reprinted eighteen times.

30 J. R. Seeley to Anne Seeley, n.d., c. late 1860s, Seeley Papers, Box 1.

31 J. R. Seeley to Macmillan, early 1866, Seeley Papers, Box 1.

32 J. R. Seeley to one of his sisters (salutation missing), n.d., Seeley Papers, Box 1.

33 Although Seeley was not aware of it, the dilemmas he recognized and some of the solutions he pursued were closer to the struggles among the Unitarians than to those of any other contemporary religious group. See R. K. Webb's subtle discussion of the complex issues addressed by the Unitarians in "The faith of nineteenth-century Unitarians: A Curious Incident," in Helmstadter and Lightman, *Victorian Faith in Crisis*, pp. 126–49.

34 J. R. Seeley, "Preface to the fifth edition" (London, 1866), *Ecce Homo*, p. xxvi.

35 Caroline Jebb, in her biography *The Life and Letters of Sir Richard Claverhous Jebb* (Cambridge, 1907), recalled that Jebb had asked Seeley why he had never written about Christ's divinity, and Seeley replied that he had, in his *Life and Times of Stein*, pp. 85–6. R. T. Shannon's "John Robert Seeley and the idea of a national church," in R. Robson (ed.), *Ideas and Institutions of Victorian Britain* (New York, 1967), p. 241, does not give *Ecce Homo* sufficient credit as a source for "understanding Seeley's application of liberal religious principles to politics."

36 J. R. Seeley, *Life and Times of Stein, or Germany and Prussia in the Napoleonic Age*, 3 vols (New York, 1968), Vol. 3, pp. 545, 547, 551, 552, 556, 549, 557, 558.

37 Seeley, *Ecce Homo*, p. 208.

38 Arnold Toynbee to J. R. Seeley, 4 June 1881, Seeley Papers, Box 2.

39 J. R. Seeley, MS notes for lecture to meeting at Cambridge to hear delegates from Toynbee Hall, n.d., but appears to be shortly after Toynbee's death in 1883, Seeley Papers, Box 2.

40 Seeley, *Ecce Homo*, p. 175.

41 In "Our insular ignorance," *The Nineteenth Century* (1885), 18, p. 861, Seeley reflected that he had been a teacher "the whole of my life, without the interruption of a single year," and had found so much satisfaction in it "that I have never even for a passing moment entertained the desire of quitting it for any other."

42 For a perceptive discussion of Seeley's "priesthood of the historian," see Shannon, "John Robert Seeley," p. 248.

43 "The Japanese Club at Cambridge," pamphlet, Seeley Papers. The club, formed in 1883, invited Seeley to address its twelfth meeting on 10 May 1893.

44 J. R. Seeley, *Classical Studies as an Introduction to the Moral Sciences* (London, 1864), p. 15.

45 Seeley, *Life and Times of Stein*, Vol. 2, p. 435.

46 J. R. Seeley, *Goethe Reviewed after Sixty Years* (New York, 1971), p. 39. The three essays, published as a book in 1894, appeared first in the *Contemporary Review*, 1884.

47 J. R. Seeley, *Natural Religion* (Boston, Mass., 1882), pp. 92, 93, 180.

48 J. R. Seeley, "From the Cambridge lecture-rooms: Bonaparte," *Macmillan's Magazine*, XLIV (July 1881), p. 179; see, too, *A Short History of Napoleon the First* (London, 1886).

49 Seeley, *Natural Religion*, pp. 187-8.
50 Seeley, "Our insular ignorance," p. 869.
51 See the following by Reba N. Soffer: "Nation, duty, character, and confidence: history at Oxford, 1850-1914," *Historical Journal*, XXX (Mar. 1987), pp. 77-104; "The modern university and national values, 1850-1930," *Historical Research*, 60, 142 (June 1987), pp. 166-87; "The Development of Disciplines in the Modern English University," *Historical Journal*, XXXI, 4 (1988), pp. 933-46; "The honours school of modern history," in *The Oxford University History of the University* (Oxford, 1991), Vol. 7; and *The University and National Values 1850-1930* (forthcoming).
52 J. R. Seeley, *The Impartial Study of Politics*, an inaugural address to the Cardiff Society for the Impartial Discussion of Political and other Questions, 18 Oct. 1886 (London, 1888; reprinted from the *Contemporary Review*, July 1888, pp. 5, 13.
53 Seeley, "Teaching of politics," Seeley's inaugural lecture as Regius Professor of Modern History at Cambridge, pp. 305, 298-9.
54 Seeley, *Introduction to Political Science*, pp. 25-6.
55 Seeley, *Impartial Study of Politics*, pp. 5, 10, 11, 15.
56 J. R. Seeley, *Education and Politics*, a presidential address to the Social and Political Education League (London, c. 1879), pp. 5, 3.
57 Seeley, *Natural Religion*, pp. 66, 106, 66, 18, 48.
58 Ibid., pp. 79, 67, 223, 224, 78.
59 The attempt by Baden Powell and Seeley to reach the gentiles and other skeptics belongs to an entirely diferent natural religion than earlier orthodox efforts to unite science and religion, especially as encoded in the eight Bridgewater Treatises of the mid-1830s. See John M. Robson, "The finger and fiat of God: the Bridgewater Treatises," in Helmstadter and Lightman, *Victorian Faith in Crisis*, esp. pp. 103-15.
60 H. G. Baden Powell, *Essays* (London, 1855), pp. 162-3. See Corsi, *Science and Religion*, p. 202.
61 Seeley, *Natural Religion*, pp. 85, 88.
62 Ibid., pp. 195, 201.
63 Ibid., pp. 202, 208, 209, 218.
64 J. R. Seeley, "The English revolution of the 19th century I," *Macmillan's Magazine*, Aug. 1870, p. 243.

Chapter 9

Christianity and the state in Victorian India: confrontation and collaboration

Ainslie T. Embree

In the remarkable proclamation addressed to the people of India in 1858 at the end of the great uprising against British rule, Queen Victoria declared that, while "Firmly relying ourselves on the truth of Christianity, and acknowledging with gratitude the solace of religion, we disclaim alike the right and desire to impose our convictions on any of our subjects."[1] Everyone in India was to enjoy the equal protection of the law; no one was to be either favored or molested because of religious faith; people in positions of authority were forbidden to interfere with the religious belief or worship of the queen's subjects, on pain of her highest displeasure. In framing and administering the law due regard was to be paid to "the ancient rights, usages, and customs of India."

All this may seem unexceptionably bland, but behind it was nearly a hundred years of debate over the nature of the responsibility of the British people for the religious, cultural, and social life of the possessions of the East India Company in the Indian subcontinent. The debate continued after the company was abolished, with the government of India being taken over by the Crown. Under both the company and the Crown rule, the relationship between Christian groups in Great Britain and the government of India was character-ized by incidents of both confrontation and collaboration that are central to many developments in modern Indian history. Like so much of that history, they are bound up with the peculiar position of the East India Company.

The East India Company was given a monopoly of the trade between India and Great Britain, although not, of course, with other countries, through a series of royal charters beginning in 1600. The Company became the effective ruler in the 1760s of the great Mughal province of Bengal (including much of what are now the Indian states of West Bengal, Orissa, and Bihar, as well as Bangladesh) but not in any sense of the Indian subcontinent. From 1773 on, the British Parliament renewed the company's charter every twenty years, with each new renewal increasing the control of Parliament. The Board of Control was established in 1784, and its president was ultimately responsible for the government of the British possessions in India. The Court of Directors of the East India Company controlled its commercial activities as well as appointing all officials, except the governor general. These officials are always referred to as "our servants," a usage that preserves a memory of their commercial origin. After 1833 the company ceased to be involved in commerce, but remained technically in charge of the government until it was abolished in 1858, after the great rebellion of 1857 had been crushed.[2]

The argument over the nature of Britain's responsibility for its Indian subjects had been especially bitter in the years just before Victoria came to the throne, but it assumed new importance with what the British called the Mutiny of 1857, which later Indian nationalists named the First Indian War of Independence. The immediate background of the language of the proclamation was that many people, including Disraeli, believed that the cause of the rebellion had been the conviction of many Indians that the British were interfering in their religious customs, with the intention of converting them to Christianity. Whether such a perception was widespread among Indians, and, if so, whether it was a significant factor in the rebellion in 1857, has been much debated; but there were people of influence, both Indian and British, who had argued for years that, in one fashion or another, before the Mutiny the religious rights and customs of India had been systematically violated by the British government in giving support to Christianity.[3]

On the other hand, there were those who argued that, so far from supporting the cause of Christianity, the government was ready, in the words of an advocate of Christian missions, to "trample on the Cross of Christ to avoid the apprehension of native jealousy."[4] Behind these extreme judgments on the relationship of Christianity to British rule in India, there were three issues that illumine some of the complexities of British imperialism in the Victorian era. One was Christian missionary activity; another was the participation by the government in the supervision and support of Hindu and Muslim religious institutions; a third was the support at state expense of a chaplaincy service and the ecclesiastical establishment of the Church of England in India. All three issues were intertwined both chronologically and in terms of those concerned in support of or opposition to them, but it is useful to look at them somewhat separately. They were all of special importance in the Victorian era when – as John William Kaye, an enthusiastic but very knowledgeable observer, noted with approval – the British government in India asserted the "national faith," that is, Christianity. Before Victoria's time, Kaye said, the people of India might have questioned if the English had a religion, but now they could have no such doubts:

> They saw Christian Churches springing up everywhere; they saw the servants of Government punctually attending public worship on the Christian Sabbath; they saw that, on that one day of seven, business and pleasure were laid aside; they saw that more Christian priests, and some of the highest dignity, were arriving to minister to Christian congregations; and they saw that, supported by the English people, though not by the English Government, the Christian missionary was itinerating in all parts of the country.[5]

One reads this in the twentieth century with some embarrassment, realizing that Kaye was not making an indictment of the British for imposing their religion on a conquered people, but praising them. There is no doubt, however, that while exuberant piety led Kaye to overstate the reality of Christian penetration into Indian life, he was stating a widely held belief both of what was and of what should be the British role in India. It is true that a century later the churches the Victorians built are falling into decay, that the cemeteries where they were buried are abandoned, that bishops and missionaries no longer count for much in the Indian scheme of things; but Kaye's assignment of a special role for Christianity in India was part of the imperial vision that sustained British rule. By the end of Victoria's reign it had ceased to be congenial to dominant groups in British political life and it was becoming abhorrent to Indian nationalists, but for at least two generations it defined for many people the meaning of the Indian Empire. And, it is worth remembering, not just for the British, but also for Americans who began their first foreign mission work in India: as an early missionary report noted, the American missionaries were partners with the British government in India in a "generous endeavour to enlighten and elevate its ignorant races."[6] One has to recognize that there were many intellectual and influential people who believed that the possession of India carried with it the moral right and duty to challenge the traditional religions of India and to replace them with the British version of Christianity. But it was also true that there were those who argued that it was both politically inexpedient and immoral to integrate Christianity, the British national ideology, with the exercise of political power.

The proclamation was, then, an attempt to take an unambiguous position on an issue that had divided those concerned with British rule in India ever since it became apparent at the beginning of the nineteenth century that the British were to be the major political power in the Indian subcontinent. Stated in the simplest terms, that issue was the relationship of institutionalized Christianity to the British government of India.

At the beginning of the 1858 proclamation, Victoria had been declared to be queen of all her possessions throughout the world by the grace of God and to be the Defender of the Faith. But by the grace of whose God had Victoria become ruler of India, and of what Faith was she the Defender? To the British, the answers might be obvious enough, but a group of Hindu priests in the great temple city of Puri in Orissa had seen the matter in a very different light. Some years before Victoria came to the throne, after the British conquest of their area, they wrote to the governor general reminding him that he owed his victory to the gods of their temple, and that he must now defend their rights.[7] What should be the attitude of a Christian government to the vast multitude of Hindus and Muslims in India who were now British subjects, far outnumbering the Christians in all the queen's other possessions? If the British government interfered in any way with the religious customs of its Indian subjects, would this not lead to the violent overthrow of the British in India? And what, after all, were "the ancient rights, usages, and customs of India" of which the proclamation speaks?

Many contemporary scholars of modern India argue that the idea of "ancient usages" is an ideological construct of the British used to maintain their rule.[8] While this line of interpretation can be pushed to absurd limits, as when it is argued that such social phenomena as caste, the position of women, untouchability, and Hindu–Muslim conflicts were the product, both intentionally and unintentionally, of British rule, nevertheless it has great relevance for understanding the complexities of the relationship of institutionalized Christianity to the state in Victorian India. Westerners who were involved with India, whether they were administrators, army officers, missionaries, businessmen, or scholars (who very often came from one of the other four groups), might have very different agendas, but it is fair to say that they shared to a remarkable degree an understanding of Indian society as peculiarly rooted in religion, and that Indians were not a political, but a religious, people. But while they would have agreed that ancient rights, usages, and customs were essentially religious in nature, they differed, often with great bitterness, over the way the government should deal with them. Modern Indians, as well as many Western scholars, would vigorously deny this characterization of India as a peculiarly religious civilization, but belief in it was fundamental for the debate over the relation of Christianity and the government of India. The Victorians believed religion was of great importance in British society as well as in India, but with the difference that British religion strengthened, rather than hindered, progress.

While there must have been sermons preached on that useful and pro-vocative text, "Go out into the highways and byways and compel them to come in," by clergy who believed that the government should use its power to convert India to Christianity, expressions of this attitude seem not to have found their way into the records. The issues that do surface in government records, tracts, books, speeches, sermons, newspapers, and private correspon-dence reflect fairly accurately the varieties of religious concerns that were dominant in Great Britain itself, with, of course, the complexity of India adding new dimensions to them. The overarching issue, the degree of responsibility of the state for the religious faith and observance of its subjects, was one that had been integral to British history for a long time, but the possession of India raised the new issue of dealing with large populations of non-Christian faiths as well as looking after the spiritual welfare of British officials and private citizens who went to India.

It is well known that the queen showed great interest in India, but she appears not to have shared the enthusiasm of many of her subjects for the spread of Christianity in India. In her communications with her viceroys, she asked about many aspects of government and she frequently expressed her very strong displeasure at reports of British mistreatment of Indians, but she seems not to have inquired about the progress of Christian missions. Her curiously personal response to India is suggested by a phrase in the speech from the throne when she opened Parliament in person in 1876. The Prince of Wales had just returned from the first royal visit to India, and the queen noted that the warm reception he had received showed that "the people are happy under my rule."[9] This conclusion led to a somewhat guarded statement on her real reason for coming to Parliament, the assumption of the title "Empress of India." When the government of India had been transferred from the East India Company to the Crown, there had been, she noted, no change in her style and titles to mark the momentous occasion, but she hoped that would soon be rectified. The fact that the people of India were happy under her rule legitimized her claim to the title.

For over fifty years, people who claimed a special knowledge of India had warned that Britain could govern India only as long as there was no interference in its religious systems by overt Christian activity. As one zealous opponent of missionary activity put it: "The people of India are not a political, but a religious people. . . . When religious Innovation shall set foot in that country, indignation will spread from one end of Hindostan to the other, and the arms of fifty millions of people will drive us from that country."[10] Over against this position was that of probably a larger, and certainly a more vocal, group, who believed that it was precisely the duty and obligation of the British to give the gospel to India. British officials, both those in Great Britain and in India, were aware of the influence of this group, which Lord William Bentinck, governor general from 1828 to 1835, once referred to as "a large class of excellent persons," who considered the protection afforded the religion of the country as "a compromise of principle," since what they wanted was a more active role in support of Christianity.[11] Although Bentinck was writing before the queen came to the throne, he was acknowledging the influence of attitudes that are conventionally associated with the Victorian era.

Long before this, Robert Dundas, the president of the Board of Control, the body that exercised the government's authority over the East India Company, had given an influential interpretation in 1808 of what he regarded as the official position of the British government, in contrast to that of the evangelicals. When the British government permitted the East India Company to take over Bengal and other territories in India, they did not merely guarantee religious neutrality; instead, he argued, they "virtually contracted an obligation . . . to support . . . those establishments which have immemorially been held in reverence and deemed sacred by their subjects."[12] This idea that a contract existed between the British and the Indians had also been formulated by Edmund Burke in his great quarrel with Warren Hastings, whom he charged with violating Indian customs. When the British had received the right to control Bengal from the Mughal Emperor in 1765, they had accepted the obligation "to preserve the people in the rights, laws, and liberties which their natural sovereign was bound to support, if he had the condition to support them."[13]

Aside from his personal predelictions for the religion of an eighteenth-century gentleman, in contrast to that of his evangelical opponents among the directors of the East India Company, Dundas was basing his position on the preamble to Regulation III of 1793, one of the fundamental documents that defined the East India Company's claims to Bengal, its relations with the British government, and its obligations to the people. Spelling out Burke's idea, the regulation stated that the British would take care that all new laws would preserve to the people "the laws of the Shaster and the Koran, in matters in which they have been invariably applied."[14]

At this time, the British had very little idea of either Hindu or Islamic laws, but in any case the regulation was meant, above all, to satisfy vociferous critics of the East India Company in England rather than the people of India. It is important to remember that statements about the views of Indians are almost wholly expressions by the British in support of their own opinions. How far they actually represented Indian opinion is conjectural, and this is true throughout most of the period with which we are concerned. There are many voices, many clashing opinions, but there is a strangeness about the discourse, because we seldom hear from the people who are its object, the people of India. But, as the historian Edward Thompson noted, because there were no Indians listening, ready to ask the really fundamental question, "What right have you to be in India at all?" the British discussion was franker, fuller, better informed, and more interesting than it was in the twentieth century.[15] The regulation of 1793 was also meant to provide guidelines for the company's servants in Bengal. This was surely the intention of a central provision, phrased in language that recalled eighteenth-century British thought, when it ensured the people of Bengal "the free exercise of their religion and the security of their persons and property." Dundas's interpretation of the preamble of Regulation III was often referred to as the "compact" made by the British with the Indians, with the clear intent of preventing attempts to convert Indians to Christianity, along with a promise that there would be no interference with Indian customs. The document was not, of course, a "compact" in any real sense, since no Indians were signatories to it and at the time they were probably unaware of its existence. It reflected instead a great deal of acrimonious and devious political maneuvering between Dundas and his evangelical opponents in Parliament, including William Wilberforce, who thought that Dundas had acted in "a most false and double way" in preventing the passage of a measure that would have required the East India Company to send schoolteachers and missionaries to "the native inhabitants of the British dominion in India" for "their advancement in useful knowledge, and to their religious and moral improvement."[16]

Evangelical Christians of all denominations rejected out of hand the idea that a self-denying "compact" existed between Great Britain and India.[17] This would have meant, according to Charles Grant (1746–1823), the leading proponent in the pre-Victorian period of active participation by the government in religious and social change in India, that Britain was determining that the situation of its Indian subjects should never change. Instead, he argued as early as 1792, the path to be followed by the British was plain:

> By planting our language, or knowledge, our opinions, and our religion, in our Asiatic territories, we shall put a great work beyond the reach of contingencies; we shall probably have wedded the inhabitants of these territories to this country; but at any rate, we shall have done an act of strict duty to them, and a lasting service to mankind.[18]

It would be difficult to find a statement that summarizes more concisely the agenda for probably the majority of British officials in Victorian India, as well as people in Great Britain, for the relationship of Christianity and the state, even though they might have been unwilling to make so uncompromising an expression public. But, as Edward Thompson said, by then Indians were "listening intently and . . . quick to take offence."[19]

In speaking of Christianity and the government of India in the Victorian era, it must be acknowledged that many of the issues that dominated the relationship throughout the period had developed long before Victoria came to the throne. During the years of Victoria's reign, however, Christianity as an institutionalized religion occupied a position in public life in India quite different from that of the early years of the century, duplicating both the weaknesses and the strengths of the churches in Great Britain itself. John William Kaye, one of the most assiduous chroniclers of British rule in India, wrote that in the eighteenth century the lax habits and coarse manners of the British in India had "blackened the face of Christianity in the eyes of the natives," whereas in Victoria's time the fruit of the evangelical revival, shown everywhere in the lives of officials, had brought about a changed evaluation of the British and their religion.[20]

The evidence of this reevaluation on the part of the Indians, however, is slight, despite the constant reiteration of judgments like that of Kaye throughout the century by the British themselves. As the history of Indian nationalism demonstrates, Indians had admiration for the British institutions they saw in England, such as a free press, representative government, and democracy, but this clearly did not extend to the British officials in India, as people, or, indeed, to their religion. This point was made in a telling fashion by Dadabhai Naoroji, the famous nationalist leader who became a Liberal Member of Parliament in 1892. He was sympathetic to many aspects of British rule, but the belief that the promises of the queen's proclamation of 1858 had been fulfilled was "the purest romance," and Indians were "deliberately and insultingly excluded" from British social institutions. As for any moral influence the British officials had on Indians, they "might just as well be living in the moon. . . . All they effectually do is to eat the substance of India, material and moral, while living here."[21] Remote from the Indian people, they were rulers but had no involvement in the life of the people or its institutions.

Very much the same criticism had been made of the British twenty years before, at the end of the Mutiny of 1857–8, by the great Muslim leader Syed Ahmed Khan, who argued that a major cause of the uprising, along with the activities of Christian missionaries, was the ignorance of the British of public sentiment because of their shutting themselves off from India's life.[22]

This criticism of the British officials for their lack of involvement in Indian life has special irony in a consideration of the relationship of Christianity to the state in India, for in the year Victoria came to the throne they were being fiercely assailed for overinvolvement in Indian religious practices. One of those who entered the controversy was Gladstone. Although up to this time he seems not to have shown much interest in Indian questions, Gladstone's comments reflect widespread views both in the Church of England and among Dissenters. In his examination of the relations of church and state, he had defended the established church in both England and Ireland on the grounds that one of the fundamental functions of government was the care and propagation of religion, the sharing in "the glorious enterprise to which the Church was committed, the universal proclamation of the Gospel."[23] He was astonished to discover, then, that in India the British government was following an utterly different course. It was alleged, Gladstone said, that it participated "in the idolatrous rites of the Hindoo worship" through "the coerced attendance of its servants at their celebration, as well as pecuniary concern with its management." If this were true, we were involved, "in the sin of having acted against the light of our own principles." The justification given for this involvement was "more monstrous than [he] could bear to contemplate."[24]

What Gladstone had discovered in 1838 was that the East India Company had for over forty years been involved in Hindu festivals through a tax on pilgrims who attended the great annual festivals at the famous temple of Jagganath (Juggernath to the British) at Puri in Orissa. They were also involved in the management of the temple, including appointment of the priests who were the financial overseers. Similar supervision of temple finances, the control of the vast crowds that gathered at festivals and other religious ceremonies, and the imposition of special taxes were common throughout the British territories in India. It was the Jagganath temple that had captured the British imagination because of the many lurid accounts that had been published about pilgrims throwing themselves beneath the wheels of the great chariot that carried the gods in procession.[25] The reasons for the company's getting involved in temple affairs were often stated in the contemporary records: previous rulers, both Hindu and Muslim, had done so; the temple authorities requested the company to do so in order to maintain order and to ensure the proper people were in charge; it was important to show the local notables that the company would protect the religious institutions; finally, the company might profit financially from the arrangement.[26]

Collection of the so-called "pilgrim tax" was begun in 1806, and almost immediately there were objections to it on the grounds that a Christian government should not be involved in the appointment of Hindu priests and should not profit from a tax on pilgrims who were as miserable and poverty-stricken in body as they were deluded in spirit by the machinations of the priests.[27] The principle enunciated in 1808 in objection to the government's supervision of non-Christian religious institutions was reiterated throughout the years: "It is improper for a Christian government to take upon itself any regulation of Heathen worship."[28] So, too, was the counterargument of 1808, that when the British took over Indian territories they had made a "compact" to maintain the existing institutions. The answer of the evangelicals was that, if there was any "compact" involved, it was to give good government, but that this was to be grounded in the moral understanding of the rulers, not the ruled.[29] It was in this spirit that Lord William Bentinck defended his abolition of the practice of suttee in 1829, saying that he consulted his own moral judgment, not that of the people of India.[30] So it was in 1838 when an order went out to India from London that all temple management be "resigned into the hands of the natives; and that the interference by the Public Authorities in the religious ceremonies of the people should cease."[31] Many people involved with India objected to the action, including Sir John Hobhouse, the president of the Board of Control, arguing that for the government to withdraw from involvement in their religious institutions would seem to Indians that protection was being taken away. It is difficult to say how widespread such a perception was among Indians, although petitions, signed not only by Hindus but also by Muslims and Parsis, were sent to the British officials at this time protesting what seemed to be a departure from former practice.[32]

The ending of the government's direct involvement in Indian religious institutions through the appointment of temple officials (often referred to as "churchwardens" in the literature) was regarded as a victory for righteousness by the evangelical groups. That there was a general change in attitude toward the responsibility of a Christian government in India was indicated when the Bishop of London and the Archbishop of Canterbury, who had previously shown little interest in the controversy, declared that the participation of the British government in temple management was offensive in the eyes of God, since it lowered the British character in the eyes of the natives, and prevented the spread of Christianity.[33]

The result of the government's withdrawal from temple management did not mean, as the rhetoric suggested, that the British would no longer be involved in non-Christian religious institutions; what happened was a movement from direct bureaucratic control to judicial involvement for the settlement of religious disputes. As Arjun Appadurai has shown in a detailed study of one important south Indian temple complex in the period after 1840, the arbitration by the courts of conflicts over temple endowments bound the temples to the legal structure in a fashion that had no precedent in previous administrations. By giving legal authority to the claims of one group, by treating the temple as if it were an English charitable trust, and by the introduction of court precedents in decision making, the British, in Appadurai's words, "generated a dynamic framework that bound the temple to the court in increasingly subtle and complicated ways."[34] One of the many ironies of the Victorian age in India is that the legislation preventing the government from giving support to non-Christian religions almost certainly strengthened Hinduism and gave it new vitality by linking it to that most potent of Victorian constructs in India, the judicial system. This involvement of the courts in religious disputes remains a major legacy from the Victorian age in contemporary India, as instanced by bitter legal disputes over the birthplace of the god Rama.[35]

While the right of missionaries to propagate Christianity in India and the issue of involvement by the government in temple management generated much debate, a third aspect of the relationship of government to Christianity evoked less discussion, although in some ways it raised even more difficult questions. This was the existence of an ecclesiastical establishment in India paid for by the government from the revenues of India. Here surely was an instance where the queen's proclamation that no one was to be either favored or molested because of religious faith was blatantly contravened. One would suppose that to many Hindus and Muslims it would have seemed intolerable that their taxes should go to support the building of Christian churches and the payment of the salaries of clergymen, including a full-fledged episcopal establishment, and yet the issue rarely surfaces in nineteenth-century Indian sources. The contrast with the present time is startling, when the government of independent India is fiercely attacked by minority religious communities, such as the Sikhs and Muslims, if it seems to be displaying any support for Hinduism, the religion of 80 per cent of the population, and, conversely, it is criticized by the Hindus if it seems to be, in a much used phrase, "pandering to the minorities." The explanation is probably that the nature of a democratic regime is to call forth such a public response, in contrast to social behavior under a despotism. Sir John Lawrence, one of the great Victorians, put this idea in another way when he said: "We have not been elected by the people, but we are here through our moral superiority, by the force of circumstances, and the will of Providence," and that "Christian things done in a Christian way will never alienate the heathen."[36] Put less grandly, it was probably true that Indians took for granted that the new rulers would have their own religious specialists to cater for their spiritual needs and that they would be paid from public funds.

The ecclesiastical establishment was sometimes referred to as the "moral police" and the term reflects its origins, which, like so much in the government of India, was located in the East India Company. Provision was made for chaplains for the company's employees, since, as the orders for the earliest voyage put it, religion "doth best bind men to perform their duties."[37] Throughout the seventeenth and eighteenth centuries chaplains were spasmodically appointed, but their chief interest was often in making money through trade. A great change came at the end of the eighteenth century, when, under pressure from evangelicals, led by Charles Grant and William Wilberforce, the first evangelical chaplains were appointed. Technically they were supposed to minister only to the British community – government officials, soldiers, and the few nonofficials who were in India – but to the annoyance of officials they soon concerned themselves not just with the European community but with Indian society.[38]

The most famous of these evangelical chaplains was Claudius Buchanan, who condemned the private lives of the Europeans while mounting violent attacks on what he considered the evils of Indian religion. His denunciations of Hinduism provided much of the material for those who opposed the company's involvement in the management of Hindu temples.[39] The line between the activities of missionaries sent out by the churches to convert the Indians and the chaplains, who were paid employees of the government, became increasingly blurred, especially after the appointment of the first Bishop of Calcutta, along with archdeacons for three Presidency towns. The bishop was well paid, getting a salary of £5,000 and £1,000 for expenses, plus travel.[40] The argument for this large expenditure was that the bishop had to maintain the dignity of his office before the Indian populace, and, despite much grumbling by the officials who would have preferred to spend the money elsewhere, the ecclesiastical establishment continued to grow. By 1852 Bombay and Madras had their own bishops, with a total of 121 chaplains. The directors of the East India Company had made it clear that this expenditure was for the spiritual instruction of its employees "according to the principles of the Church of England," but, under pressure from Dissenting forces in England, grudging provision was made for a few sectarian chaplains. Even the Roman Catholics were included, with about £5,000 being distributed among seventy-eight priests, with a £20 allowance for their bishop.[41]

To a much greater extent than in England itself, the bishops and clergy were government employees, and, according to an authoritative history of the Anglican Church in India, the control by the state over the church was much more rigid than in England.[42] This led many people, both within and without the ecclesiastical establishment, to conclude that it was the established church of India. But the governors general at various times argued that this was not so; it was simply a department of the government, as Lord Northbrook pointed out, that "recognizes the duty, within reasonable limits, of providing the ministration of religion for British-born European servants of the Crown."[43] This was a careful statement, intended to emphasize that the ecclesiastical establishment served only Europeans, not Indian Christians, but it also stated racial reality. Indians were not welcome in "white" churches, in contrast to the "Indian" churches founded by the missionaries.

As governor general, Lord Ripon was especially sensitive to the issue of support of the church establishment, since as the first Roman Catholic governor general he would have been accused of anti-Protestant sentiments if he had supported any diminution of the privileges of the Church of England. He was also uneasy about curbing the activities of missionaries, and when Protestant street preachers caused trouble in Calcutta, he made the ingenious suggestion that instead of forbidding them to preach they be charged with trampling the public flower gardens.[44]

After 1880 the question of disestablishing the church in India was frequently raised, but when there was a discussion in the cabinet of the issue, and Ripon was asked for his comments, he did not reply.[45] He later suggested, however, that the salaries of the bishops and clergy should be paid from the accounts of the Public Works Department to make clear their relation to the government. On the basis of meeting the spiritual needs of the handful of Europeans, there was little need for bishops and cathedrals, but he did not push his argument to its logical conclusion. The editorial writer in the *Friend of India*, the newspaper of the Dissenters that acted as a goad to both church and state, did, however. Why should the principle that was used to defend the church establishment not be extended to all areas of life? "It would be equally pleasant, and we may add equally defensible, if the heathen could be made to pay for the doctors' and lawyers' bills of the privileged ruling class."[46] When an MP raised the issue of disestablishment in the House of Commons in 1897, the secretary of state's only defense of the practice was that it had been in existence for 200 years.[47]

The end of the Victorian era coincided with the rise of Indian nationalism, and the identification of church and state became an increasing embarrassment to both; but it was not until 1927 that the Indian Church Bill was passed by the House of Commons, and in 1930 an independent Anglican church, the Church of India, Burma, and Ceylon, came into existence. The constitution of the new church declared that it was "free in all spiritual matters from the direction or interposition of any civil government."[48] One suspects that this was not only a declaration of independence from the British government of which it had for so long been a dependent, but also from the new government of India that by then was looming on the horizon. Looking back on the glories of the Victorian age in India from the vantage point of the 1920s, Arthur Mayhew, a former official who was very knowledgeable about the period, could declare with a self-satisfaction that must now seem astonishing that "our government of India has earned the title of Christian by the character of its activities . . . and still more by the essentially Christian vigour and hopefulness that have inspired them." He hoped he would not give offense if he expressed a fear that with the entrance of what he called "the non-Christian factor" into government this situation would change.[49]

Except for a few ardent spirits in Hindu organizations that were dismissed as marginal by such leaders of the mainstream of Indian nationalism as Nehru and Gandhi, there was little sense that after independence India would be a Hindu country. Quite the reverse, the commitment was to what Indians call "secularism," meaning that no religion would be favored over another. It is said that when the queen was shown what was to become the great proclamation of 1858, she saw that it used the word "neutrality" to describe the stance of the government in relation to religion; the queen struck it out with her own hand, on the grounds that she was tolerant, not neutral.[50] Nationalist leaders like Nehru, on the other hand, wanted the government to be neutral; they did not, as did Victoria, say they were firmly convinced of the truth of any one religion. Yet by the last decade of the twentieth century, powerful forces in India were arguing, often through violent confrontations, that India could only be true to itself if its laws, education, and national ideology reflected the religious compulsions of the Hindu majority. The arguments of the spokesman for a Hindu India duplicated in a curious fashion those of the champions of a Christian government of India in the Victorian period.[51] To a considerable extent, this is a reaction against activities of individuals and groups, both public and private, who in the nineteenth century so vigorously asserted the claims of Christianity. In a deeper sense, however, it is an expression of the logic of ideological commitment, whether religious or secular, to demand an integration of the public and private spheres. On balance, one can conclude that the attempt to do so during the Victorian age in India, to establish a government informed by Christian – perhaps one should say Protestant – ideals, was doomed to failure. But then so were similar attempts elsewhere, notably in the United States and in Great Britain.

NOTES

1 *Parliamentary Papers*, 1876, Vol. 61, paper 117.
2 For an authoritative brief account of the complicated history of the East India Company, see the article by K. C. Chaudhuri, "East India Company," in *Encyclopedia of Asian History* (New York, 1989). Lucy Sutherland, *The East India Company in Eighteenth Century Politics* (Oxford, 1952); and C. H. Philips, *The East India Company, 1784-1834* (repr. Manchester, 1961), are detailed studies of the interaction of the company and various British administrations. Ainslie T. Embree, *Charles Grant and British Rule in India* (New York, 1962), gives special attention to the religious issues in the period from 1780 to 1820.
3 V. D. Savarkar, *The First Indian War of Independence* (Bombay, 1960). For the various explanations given for the uprisings, see Ainslie T. Embree, *India in 1857* (New Delhi, 1987).
4 University of Nottingham, Portland Papers, 110, Charles Grant to Lord William Bentinck, 17 Apr. 1807.
5 John William Kaye, *Christianity in India: A Historical Narrative* (London, 1859), p. 478.
6 Quoted in Sushil Madhava Pathak, *American Missionaries and Hinduism* (Delhi, 1967), p. 43.
7 Letter from Puri priests to Lord Wellesley, 24 July 1804, in Nancy Gardner Cassels, *Religion and Pilgrim Tax under the Company Raj* (Riverdale, Md, 1988), pp. 160-2.
8 Edward Said, *Orientalism* (New York, 1979), states the general theoretical case for this position.

9 *Parliamentary Debates*, 1876, Vol. 227, 8 Feb.

10 Thomas Twining, quoted in Cassels, *Religion and Pilgrim Tax*, p. 50.

11 Quoted in *Anti-Conversion Petitions Addressed to the Governor in Council of Bombay* (Bombay, c. 1839), p. 5.

12 *Parliamentary Papers*, 1812–13, Vol. 8 (iii), paper 194, p. 510.

13 Quoted in David Lelyveld, "Of kings and kings of kings: ideologies of ruling power in Indian history," unpublished paper, Harvard China India Seminar, 18 Oct. 1985.

14 J. W. Kaye (ed.), *Memorials of Indian Government: Being a Selection from the Papers of Henry St George Tucker* (London, 1853), p. 354.

15 Edward Thompson and G. T. Garratt, *The Rise of Fulfillment of British Rule in India* (Allahabad, 1958), p. 597.

16 Quoted in Embree, *Charles Grant*, pp. 152, 155.

17 I am using "evangelical" in the way it tended to be used in the nineteenth century, that is, for people in all denominations, but particularly in the Church of England, who had been members of a church but who previously had not, as they were inclined to phrase it, taken seriously the implications of Christian discipleship as a personal commitment. It did not imply "conversion" or being "born again," but, as a writer in the *Edinburgh Review* (XI, 1801, p. 342) remarked, evangelicals were "one general conspiracy against common sense and rational orthodox Christianity."

18 "Charles Grant's first manifesto," in Kaye, *Christianity in India*, pp. 510–13.

19 Thompson and Garratt, *Rise and Fulfillment*, p. 597.

20 Kaye, *Christianity in India*, p. 476.

21 Dadabhai Naoroji, "Memorandum," in Stephen Hay (ed.), *Sources of Indian Tradition*, Vol. 2, pp. 94–6.

22 Sir Syed Ahmed Khan, "The rulers were ignorant of the people's feelings," in Embree, *India in 1857*, pp. 47–58.

23 William Ewart Gladstone, *The State and its Relations with the Church* (London, 1839), p. 281.

24 Ibid., pp. 274–7.

25 The point of view of two of the best known are indicated by their titles: Claudius Buchanan, *An Apology for Promoting Christianity in India* (London, 1813); and James Peggs, *India's Cries to British Humanity* (London, 1832).

26 Much of the relevant material can be found in *Parliamentary Papers*, 1812–13, Vols 7, 8, 10; and in the India Office Library (hereafter IOL) Home Miscellaneous Series, Vols 59, 690.

27 Cassels, *Religion and Pilgrim Tax*, is the most detailed study of the issue.

28 Charles Grant to William Wilberforce, 30 August 1808, in Robert Wilberforce and Samuel Wilberforce (eds), *The Correspondence of William Wilberforce* (Philadelphia, Pa, 1841), Vol. 2, p. 37.

29 IOL, Home Miscellaneous Series, Vol. 59, p. 489, Edward Parry and Charles Grant, notes on Dundas's letter of 6 Sept. 1808.

30 A. B. Keith (ed.), *Speeches and Documents on Indian Policy, 1757–1921* (London, 1922), Vol. 1, pp. 211–12, Minute of Lord William Bentinck, 1829.

31 IOL, India and Bengal Despatches, E/4/756, f. 362, 8 Aug. 1838.

32 *Anti-Conversion Petitions Addressed to the Governor in Council of Bombay.*

33 *Parliamentary Debates* (Lords), 1838, Vol. 41, cols 1210–15.

34 Arjun Appadurai, *Worship and Conflict under Colonial Rule: A South Indian Case* (Cambridge, 1981), p. 211.

35 Ainslie T. Embree, "Religion and politics," in Marshall M. Bouton (ed.), *India Briefing, 1987* (Boulder, C, 1987), pp. 49–76.

36 Quoted in Arthur Mayhew, *Christianity and the Government of India* (London, 1929), pp. 214, 122.

37 Quoted in M. E. Gibbs, *The Anglican Church in India, 1600-1970* (New Delhi, 1972), p. 3.
38 Embree, *Charles Grant*, pp. 239–51.
39 Claudius Buchanan, *An Apology for Promoting Christianity in India* (London, 1813).
40 *An Analysis of the Evidence before the Select Committee of the House of Commons in 1852* (London, 1853).
41 Ibid.
42 Gibbs, *Anglican Church in India*, p. vii.
43 Quoted in *Friend of India* (Calcutta), 3 Mar. 1897.
44 British Museum, Add. Mss 43475, Ripon Papers, Vol. 75, pp. 481–3.
45 IOL, European Mss, Northbrook Collection, C144/4, Vol. 4, Northbrook to Ripon, 4 Jan. 1884.
46 *Friend of India*, 3 Mar. 1897.
47 Ibid.
48 Quoted in Gibbs, *Anglican Church in India*, p. 357.
49 Mayhew, *Christianity and the Government*, pp. 234, 237.
50 Ibid., p. 187.
51 H. V. Seshadri, *Hindu Renaissance under Way* (Bangalore, 1984).

Chapter 10

Independent English women in Delhi and Lahore, 1860–1947

Jeffrey Cox

Between 1857 and 1947 at least 312 women, mostly English, mostly unmarried, served as Anglican missionaries in Delhi and Lahore with the Society for the Propagation of the Gospel.[1] These two cities had special significance for the Church of England's missionary enterprise. Anglican missionary theorists, who thought in quasi-military geo-religious metaphors, regarded the Christianization of the Punjab as one of the providential tasks thrust upon them by God. Just as God had arranged the Roman Empire with unified channels of communications, preparing the way for the spread of the Christian message, so had God provided in the Punjab a strategic window of opportunity in Asia, an opportunity for which the Church of England would be held eternally responsible.

God provided the opportunity, but no detailed plan of action. How to exploit this opening was a matter for spirited debate among some evangelical administrators in the government of India and missionary theorists in the two rival Anglican missionary organizations, the evangelical Church Missionary Society and the high-church Society for the Propagation of the Gospel. Faced with a government that refused to proselytize directly, and embarrassed by competition from Presbyterians, who had already "occupied" Lahore, the Church Missionary Society (CMS) established a mission in Amritsar in 1852. Expanding throughout central Punjab, CMS missionaries sought to apply their own optimistic missionary theories, and in particular to promote the rapid development of a self-governing native Indian church.[2]

After 1860 a missionary from the Society for the Propagation of the Gospel (SPG) maintained an Anglican missionary presence in Delhi. The SPG work in Delhi changed rapidly in the 1880s, when the married male missionary there was displaced by an aggressive new team of unmarried Cambridge graduates associated with the Cambridge Mission to Delhi, which operated in close cooperation with the SPG. In the 1870s B. F. Westcott, the Regius Professor of Divinity and a well-known New Testament scholar, had delivered a series of lectures to missionary meetings at Cambridge in which he encouraged undergraduates to think in terms of a special mission to the East, modeled on the Alexandrian school of the second and third centuries.

The Alexandrian school was distinguished, according to Westcott, by its acknowledgment of truth in Greek philosophy. The Alexandrian theologians, Clement and Origen, believed that the incomplete truth apprehended by Greek philosophers found its fulfillment in Christ. Thus, God's revelation of truth had been partially revealed to the Greeks as well as to the Jews in preparation for the full revelation in Christ.

Early Protestant missionaries in India had treated both Hinduism and Islam as systems hopelessly mired from the beginning in utter falsehood. Missionaries had hoped to destroy both through a demonstration of the complete truth of Christianity. The Alexandrian model, anticipating later liberal Protestant approaches, provided another way forward. In Westcott's view, missionaries should look for truth in Hinduism and identify ways in which the lesser truth pointed to the greater truth in Christ. "And is it too much to hope," Westcott asked, "that we may yet see on the Indus, or on the Ganges, some new Alexandria?"[3] Working together at this new Alexandria, western and Indian theologians would incorporate the best of Indian culture into a new Christian theological statement, which in turn would provide the basis for the conversion of India and ultimately all of Asia to Christ.

Before dismissing Westcott entirely as nothing more than a Victorian orientalist fantasizer, for whom the Nile, the Indus, and the Ganges, and Greek thought, Muslim thought, and Hindu thought were all jumbled together in a timeless Orient, it is important to recognize the genuine liberal appeal of his ideas. Westcott was one of many nineteenth-century British and American missionary thinkers who tried to disentangle Christianity from western culture. His ideas offered a way around the missionary triumphalism that declared Hinduism depraved and Islam fraudulent. At a time when the superiority of western culture was axiomatic in England, and when racist ideas were growing more prevalent and more virulent, Westcott encouraged potential missionaries at Cambridge to listen for things of value from people in other cultures rather than merely preaching at them.

In practice, however, Westcott knew very little about Hinduism. In the discourse of the Cambridge Mission to Delhi, Indians appeared, not as Indians, but as Egyptians – or, to be more specific, as Greek-speaking inhabitants of the Roman Empire living in second-century Alexandria. Women appeared not at all, not even as wives, since the Cambridge Mission to Delhi was committed to clerical celibacy. Even from a missionary point of view, Westcott's ideas provided no practical guidance about what to do in a mission that involved Indian men and women, and large numbers of European women, as well as clerical missionary heroes from Cambridge.

In 1878 two Cambridge graduates sailed for Delhi to establish a new Alexandria, not on the Indus or the Ganges, but on yet another oriental river, the Yamuna.[4] As colleagues dedicated to a common life of service and thought joined them in subsequent years, they discovered that the Indian Christians of Delhi were not potential Clements or Origens, but instead a community of outcaste leatherworkers (Chamars). An obstacle to their hopes of converting upper-caste Indians, these despised Christians embarrassed the Cambridge missionaries, who subjected them to a program of discipline and excommunication that reduced their numbers to a handful by 1890. The Cambridge missionaries abandoned the Westcottian theory, and began to behave as Anglican clergymen behaved everywhere in the world in the nineteenth century, as chaplains to influential and prosperous people. That the influential and prosperous people of Delhi were not Christians bothered the clergymen very little. They began to create a set of institutions designed to serve non-Christians, notably St Stephen's College, which they justified as preparing the way culturally for an eventual conversion of India.

The unrealistic orientalist view of Indians had created a crisis for the Cambridge Mission when its members encountered the actual Indian Christians of Delhi. The male clericalist attitudes that also shaped their work did not lead to any comparable crisis in the missionaries' dealings with their female counterparts, even though the mission was from the first predominantly female. At home there was a variety of alternative roles, some old and some new, for women in the Church of England. By the time the first Cambridge missionaries arrived, in 1878, women's work was already well developed in Delhi under the direction of Priscilla Winter, the wife of the SPG clergyman Richard Winter. The Winters had run the mission in Delhi very much on the lines of a large, well-funded, urban parish in England, with parochial work, schools, relief work, and visitation – emphasizing the value of the personal presence of a clergyman as a civilizing influence on a neighborhood. The characteristic form of women's mission work was known as zenana work, an Indian adaptation of the extensive visitation of parishioners at home, either by the clergyman if the parishioners were prosperous, or by volunteer ladies or paid visitors if they were poor.

The British view of Indian women was powerfully shaped by visions of the zenana, the women's household quarters to which men were admitted only if they were family members.[5] Consequently, women missionaries were required for the private visitation of Hindu and Muslim wives who were thought to live in purdah, a state of seclusion that precluded visits from European men but not from European women. SPG literature often portrayed Richard Winter as being alone in Delhi before the arrival of the Cambridge missionaries. But before 1878 at least thirty-four women helped out in one way or another as missionaries with the Winters' mission, and ten additional recruits were added in 1878 and 1879.

How would the celibate Cambridge missionaries organize zenana work without the help of clergymen's wives? The revival of monastic life in the Church of England was proceeding amid much controversy, and the high-church missionaries of the Cambridge Mission regarded the new Protestant brotherhoods and sisterhoods as ideal missionary institutions. They organized their own brotherhood for men, and when they took charge of women's work in Delhi they naturally organized the unmarried women missionaries into the St Stephen's Community of Anglican sisters, many of them ordained deaconesses, committed to a common life of prayer and service in the heart of Delhi. This meant, almost at once, a new institutional autonomy for women living with other women in a community that, for the most part, excluded men much more thoroughly than did purdah. Despite the formal administrative control that men continued to exercise, they rarely entered St Stephen's Community except to celebrate Holy Communion in chapel.

The male head of the mission in the 1880s and 1890s, G. A. Lefroy, was also head of the women's mission, but he was never very eager to interfere in its internal administrative affairs. In the late 1890s Lefroy recruited the first outsider to come to Delhi to direct the women's work, Christine Byam, daughter of Colonel Byam of Brighton. The *Delhi Mission News* described her first mission work abroad as "among the communists at Belleville, Paris."[6] One of her first acts as head of St Stephen's Community was having the horses in the mission compound stables freed of their heel ropes.

The ruling body of the mission, the Mission Council, was all male and in 1902, after Christine Byam's departure to become the head of the Soldier's Church Home in Peshawar, women requested but were denied representation. The mission was reluctant to abandon the principle that women's work in India, as in England, should be under at least nominal clerical control. As the Mission Council spent its time wrangling over issues of ecclesiastical discipline that were of very little concern to women missionaries, and as successive male heads of the mission were never eager to interfere in the internal administrative affairs of the women's institutions, this formal exclusion does not appear to have generated much sense of grievance among women. Even more important, it did not prevent the share of the mission budget dedicated to women's work from growing steadily. A storm of controversy surrounded the mission over the question of the appointment of an Indian principal of St Stephen's College in 1907, but the granting in 1918 of formal administrative autonomy to the head of women's work, along with representation on the Mission Council, passed with little comment from men or women missionaries.

St Stephen's Community in the 1890s was centered in a five-acre compound outside the old city walls in the civil lines, with a home for missionaries, boarding school for Christian girls, St Mary's Refuge for women, and four closed carriages for transporting women in purdah. In the cold weather the daily routine began at six with *chota haziri*, an early small breakfast, followed by service at seven in the mission church, St Stephen's in Old Delhi. After returning to the compound, the women would have prayers with the servants, then their own service in the chapel, then breakfast. The school and zenana workers would depart for five hours of teaching; those learning Urdu would join their *munshis*. The work day ended with mid-afternoon prayers, then a walk or a drive before dinner at seven. After spending an hour with each other in the drawing room, the women would say compline at nine and retire.[7]

St Stephen's zenana work fitted in nicely with one dimension of the Cambridge Mission's work: its snobbery. The Cambridge Brothers attempted to meet distinguished Indian men in Delhi and persuade them to send their sons to St Stephen's College, and to allow zenana workers to visit their wives and teach the rudiments of reading, embroidery, personal and family hygiene, and, if possible, Christianity. The male missionaries assumed that the Indian man's motive was a desire to raise his wife's standard of housekeeping or to give her some social graces or education in order to make her a more suitable companion. From their male clerical point of view, zenana and other women's work was auxiliary to the main task. This view dominates the historical writing about the Cambridge Mission and its archival records to an extraordinary degree. I worked in their archives for months before realizing that the mission was predominantly female.

From the European women's point of view, work with Indian women was not marginal at all, but the central missionary task. Excluded from the clerical model of missionary heroism that dominated the Cambridge Mission – excluded in some cases even from the statistical tables used to describe missionary work[8] – women missionaries promoted their own ideal of a special bond of sympathy between English women and Indian women, a bond that would eventually lead India to Christ or, if not to Christ, to Western standards of hygiene.

Missionaries, portraying themselves as advocates for Indian women to an audience of enlightened Indians, Europeans in India, and people in England, tended to give grim accounts of the conditions in the living quarters of Indian women – accounts not always confirmed in nonmissionary sources.[9] A zenana missionary working at the Hissar outstation reported that "I can only teach work, as her husband, an educated man and accountant in the canal office, attributes his first wife's death to her learning to read."[10] Jenny Muller, the first fully qualified doctor in the Cambridge Mission, claimed that women's apartments in wealthy homes were often cold and filthy:

> So many of the men have come into contact with western methods of living that they generally have their own apartments fitted up more or less like ours. In one case . . . the man asked me to see his own apartments, which were very finely got up with carpets and chairs and tables and chandeliers of enormous size, but when I asked if the ladies of the house kept the rooms in order, he said "I do not so much as allow them to come in, lest they should dirty them."[11]

Emily Pilkington spent two years in Delhi in the early 1890s, and reported on her zenana visit in this way:

> One woman I [was] teaching Bible verses; her husband became angry and sat in on lessons, contradicting what I said. When he saw that I would not become angry he forbade me to do more than come talk to her of general

things, which I do so as not to lose touch. She is 28 with no children, and presented me with a little fan.[12]

Indian women may have regarded the zenana workers as amusing, but they certainly went to considerable length to be courteous. Missionaries were somewhat reluctant to proselytize directly, not from any doubts about the truth of Christianity, but from a fear of endangering their rights of access, and from a conviction that the spread of Christianity would involve a slow process of diffusion from Christian institutions. When Christian themes were introduced into teaching, some Hindu women reassured their missionary visitors that they were Christians at heart in some obscure sense, presumably out of a desire to be courteous and avoid embarrassment for both sides. Missionaries were not well equipped with the knowledge of Hinduism necessary to interpret what they were being told.

Emily Pilkington reported another woman who prayed for the conversion of India but could not pray

for the sake of Jesus Christ, according to his word. "I can't do that yet, Miss Sahiba, not till my heart is quite sure." I told her certainly not to say one word that she did not believe with her whole heart and soul. This pleased me too as a proof of sincerity, a priceless virtue, especially here. I love this woman so truly, and am so deeply interested in her, that I could go on writing about her and her sayings, but I must not.[13]

Women missionaries encountered not only a courteous attempt to please but also bemused questions about Christian exclusivism. Indian women very reasonably asked, for instance: "Why did not God make us all Christians, and why does not God use His power and convert the whole world at once, so that there need be no leaving of one's loved ones to confess Him?"[14] Miss Hooper reported a list of objections to conversion:

Besides the persecution they would suffer. . . . One is the conviction they have that it is wrong to change one's religion, whatever it be, and that if God caused them to be born Hindus, He meant them to remain Hindus. Another obstacle I have to get over in every new house is their idea that our religions and theirs are really the same, only we call God by a different name.[15]

One question asked several times, according to Frances May, was: "If God is so good, why does he let us suffer so?" – a question that missionaries themselves often asked when doing famine relief.[16]

English women missionaries had little understanding of Indian women, proceeded on the basis of stereotypes drawn from western discussions about what they were like, and contributed to western images of Indian women as oppressed, dependent, and helpless. Furthermore, as missionaries they were too entrenched in Christian institutions, and too hemmed in by European and

Indian men, to act as facilitators of the sort of progressive, modernizing Indian-led women's movement that existed in Calcutta.[17] Recruited into mission work through Anglican churches and schools in England, women missionaries often came from a socially conservative ecclesiastical world. Many of them were daughters, nieces, or sisters of clergymen, others from families with a tradition of missionary service.[18] In India they moved into missionary institutions that, if not actually isolated, certainly constituted a separate world from that of other Europeans. The women of this mission were for the most part isolated from British feminists and other reformers both in England and India, although it is significant that the portrayal of Indian women in the British feminist press and in missionary literature displayed the same predictable images of dependency and helplessness.[19]

Unlike many British feminist advocates of Indian women, missionaries actually knew Indian women and could converse with them, with varying degrees of success, in Urdu. Orientalist discourse and Christian exclusivism were not entirely effective in preventing missionaries from establishing affectionate relationships with some of their zenana students, a relationship that often reflected a sense of personal sympathy and self-consciousness about their position or a straightforward and acute frustration with the plight of Indian women. Emily Pilkington wrote: "I think that I grow more and more alive to the funniness of these people, probably the feeling is mutual. I don't know what they think most peculiar in me – myself, my clothes, or my manners."[20] Frances May wrote in 1903 that "I think one gets a kind of passion for one's own sex out here; it is so downtrodden, and so much nicer than the other, in spite of everything."[21]

Whatever the merits of zenana visitation, it was gradually displaced after 1880 by other kinds of work. As with St Stephen's Community, women and men cooperated actively in the creation of new medical and educational institutions, although they were operated by English and Indian women for Indian women. A passion for one's own sex led to a passion for improving women's medical care well before the Cambridge Brothers arrived. In 1875 Miss Engellmann began medical zenana work in Delhi. In 1877 she began to concentrate on midwifery. When the first Cambridge Brothers arrived in Delhi in 1878 she was delivering babies by the hundreds. With a passion for Christianity embodied in institutions, Miss Engellmann and the Cambridge Brothers established St Stephen's Hospital for Women. By 1888 she and her Anglo-Indian assistant, Alice King, lived in a new thirty-bed hospital overlooking the Queen's Gardens in Delhi, and a branch hospital had been established in Karnal. In 1888 the aggregate number of patients seen at Delhi and Karnal (including outpatients) was reported as 19,790.[22] Zenana pupils at that time numbered a couple of hundred, a striking contrast for readers in England who were concerned with measuring missionary productivity.[23]

St Stephen's Hospital became the heart of the women's missionary effort in Delhi in the 1890s. With the new hospital came a new emphasis on professionalism, and a new emphasis on the missionary value of the sheer presence of western institutions in India. Another medical zenana worker, Jenny Muller, went for training to Calcutta Medical College in 1888, and returned in 1891 to serve as the hospital's first qualified doctor. Probably born in India, she had been educated at the Lawrence Military School at Sanawar Asylum. The progression from unqualified local medical missionary to qualified medical missionary from Europe is neatly demonstrated by the arrival from England in 1893 of St Stephen's second qualified doctor, Mildred Staley (MB, London), a bishop's daughter who "gave up a lucrative practice for Christ's sake, at first in order to fill the need in Karnal."[24]

In 1896 she was joined by Charlotte Hull (MB, BSc., London), who returned to London in 1901 to deliver a speech to women in medical training – an appeal to join her in mission work in Delhi. Forget about the old and already unfashionable image of the missionary, she argued, the "unconscious survival of our childish picture of the pith hat and the big Bible under the palm tree." At a time when the number of unmarried women physicians, surgeons, and general practitioners in England and Wales amounted to only 167, she argued that India offered an opportunity to exercise the highest level of medical skill.[25] "There are few places where such a variety of practice, and especially surgical practice, can be obtained by a medical woman as in our Delhi Hospital." Furthermore, there need be no worries about being forced to proselytize. "Is not the spirit and aim with which the work is done more than the actual work itself, more at any rate than the actual preaching, which constitutes its missionary aspect?"[26]

In 1904 women's work took only 37 per cent of the Delhi missions' budget, even though there were twice as many European women as men in Delhi. But in 1906 the foundation stone was laid for a new hospital in the civil lines north of Old Delhi, paid for in part by the sale of the old buildings. In 1916 St Stephen's Hospital had a European staff of 5 doctors, 2 evangelists, 2 housekeepers, 5 nursing sisters, and an Indian staff of 27. By 1919 women's work accounted for 56 per cent of the SPG and Cambridge Mission budget, and women's medical work 29 per cent.[27]

Published and manuscript reports of the missionaries display little information about, and even less sympathy with, Indian medical practices, which were diverse and changing rapidly in the late nineteenth century. Designed to serve the rhetorical purposes of the missionary movement, the reports stress the mistreatment of women in Indian society and fulminate against the enemies of western-style medicine: "the fearsome old mother-in-law, the filthy old family mid-wife, and the foolish old family medicine men."[28] "This is the place to see miserable babies," Jenny Muller wrote of St Stephen's dispensary, while lamenting the small number she saw that day because of an eclipse of the sun and fear of new plague regulations.[29] In 1894 the civil surgeon at Karnal assembled the local *dais*, Indian midwives, for a lecture from Miss Muller on hygiene. "Anything more gruesome and horrible for a person trained in antiseptic principles to behold than that crowd of dirty women can hardly be conceived," she wrote.[30] Medical missionaries made no attempt to identify the good in Indian medical knowledge, which they portrayed as a static, traditional monolith, in practice either quaint or lethal. Their ability to effect visible good for Indians very quickly gave them an impregnable sense of the superiority of their own approach.

By the turn of the century the institutional emphasis of the mission meant that women were not concentrated in St Stephen's home in the mission compound, but dispersed in medical and educational institutions. In 1898 there were 29 women missionaries working in Delhi (compared to 11 European men), but only 8 to 10 of the women lived in the mission compound, the remainder living in St Stephen's Hospital or one of the outstations at Hissar, Karnal, and Riwari. At that time educational work was focused on zenana work and two institutions for Indian Christian women. A boarding school, later named the Victoria School for Girls, served the daughters of the Indian catechists and other educated Indian Christians. St Mary's Home, described by one missionary with the telling phrase, the "wastepaper basket of the mission," was a home for women and girls who had no place else to go: orphans, convalescents, converts abandoned by their husbands or families, runaway wives, "waifs and strays."[31]

In the early twentieth century the mission's educational strategy was refocused on Queen Mary's School, opened in 1912 with twenty-five students under the direction of Helen Jerwood, a clergyman's daughter and graduate of Cheltenham Ladies College who donated £1,000 toward the cost of a new building.[32] The school's purpose was to give "an education which will fit the girls to be companions of 'English educated' men."[33] It was so thoroughly under the direction of women that "Miss Jerwood's School" allowed no men on the premises at all, except on one occasion, an official visit by the viceroy. In 1916 zenana work was officially abandoned altogether in Delhi.[34]

In 1899 one of the Cambridge Brothers, G. A. Lefroy, became Bishop of Lahore. In cooperation with an English deaconess, Katherine Beynon, he oversaw the creation of a new women's community, St Hilda's. Beynon used her personal wealth to subsidize the construction of a large new deaconess house on the cathedral grounds (each room named for a single virtue, such as honesty, truth, and courage). The SPG began to send qualified teachers and trained deaconesses to St Hilda's, where they emphasized educational work with non-Christians in a new cathedral school system at the expense of parochial work with the Eurasian Christian community in Lahore.

Of the 312 women who worked in Delhi and Lahore in connection with the SPG after 1860, 260 were recruited after 1880 and roughly 200 in the first half of the twentieth century, the heyday of British missionary work in India. By way of contrast, the Cambridge Brotherhood recruited fewer than fifty male missionaries for the entire period 1878–1947.[35] In any given year between 1910 and 1930, roughly sixty European women were at work in Delhi and

Lahore. The characteristic missionary was an unmarried career woman, from London or a small city in the south of England, who arrived in India in her late twenties and either returned quickly, within a year or two, or served a lengthy term, the mean being twelve years. Those who did not die in India (at least 24 did), or marry while in service (at least 23), or move on to missionary service elsewhere (at least 15), resigned to return to England. A few were dismissed from service for a variety of reasons including "broke down," "unfit for work in India," or (most ominous of all to me) "too old to learn the language."

As women came into this institutional setting, they were increasingly likely to have formal educational qualifications. Forty women had a BA or MB (medical) degree or its equivalent. As many as 113 mentioned some kind of secondary education, usually a girls' high school.[36] At least 81 had some instruction at one of the Church of England deaconess training institutions.[37] Twenty-four women were doctors.[38] At one time just after the First World War there were nine women doctors affiliated with the mission, although not all were in residence in India at once.

It is clear that the missionary movement gave English women important opportunities, especially as medical doctors, which in some ways went beyond those in England discussed in Martha Vicinus's *Independent Women*, a book that has given me considerably more than a title for this essay.[39] That their behavior and achievements in India throw an interesting light on the nature of English religion is also clear. That the women of the Cambridge Mission created important institutions for Indian women in Delhi is beyond dispute as well.

The story of the Cambridge Mission certainly gives no support whatsoever for the literary tradition – exemplified in Kipling, Forster, and Paul Scott – of treating women as sources of racial antagonism in India. Nor does it support the frequently encountered historical generalization that the advent of women in India, in the words of Eric Stokes, "diminished contact between the races."[40] But recent historical writing on women in the empire has produced several case studies of the pitfalls of taking western historiographical approaches into a non-Western context, for the attempt to restore women's agency in imperial history often succeeds in establishing only that women too were successful imperialists or in generating exaggerated claims for the racial tolerance of European women.[41]

If the entire missionary presence is condemned wholesale, and men and women missionaries dismissed as nothing more than particularly offensive manifestations of imperialism, many problems are solved. But Edward Said's comments on orientalist scholarship are, I believe, equally applicable to the missionary movement: "To say simply that modern orientalism has been an aspect of both imperialism and colonialism is not to say anything very disputable. Yet it is not enough to say it; it needs to be worked through analytically and historically."[42] If we are to understand St Stephen's Hospital and Queen Mary's School, we must try to understand the people who created them. In order to understand imperialism or the missionary movement we must do more than challenge the moral credentials of imperialists and missionaries, however distasteful such people may be in a postcolonial and largely secular intellectual world. It is important to judge historical actors by their own standards, among others. It is precisely because missionaries were not exactly like other imperialists, but had different motives and goals, that we are in some ways justified in holding them to very high standards of judgment, that is, their own.

The initial male rhetoric of the Cambridge Mission involved a commitment to view Indian culture with a new sympathy. There was a corresponding strain of egalitarianism in the women missionaries' commitment to a personal bond of sympathy between themselves and Indian women. This special bond of sympathy was elitist in terms of class relationships, based upon a narrow and distorted knowledge of Indian women, and easily corrupted by the inequality of the relationship between Europeans and Indians. Enough has now been written on the imperial and dominating uses of what appears to be the feminist rhetoric of missionaries and others to make us skeptical of its deployment in India.[43] The mistreatment of Indian women by Indian men was used repeatedly to justify the British, and the missionary, presence in India, and such arguments helped to stir up distorted views of India in Europe and North America.

However impossible the ideal of a special bond of sympathy might have been in the imperial setting, it is nonetheless true that women's work initially operated in a different moral world from men's work. European women were freed from the blight of clerical professionalism, which forced male clergy into the role of ecclesiastical disciplinarians. Women did not have to manipulate, mold, evict, and excommunicate Indian Christians. But as the character of missionary work changed, the egalitarian elements of women's work were for the most part lost in the setting of school and hospital. In the Cambridge Mission and the SPG mission in Lahore, the relationship of English woman to Indian woman was one of English doctor and Indian patient, English nurse and Indian patient, English teacher and Indian student, English matron and Indian orphan, English employer and Indian employee, English supervisor and Indian subordinate. Instead of encountering Indians as colleagues in mission work or as social equals in zenana work, missionary women encountered them as patients, students, or employees. In India as in England, patients, students, and employees were people to be managed, disciplined, or discharged.

Although the missionary movement for the most part worked against thinking of Indians in terms of racial as opposed to cultural difference, the institutional emphasis of the Cambridge Mission nevertheless tended to exclude Indians from the mission. At least 6 (14 per cent), and probably more, of the 43 women designated as missionaries before 1880 were from Eurasian or Indian families. Only 7 (3 per cent) of 260 recruited after 1880 fitted that category. As late as 1899 one of the sisters living in St Stephen's Community was an Indian, Mary Tara Chand, the daughter of one of the Indian clergymen ordained before the arrival of the Cambridge Brothers. The head doctor at St Stephen's Hospital in 1899 was also an Indian: Martha Francis, a surgeon whose formal qualifications were listed only as "Indian doctor" but who served as a surgeon at Delhi or Riwari until 1932. As English women with formal qualifications arrived, she was put into a subordinate position and new Indians were not recruited except for temporary service. From the Indian woman's point of view, exclusion was exclusion whether based on race, culture, or educational qualifications.

Most galling of all for Indian women was the recruitment of European missionary doctors into secular imperial medical institutions for women, where they took up places as doctors and medical teachers that could have been held by Indians. In 1916 Dr Agnes Scott became assistant to the Inspector General of Civil Hospitals, an appointment that allowed her to live in the hills during the hot weather.[44] In 1918 Helen Franklin, the head of St Stephen's Hospital, was appointed professor of surgery at the government's new Lady Hardinge Medical College and Hospital in Delhi; in 1920 she became vice principal.[45]

The institutional emphasis worked in another way to elicit explanations of difference based upon the allegedly superior cultural characteristics of Europeans. As English missionaries devoted more and more time to working with Indian staff, the frustrations of management found an outlet in British stereotypes about Indian national character. In 1893 Jenny Muller reported that "We are obliged to use uneducated women for nurses, and though we try to train them, yet the lax ideas which prevail in India in regard to truth and cleanliness stand very much in the way of their being good trustworthy nurses."[46] Hospital and school routines were operated naturally and unselfconsciously as they would be in London, and problems with recalcitrant patients or students were attributed to their Indianness, as Mildred Staley's description of how patients were treated shows:

> [The patient is] attired in petticoat, jacket, and redbordered sheet for the head. Thus attired and cleaner probably than she has been for many a long year, she is put to bed in a ward, and then begins the struggle to instill something of the meaning of the words obedience, regularity, cleanliness and decency into those who have up till now done as they pleased, slept, eaten etc. when and where they pleased, without an idea of consulting the comfort of others. Those from the most secluded families often find the restraints most irksome.[47]

In this institutional and managerial setting, the rationale for women's missionary work changed. Indian women would be led to Christ, not through personal conversations, but through the observation of sacrificial service by English women in teaching, medical practice and nursing. This rhetoric of sacrificial service generated its own frustrations for missionaries, who were less alarmed about Hindu idolatry among their patients than they were about Indian misunderstanding of their own missionary motives. Dr Jenny Muller complained that Indian women "appear to have a deep rooted conviction in their minds that all we do for their bodies is for our own gain either in this world or in the next."[48] Indian patients sometimes responded to a request for a fee by pointing out to the exasperated doctor that she had gained merit for herself by doing good. Despite the fact that missionaries in India had opportunities that they might not have had in England, they were convinced that the missionary life involved great sacrifice, in particular the sacrifice of living away from England. It is easy to understand why Indian women missed the theological significance of that sacrifice, or even failed to notice that it was a sacrifice.

The special bond of sympathy, the passion for one's own sex, that characterized the zenana relationship was gone, replaced by a managerial and professional relationship with Indian women. They encountered missionaries at a distance, as teachers, nurses, or doctors whose qualifications for their position reinforced the notion of western superiority. "The English people I knew as a child," wrote Anita Desai,

> were the teachers in my school, Queen Mary's in Old Delhi. They were the Grey Sisters (in grey cotton dresses with white collars and buttons, unmarried and austere) of the Cambridge Mission that had founded the school, as well as St Stephen's Hospital over the wall. These teachers and doctors lived busy lives inside the grey walls of their institutions, and did not go much beyond their compound except to service at St James's Church in Kashmere Gate.[49]

There is another view of them through the eyes of a schoolgirl, Tara, in Desai's novel *Clear Light of Day*:

> The missionary ladies who ran the grey austere mission school . . . were all elderly spinsters – had, in fact, taken the vow of celibacy although not the nun's habit – awesomely brisk, cheerful and resourceful. Having left the meadows and hedgerows, the parsonages and village greens of their homes behind in their confident and quixotic youth, they had gone through experiences of a kind others might have buckled under but they had borne and survived and overcome like boats riding the waves – wars and blitzes, riots and mutinies, famines and droughts, floods, fires and native customs – and had then retired, not to the parsonages and village greens, but to the running of a sober, disciplined mission school with all their confidence, their cheerfulness and their faith impeccably intact. Tara could not suppress a baleful look as she observed them bustling about the classrooms, cracking open the registers or working out algebraic problems across the blackboards, blowing whistles and rushing across the netball fields, organizing sports days and annual school concerts, leading the girls in singing

hymns and, every so often, dropping suddenly to their knees, burying their faces in worn and naked hands, and praying with most distinguished intensity. Tara wondered uneasily if hers were one of the lost souls they prayed for.[50]

From the point of view of the majority of Indian women associated with the Cambridge Mission, there is good reason to believe that the new distance in missionary work was a positive advantage. Leslie Flemming, in her study of American Presbyterian mission work in the United Provinces, argues that women missionaries provided valuable role models for Indian women, especially as nurses and teachers.[51] There is some evidence for that argument in the records of the Delhi mission as well, although it was clearly not the case for Indian women doctors, who did not need missionaries to provide role models. Indian women could receive training as doctors as early as English women and, as we have seen, English doctors in some cases displaced Indian doctors in the mission.

For some Indian nurses, teachers, and students, however, the situation was different. The influence of role models is difficult to measure, and presumably Indian role models would have been preferable to English ones. But the mission supplied employment and training alternatives that provided some degree of independence for many Christian and non-Christian Indian women. Although I cannot reconstruct the numbers employed or trained for the entire period, in 1929 the hospitals in Riwari and Delhi employed forty-seven Indian nurses.[52] The mission appears to have recruited nurses from the Chamar community in Delhi and other outstations. In 1928 when the government launched a scheme for village dispensaries with a subassistant surgeon and midwife nurse, a missionary claimed that most of the nurses hired were poor Christian widows of outcaste origins. Insulted by Hindus because of their caste, and subject to attempts at conversion or reconversion from Arya Samaj missionaries, they nonetheless had marketable skills derived from the mission.[53]

Missionaries could not do all the teaching in mission schools, and depended upon Indian teachers. Government schools paid more, and hired away Indian Christian teachers from the mission schools. The mission was competing in a tight labor market for nurses and teachers, especially after 1900 as the government and the Delhi municipality became more involved in women's education and medical care. Missionaries tried to hire as many Indian Christians as possible, but they were often forced to hire non-Christians, especially as teachers. Consequently both Christian and non-Christian teachers and nurses were not only being paid for their work, but could escape the kind of domination and control that missionaries no doubt wished to exercise over their private lives.

From the point of view of Indian students, whatever the value of old-style zenana work in providing moral advantages to women missionaries, it is difficult to see that it did much good for Indian women, many of whom regarded their visitors as amusing intruders in need of humoring. The education provided to the students at Queen Mary's was of genuine value to them, and they were not bothered with direct proselytization, which would have destroyed the school's effectiveness. They were freer from missionary interference in their private lives than the lower-status Christian girls at the Victoria School for Girls, who faced missionary dictation of the details of their diet, clothing, and demeanor. Facing competition from Theosophist and later Hindu schools, European missionaries were unable to dominate Indian students at Queen Mary's School, who were in turn freer to pick and choose those aspects of missionary institution-building that served their own interests.

In Desai's *Clear Light of Day*, it is perhaps significant that the major character is a woman, Bim, who is determined against all odds to resist marriage and be a teacher. Indian men and women had every right to ransack the British presence and appropriate what they found useful. Not all westernized Indians, or Indians who were interested in making use of western education – or even, in some cases, in becoming Christians – were pale shadows of orientalism or collaborationists. The relationship between Chamar nurses and European doctors and nurses, or relatively prosperous Muslim and Hindu girls and their teachers at Queen Mary's School, was more complicated than that.

The largest number of Indian women came into contact with the mission as medical patients. The mission provided medical care for nearly forty years before the government and municipality began to open clinics for women, and St Stephen's Hospital opened forty years before the government's Lady Hardinge Hospital for Women opened in 1916. Early surgical reports from St Stephen's and St Elizabeth's Hospital in Karnal report, along with the usual bones set, abscesses drained, and cataracts removed, an emphasis on gynecological and obstetric operations that were probably available nowhere else.[54] A woman whose pain was relieved, or whose baby was saved from death or disfigurement, would no doubt have found it very bewildering to be told that the lady sahiba was really involved in the construction of a complex discourse of subordination whose ultimate purpose was the maintenance of Western superiority.

In the final analysis, however, this kind of utilitarian balance sheet, which measures the good against the bad in missionary work, is not a standard that can be used to justify, or even judge the significance of, a missionary presence that was part of a larger colonial and imperial presence. Furthermore, it is not the basis upon which missionaries themselves would wish to be judged. They reasonably argued that the mission should not be judged only by conversions, which were few in Delhi and Lahore when compared to parts of village Punjab. But missionaries acknowledged that the ultimate purpose of the mission was rhetorical. Any good that they might be doing, or not doing, was worthwhile in and of itself; but it had a larger theological purpose, which was to bear witness to the Christian faith of the missionaries.

In this mission, the institutions were the message. Emily Pilkington took her zenana pupils to see the hospital, private rooms and all: "I feel that to see the hospital is a practical lesson to them, more lasting and effective than words. There they see an outcome of our faith. The Hospital, as it stands in the midst of this great city, is a witness to Christ."[55] But St Stephen's Hospital and Queen Mary's School taught Indian women less about Christianity or compassion or sacrifice than about the allegedly superior organizational, technical, and professional abilities of English women. Mission institutions were part of a larger western institutional presence in India that defined organizational and managerial skills as superior to compassion and self-sacrifice. It was a definition that many Indians accepted enthusiastically, but it was not the point of the missionary movement.

The missionary movement was a channel for a large outpouring of goodwill by ordinary English people toward the people of India, and by English women toward the women of India. The English men and women of the Cambridge Mission had special ideals about a unique relationship with the people of India. The male ideal was subverted almost at once by clerical professionalism.[56] The female ideal took longer to abandon, but by the early twentieth century it too had been submerged, not in racism or ethnocentrism, but in a more complicated strain of imperialism, the heritage of late Victorian Christianity, with its conviction that the progress of Christianity is intimately related to bricks, mortar, and educational qualifications. Whatever the original goals of the missionary movement, or the individual intentions of missionaries, St Stephen's Community and St Hilda's Community provided, among other things, a subtle but powerful sanction for the British imperial presence.

NOTES

For helpful comments on and criticism of this paper, I am especially grateful to Roger Draper, Geeta Patel, Linda Kerber, Janaki Nair, Gail Malmgreen, Paul Greenough, and Antoinette Burton. Susan Lawrence explained to me some of the intricacies of nineteenth-century medical practice and training. Susan Tarm, Russell Friedman, and Alex Nichols helped extract information from my chaotic notes, and arrange it into neat statistical tables.

1 Lacking a central source of biographical information I put together a card file from a variety of sources including the annual reports of the Society for the Propagation of the Gospel and the Cambridge Mission to Delhi, the SPG's Committee on Women's Work manuscript reports from Delhi, the SPG's manuscript Roll of Women Missionaries, F. J. Western, "The early history of the Cambridge Mission to Delhi" (unpublished typescript, 1950), *Delhi Mission News*, and the memorial brasses on the wall of St Hilda's deaconess house in Lahore. Any centralized Western source of biographical information about missionaries will undercount their numbers, especially for the nineteenth century when direct recruitment in India was more common.

2 On the Americans, see John C. B. Webster, *The Christian Community and Change*

in Nineteenth-Century North India (Delhi, 1976); on the CMS, see Jeffrey Cox, "On redefining crisis: the Victorian crisis of faith in the Punjab, 1870–1900," in R. J. Helmstadter and B. Lightman (eds), *Victorian Faith in Crisis* (London, 1990).

3 B. F. Westcott, *On Some Points in the Religious Office of the Universities* (London, 1873), p. 41.

4 See *The Story of the Delhi Mission* (London, 1908); Western, "Early history"; and *One Hundred Years in Delhi: The Brotherhood of the Ascended Christ* (Delhi, 1977).

5 See Janaki Nair, "Uncovering the zenana: visions of Indian womanhood in Englishwomen's writings, 1813–1940," *Journal of Women's History*, 2, 1 (spring 1990), pp. 8–34.

6 *Delhi Mission News*, Jan. 1898.

7 This description is taken in part from an account in *Report of the SPG and Cambridge Mission to Delhi* (Delhi, 1898), and from other sources. Unlike many other European women, missionaries remained in Delhi during the hot weather, but did little during the day. After dinner at eight the women would then go "up to the roof to study the stars and hope for some slight breeze."

8 The annual statistical tables published by the SPG on its work in Delhi in 1909 list the number of "ordained" missionaries, outstations, churches, chapels, catechists, readers, adult baptisms, infant baptisms, Indian Christian communicants, confirmations, marriages, and burials. The word "ordained" neatly excludes women missionaries, who do not appear in the statistical tables at all: *Annual Report of the SPG and Cambridge Mission to Delhi* (Delhi, 1909).

9 See Meredith Borthwick, *The Changing Role of Women in Bengal, 1849–1905* (Princeton, NJ, 1984), pp. 7–8.

10 *Report of the SPG and Cambridge Mission to Delhi* (Delhi, 1898), pp. 20–1.

11 Ibid., p. 25.

12 *Report of the SPG and Cambridge Mission to Delhi* (Delhi, 1892), p. 10.

13 Ibid.

14 Miss Heming, in *Report of the SPG and Cambridge Mission to Delhi* (Delhi, 1894), p. 18.

15 Ibid.

16 *Report of the SPG and Cambridge Mission to Delhi* (Delhi, 1903), p. 47.

17 See Borthwick, *Changing Role*.

18 My sources do not allow me to be more precise about exact numbers or percentages.

19 I am grateful to Antoinette M. Burton for calling my attention to her article, "The white woman's burden: British feminists and the Indian woman, 1865–1915," *Women's Studies International Forum*, 13, 4 (1990), pp. 295–308, which includes an analysis of the image of Indian women in feminist periodicals. Cf. Barbara Ramusack, "Cultural missionaries, maternal imperialists, feminist allies: British women activists in India, 1865–1945," ibid., pp. 309–21.

20 *Report of the SPG and Cambridge Mission to Delhi* (Delhi, 1892), p. 10.

21 *Report of the SPG and Cambridge Mission to Delhi* (Delhi, 1903), p. 47.

22 See *Delhi Medical Mission to Women and Children: Report and Accounts for the Year 1888* (Delhi, 1888).

23 *Report of the SPG and Cambridge Mission to Delhi* (Delhi, 1899) reported 170 zenana students, roughly the same number as in the 1880s, but only 40 were in Delhi, the rest in Simla or the outstations of Riwari, Karnal, and Hissar.

24 *Report of the SPG and Cambridge Mission to Delhi* (Delhi, 1893), Miss Scott's report.

25 Census of 1901, England and Wales – summary tables, *Parliamentary Papers*, 1903, Vol. 84, p. 187. Taking as an index of the number of career doctors the number of

unmarried women doctors over 45, Martha Vicinus points out that there were only 20 in 1901, only 60 in 1911. See Martha Vicinus, *Independent Women: Work and Community for Single Women, 1850-1920* (Chicago, 1985), pp. 28–9.

26 *Report of the SPG and Cambridge Mission to Delhi* (Delhi, 1901), p. 28.

27 Figures summarized from annual reports.

28 *Report of the SPG and Cambridge Mission to Delhi* (Delhi, 1897), p. 23, Miss Staley's report.

29 *Report of the SPG and Cambridge Mission to Delhi* (Delhi, 1898), p. 25.

30 Ibid.

31 *Annual Report of the SPG and Cambridge Mission to Delhi for 1904* (Delhi, 1904), p. 82.

32 See *Queen Mary's School, Delhi: Golden Jubilee, 1912-1962* (Delhi, 1962).

33 *Report of the SPG and Cambridge Mission to Delhi* (Delhi, 1912), p. 38.

34 *Report of the SPG and Cambridge Mission to Delhi* (Delhi, 1916), p. 20.

35 A few additional missionaries were connected with the SPG but not the Cambridge Brothers.

36 The most popular were Alexandra College, Dublin (2), Alice Otley School, Worcester (2), Bedford High School (4), Cheltenham Ladies College (5), Clapham High School (3), Convent of Sacred Heart, Aberdeen (2), Godolphin School (4), Leeds Girls High School (3), Lincoln High School (2), St Mary's, Abbott's Bromley, (2).

37 These included the SPG's own deaconess house in south London, the College of the Ascension in Birmingham, and the high-church sisterhoods at Portsmouth, Truro, Warminster, and Wantage.

38 Six trained at the Royal Free Hospital, three at Guy's Hospital, and two at the London School of Medicine for Women; the rest at various hospitals. Nineteen received an MB or MD.

39 Vicinus, *Independent Women*, cited above, note 25.

40 Eric Stokes, *The English Utilitarians and India* (Oxford, 1959), p. 27. Stokes's authority for that comment is Percival Spear, who was a missionary with the Cambridge Mission and teacher at St Stephen's College before returning to England and a distinguished career as a historian of India. On this subject, see the discussion in Claudia Knapman, *White Women in Fiji, 1835-1930: The Ruin of Empire?* (Boston, Mass., 1986), ch. 1.

41 See Caroline Oliver, *Western Women in Colonial Africa* (Westport, Ct, 1982); Mary Ann Lind, *The Compassionate Memsahibs: Welfare Activities of British Women in India, 1900-1947* (New York, 1988); Helen Callaway, *Gender, Culture and Empire: European Women in Colonial Nigeria* (London, 1987). For a judicious overview of this problem, see Margaret Strobel, "Gender and race in the nineteenth- and twentieth-century British Empire," in Renate Bridenthal, Claudia Koonz, and Susan Stuart (eds), *Becoming Visible: Women in European History* (Boston, Mass., 1987), pp. 375–95.

42 Edward Said, *Orientalism* (New York, 1978), p. 123; cf. Said's own comments on missionaries, p. 100, dismissing them as part of a complex apparatus devoted to tending the interests of British state power.

43 See Joanna Liddle and Rama Joshi, "Gender and imperialism in British India," *Economic and Political Weekly: Review of Women's Studies*, 26 Oct. 1985; Lata Mani, "Production of an official discourse on sati in early nineteenth century Bengal,' *Economic and Political Weekly: Review of Women's Studies*, 26 Apr. 1986; Lata Mani, "Contentious traditions: the debate on sati in colonial India," *Cultural Critique* (1987), pp. 119–57.

44 *Annual Reports of the SPG and Cambridge Mission to Delhi* (Delhi, 1916), p. 16.

45 *Report of the SPG and Cambridge Mission to Delhi* (London, 1918, 1920).
46 *Report of the Delhi Medical Mission to Women and Children for 1893* (Delhi, 1893).
47 *Report of the SPG and Cambridge Mission to Delhi* (London, 1895), p. 17.
48 *Report of the SPG and Cambridge Mission to Delhi* (London, 1894), p. 32.
49 Anita Desai, "The rage for the raj," *New Republic*, 3697, 25 Nov. 1985, pp. 26–7.
50 Anita Desai, *Clear Light of Day* (New York, 1980), pp. 124–5.
51 See Leslie A. Flemming, "New models, new roles: US Presbyterian women missionaries and social change in north India, 1870–1910," in Leslie A. Flemming (ed.), *Women's Work for Women: Missionaries and Social Change in Asia* (Boulder, Col., 1989), pp. 35–58.
52 *Report of the SPG and Cambridge Mission to Delhi* (Delhi, 1929).
53 *Report of the SPG and Cambridge Mission to Delhi* (Delhi, 1928), p. 21.
54 *Report of the SPG and Cambridge Mission to Delhi* (Delhi, 1894), pp. 27, 29. St Stephen's reported 431 operations, including 103 obstetric and 45 gynecological.
55 *Report of the SPG and Cambridge Mission to Delhi* (Delhi, 1892), p. 12.
56 For an account of how some of the liberal ideas of the Cambridge Mission resurfaced in the twentieth century, see Daniel O'Connor, *Gospel, Raj and Swaraj: The Missionary Years of C. F. Andrews 1904–1914* (Bern, 1990).

Chapter 11

Spiritualism and the First World War

J. M. Winter

There is a vast, and still growing, historical literature on the subject of "how English culture was transformed, and English imaginations were altered, by what happened between 1914 and 1918."[1] Much of this research celebrates the birth of "modernism" (however defined) during the war or as a consequence of the war.[2] Whatever the truth of this argument with respect to the art of the avant-garde, it is difficult to accept it as a judgment about other facets of European cultural history in general, or about English cultural history in particular. The major problem is that the "modernist" interpretation of the war tends to obscure the profoundly traditional and archaic nature of cultural responses to the 1914–18 conflict, among both elites and masses.

In this context, the study of religious beliefs and practices is of some significance. This essay examines one facet of this issue. We have valuable studies of religious institutions and religious dissent during the war.[3] But a subject largely unexplored is the effect of the war on the religious imagination, broadly defined, both within and outside the confines of the traditional churches. Here it may be useful to highlight the history of the somewhat unconventional, but by no means insignificant, community of English spiritualists, whose number grew during the war and because of the war, and whose beliefs and practices carried much of the Victorian temperament into the war period and beyond. Continuity, not transformation, and reiteration, not alteration, are the key features of the wartime and postwar history of what may be described as the spiritualist communion.

Spiritualism may be defined in two ways. First, secular spiritualism encompasses the views of those who explore the existence of human personality after death and the possibility of communication with the dead. It makes little difference whether or not such people believe in God; their quest is psychological, not theological. Secondly, religious spiritualism describes the attitudes of people who see apocalyptic, divine, angelic, or saintly presences in daily life, and do so at the margins of or outside the confines of the traditional churches. The best way to understand spiritualism is as a family of men and women who were prepared to go beyond conventional materialism or theology and did so in societies, seances, and a host of publications.

Spiritualism was indeed a house of many mansions, including many who simply wanted to converse with the dead. This last category, of course, grew rapidly after 1914. Nevertheless, we should not restrict the spiritualist communion to those bereaved during and because of the war. Most either continued their prewar search for psychical experiences or embarked on spiritual quests of a kind they had undertaken time and again in the prewar period.

Some spiritualists were unbalanced; others, charlatans. Most were honest true believers. Their activities were, to say the least, controversial and occasionally bizarre, but the social and intellectual prominence of leading spiritualists, as well as the widespread belief in the paranormal among soldiers who served in the Great War, made it difficult to brush them aside simply as crackpots and cranks.

This essay presents some of their wartime history. First, we examine spiritualism on the home front, through the work of two prominent figures, Sir Arthur Conan Doyle and Sir Oliver Lodge, who popularized spiritualism in this period, and the reaction of both scientists and churchmen to their belief in communication with the dead. Secondly, we explore the uncanny world of the soldiers' war, recreated in the stories of those who were there, as soldiers, chaplains, nurses, or writers. Thirdly, we examine the spiritualist dimension of the commemoration of the fallen in the postwar years.

In the Victorian period, the spiritualist movement both in Britain and on the Continent was socially and politically more a radical than a conservative phenomenon. Many Victorian spiritualists were freethinkers who rejected mainstream religious practice and belief. But the cold certainties of positivism, the search for laws of behavior and development, left many radicals untouched or dissatisfied.[4] One impulse was to turn to spiritualism as a means of reconciling science, deism, and socialism. This Utopian project took many forms, from an exploration of autokinesis (moving objects) to automatic writing to seances. These manifestations were treated as serious scientific matters by a variety of eminent writers, scholars, and public figures, both in Britain and France. Among them were Hugo, Ruskin, Tennyson, as well as Faraday, Flammarion, Alfred Russel Wallace, and William Crookes.

Women played an important role in the spiritualist community. It is, therefore, not surprising that spiritualists were advocates of feminism and that the Catholic Church repeatedly anathematized the movement and especially the women within it.[5] The opposition of the Roman Catholic Church had a strong scriptural basis. Leviticus 20: 6 and Deuteronomy 18: 10–12 left no doubt about the sin of communion with the dead. In 1864 spiritualist writings were placed on the Index. The movement was denounced by the Holy See in 1898 (and in 1917); and to identify the enemy still more precisely, Pope Pius IX himself condemned the twin evils of spiritualism and socialism.[6]

Many spiritualists did indeed combine a subversive outlook on social questions with a taste for the unexplained and the occult.[7] Some were poets of the paranormal; some meditated on the afterlife; others were fascinated by contemporary psychological research. The work of Charcot on hypnotism and trances helped popularize the paranormal, as, in later years, did Freud's theory of the unconscious.

In the early twentieth century British scientists who entertained at least a suspension of disbelief about spiritualism did so for many different reasons. Some tried to translate traditional theology or the poetry of ancient metaphors about human survival into the language of experimental science. They pointed to magnetism, electricity, and radio waves as constituting unseen yet real phenomena of distant communication. Thought waves or other forms of human feeling or expression conceivably did the same. These speculations were the stuff of which experiments could be and were made.[8]

The home for many scientists whose minds were open to the possibility that spiritualist phenomena were worthy of investigation was the Society for Psychical Research, founded in 1882. Its membership was far from undistinguished. Sir Oliver Lodge, Professor of Physics at Liverpool and later Principal of Birmingham University, was president of the society between 1901 and 1903. He was succeeded by the physicist Sir William Barrett and by Charles Richet, Nobel prizewinning physiologist. A few years later Henri Bergson presided over the society.[9] Other eminent scholars who openly explored psychical phenomena before the war were William McDougall, the Oxford and (after the war) Harvard psychologist, the Oxford classicist Gilbert Murray, the Harvard philosopher William James, and Lord Rayleigh, Cavendish Professor of Physics at Cambridge and Nobel prizewinner in 1914.

It would be wrong, therefore, to locate such views on the lunatic fringe. Yes, there were sharks who swam in these troubled waters, and who fed off the gullible and the weak. But in appreciating the sources of the spiritualist revival during and after the First World War, we must accept that many prominent individuals earnestly believed in the paranormal or in communication with the dead, and did so because they had taken psychical phenomena seriously before the war.

David Cannadine has called spiritualism the "private denial of death."[10] But the spiritualist movement was anything but private, and spoke with renewed confidence after the First World War. During and after the war, interest in the paranormal and the afterlife naturally deepened. It was inevitably and inextricably tied up with the need expressed by many to communicate with the fallen. One French observer reversed the point. "After a murderous war," he wrote, "who would doubt that the dead would try to communicate again?"[11]

Just as in the Victorian and Edwardian period, the cause of spiritualism was promoted by prominent public figures. The continuities in English spiritualism in the period of the 1914–18 conflict, as well as the traumatic effect of the world war, appear clearly in the indefatigable efforts of two men, Sir Arthur Conan Doyle and Sir Oliver Lodge.

Let us first consider the case of Conan Doyle. The creator of Sherlock Holmes lost his son and his brother in the war. But he claimed that these losses did not change his views: on the contrary. Writing in the third person of his own experience, Conan Doyle reflected that

> the sight of a world which was distraught with sorrow, and which was eagerly asking for help and knowledge, did certainly affect his mind and cause him to understand that these psychic studies, which he had so long pursued, were of immense practical importance and could no longer be regarded as a mere intellectual hobby or fascinating pursuit of a novel research. Evidence of the presence of the dead appeared in his own household, and the relief afforded by posthumous messages taught him how great a solace it would be to a tortured world if it could share in the knowledge which had become clear to himself.[12]

In 1918 Conan Doyle wrote *The New Revelation*, a title bound to offend conventional religious sensibilities. In its preface he cited the prediction of "a celebrated Psychic," Mrs Piper, that "there will be a terrible war in different parts of the world" that would "cleanse and purify" it before the truth of spiritualism would be revealed for all to see. The meaning of the war was therefore "essentially religious, not political." It was a cataclysm set in motion to "reform . . . the decadent Christianity of to-day" and to reinforce it "by the facts of spirit communion and the clear knowledge of what lies beyond the exit-door of death."[13] In the next year, he embarked on a full and successful lecture tour of the United States,[14] and continued to speak to packed international meetings about his experience of psychical phenomena. In 1923 he helped found a spiritualist church in London, the outcome, as Sir Oliver Lodge disapprovingly put it, of decades of "missionary activity."[15]

Conan Doyle highlighted the visionary and emotional attraction of spiritualism. Oliver Lodge represented its scientific and rational appeal. His work as a physicist brought him a knighthood, international recognition, and popular notice as the man whose work had helped create the electrical ignition spark for the internal combustion engine.[16] He was a pillar of the Society for Psychical Research, publishing in its journal learned articles both on spiritualist phenomena and on the physics of wireless telegraphy.[17] Before the war, he had had wide experience of telepathy, trying to see them as experiments in paranormal psychology. The same Mrs Piper who had prophesied the disaster of the war to Conan Doyle was introduced to Lodge by the Harvard scholar William James.

Lodge's youngest son Raymond was a 26-year-old engineer serving in the Ypres salient. He was killed on 14 September 1915. A few days after his father had received the tragic news, he picked up a scrap of paper on which his wife had written these words: "To ease the pain and to try to get in touch." The bereaved couple attended a seance led by a celebrated medium, Mrs Osborne Leonard, who spoke in the voice of a young Indian girl called Feda. She normally had several sittings a day, but after 1914 she "declined all those who came to her only out of commercial or fortune-telling motives" in order "to help those who are disturbed by the war." Among those convinced of Mrs Leonard's uncanny powers to reach the dead was the radical journalist Robert Blatchford, editor of the *Clarion*.[18]

In the following weeks the Lodge family – father, mother, and at least two of the eleven children – continued the sessions and built up a detailed picture of Raymond's life in what they called "Summerland." Raymond's guide and comforter, indeed his surrogate father, was Sir Oliver's friend and fellow spiritualist intellectual, F. H. S. Myers, a Fellow of Trinity College, Cambridge, who had died in 1902. The details of this supernatural Odyssey were published in a book entitled *Raymond*, which went through a dozen printings between 1916 and 1919 and was republished in abridged form as *Raymond Revisited* in 1922.[19]

The interest in and controversy surrounding this book tell us much about the spiritualist revival during the war. *Raymond* is both a personal memorial and a scientific exposition. It is divided into three parts. The first is a memoir in the form of Raymond Lodge's letters home from the front. The second is entitled the "Supernatural portion" and describes the means through which Raymond communicated with his family. The emphasis is on a sober recounting of "the evidence . . . for the persistent existence of one of the multitude of youths who have sacrificed their lives at the call of their Country when endangered by an aggressor of calculated ruthlessness."[20] The third part considers the philosophical implications of psychical phenomena, and makes out a case for the compatibility of spiritualism with a belief in the divinity of Christ.

What gave the book its power was partly the vivid description of Raymond himself. Once we read his letters it becomes easier to imagine what Lodge and millions of others dreamed of: the continued development and growth of those whose lives were brutally cut short. But the book demonstrates another powerful source of the spiritualist appeal. It shows the dead themselves attempting to reach the living in order both to help them cope with the pain of bereavement and to help establish the truth of the spiritualist message. War service, in this context, carried on in the afterlife as well. Indeed, in the words of one writer in the *Occult Review*, which published testimonies of those who spoke to dead soldiers, the fallen were "helping to form a Britain or Empire beyond the grave, a better Britain or Empire than exists now on the material plane."[21]

Raymond was a bestseller during the war, but it was not uncritically received. Even some allies were skeptical of the strength of its findings. The French scientist Charles Richet did not believe that the case of Raymond had proved the existence of survival after death.[22] Neither did Dr Charles Mercier, who lectured on insanity to medical students in London teaching hospitals. He considered *Raymond* debased science. In his view Lodge was simply the "high priest of telepathy," who uncritically accepted as evidence the flimsiest material provided by unscrupulous mediums, profiting from the wartime "epidemic of the occult."[23]

Equally scathing in their criticism of spiritualism were some prominent Anglicans, both lay and clergy. Viscount Halifax, the author of popular volumes of ghost stories, spoke about Raymond at St Martin-in-the-Fields in February 1917. He condemned its defense of spiritualism as a snare and a delusion, leading some to disappointment and despair, others to "ruin," "madness," or "diabolical possession." To claim communication with the dead is to attempt "to draw a curtain which He has not withdrawn," and to do so without reference to sin or judgment or the gospel. "Such books as those of Sir Oliver," Halifax intoned, "are the Nemesis which comes from our neglect of the dead."[24]

J. N. Figgis, the political philosopher and theologian of the Community of the Resurrection, repeated the denunciation. Spiritualism, he claimed, had increased "by leaps and bounds" during the war, because those "crying for light" had been turned away by the church, and had been succoured instead by "practitioners in the occult who could assure them that all was not lost." Spiritualism was therefore "a Nemesis on the Church for its neglect" of those in search of the departed. What could be done in this area, Figgis noted, was limited by Anglican hostility to "noxious" Catholic practices of praying for the dead. Somewhat obstinately, he asserted that the answer to "all exaggerated spiritualism is the doctrine of angels."[25] By this he meant that the belief in the supernatural world could be tolerated if it was constrained by a belief that the human and divine orders were separate. Within this theology, angels could exist and appear; dead spirits could not.

Soldiers, it appears, had their own "doctrine of angels." *Raymond* was read at the front, and provoked a mixed reaction among clergymen in uniform. Some chaplains discussed the book sympathetically, as presenting a challenge to Anglicans to accept that some could arrive at Christian beliefs in unconventional ways.[26] Others were more hostile. F. W. Worsley considered it "a wee bit unhealthy."[27] G. K. A. Studdard Kennedy wrote that it could never "take the place of the lively hope which comes of faith in a communication with God."[28]

The problem for other chaplains was that wartime spiritualism was in vogue as much among serving men as among the families they had left behind. As one chaplain told David Cairns, the Aberdeen theologian: "The British soldier has certainly got religion; I am not so sure, however, that he has got Christianity."[29] To Geoffrey Gordon, soldiers' prayers – "petitions from the trenches" – were liberally mixed with "large numbers of idle and sometimes degrading superstitions which men hold side by side with a vague belief in God." Spiritualism was a form of superstition and had to be combated, he argued. "The superstitious man must either be a polytheist or a devil-worshipper, or, more probably, just a fool."[30] There are few statements that better illustrate why so many soldiers simply ignored what chaplains had to say.

What Gordon missed was that the experience of the trenches could not easily be explained in conventional theological (or indeed in any other) rational terms. For this reason a host of spiritualist images, stories, and legends proliferated during the conflict among British, as among all other, troops. Some were about the dead, others about magical forces affecting the living. The sense of the uncanny, of the overdetermined nature of survival in combat, can be found in many memoirs and letters written by serving men. Many maintained and occasionally celebrated the robust paradox of a belief in their personal invulnerability and also in the power of fate in determining whether a sniper's bullet or shell "had their name written on it." The reversion to pagan or prerational modes of thought under the appalling stress of combat should surprise no one.

The popular art of all combatants included images of saints or Jesus on the field of battle, and a brisk business in religious bric-a-brac grew during the conflict.[31] Soldiers' spiritualism in the British army did not reach the levels of popularity it apparently enjoyed among French, Italian, or Russian soldiers. Partly this was a reflection of the pagan elements of Catholic and Orthodox imagery, of the prewar wave of sightings of the Virgin Mary, and of the tastes of a rural population much larger on the Continent than in Britain. For similarities to continental Catholic spiritualism, one must go across the Irish Sea. There we can find to this day images and objects similar to those produced widely during the 1914–18 war.[32]

Soldiers' tales were important in deepening popular spiritualism, in that they added the prestige of the Tommy and the weight of his experience to those who lived within or on the fringes of the spiritualist community. It is not that most soldiers were avowed spiritualists. It is rather that the bizarre and unnatural world in which they fought was the perfect environment for the spread of tales of the supernatural.

As Eric Leed has noted, given the noise and disorientation of battle, myths and stories tend to quieten and reorder the world.[33] This occurred from the earliest days of the conflict, when the shock of war was greatest and the nearness of Allied defeat was hard to deny. When the British army suffered heavy casualties trying to slow the German advance in Belgium in 1914, stories began to circulate about supernatural phenomena on the field of battle.

The most celebrated of these tales concerns the appearance of angelic figures over British soldiers at Mons. The popular writer Arthur Machin claimed he made it up while daydreaming during a sermon on a Sunday early in the war. He recalled Kipling's tale of a ghostly Indian regiment, added his own "medievalism that is always there," and produced an army of Agincourt bowmen to help defend the British army at Mons. The story appeared in the *Evening News* on 29 September 1914, and then took on a life of its own.[34] But this admission of authorship was fiercely contested by others convinced that soldiers really did see angelic figures on the battlefield. Harold Begbie recounted the evidence of British nurses who had heard wounded soldiers speak of having seen "strange lights" at Mons or phantom cavalrymen. Others recalled strange figures tending the wounded, whose gentleness was as remarkable as the fact that they vanished as soon as others started to seek them out. Perhaps, Begbie suggested, Machin had received a telepathic message from a wounded soldier who wanted the word to go forth that the forces of good were arrayed against the forces of evil.[35]

The emotional mood of the first months of the war created the perfect atmosphere for such eschatological images incorporated into sermons and religious publications in 1915.[36] The same minds that conjured up angels had little difficulty in seeing demonic forces at work on the other side. Popular spiritualism, mixed abundantly with shock and fear, was the real source of the proliferation of atrocity stories during the first two years of the war.

The mix of the angelic and demonic in direct accounts of the war may be illustrated by the memoirs of an English nurse, Phyllis Campbell, who had studied music in Germany before the war, and had been trapped in France by the outbreak of hostilities. She saw cartloads of Belgian refugees passing by, the carts filled with what she said were civilian victims of German atrocities: women whipped or whose breasts had been cut off, children without hands and feet. During this terrible "Week of Terror and Faith" she also saw the other side of the supernatural struggle. "The wounded were in a curious state of exaltation," she wrote. They said that the Germans were "devils – that's why St George is fighting for us." Others described a "golden cloud," a "luminous mist" protecting the British and French. "Is it strange," Campbell noted, "that the torment of these has dragged at the feet of the Ruler of the Universe till he sent aid?" "I have seen no visions," she admitted. "But in my heart I believe that the Captains of God are leading the Allies to victory."[37]

Another way in which the supernatural appeared in the language of soldiers was in the metaphor of the trenches as hell on earth. Ford Madox Ford offered these words after peering down on the landscape of the Battle of the Somme:

> in the territory beneath the eye, or hidden by folds in the ground, there must have been – on the two sides – a million men, moving one against the other and impelled by an invisible moral force into a Hell of fear that surely cannot have had a parallel in this world.[38]

Henri Barbusse spoke the same language when, in his trench novel *Under Fire*, published in 1916 and translated into English in 1917, he spoke of the hell of trench warfare. This anticipates Ezra Pound's now-clichéd litany of soldiers walking "eye-deep in hell / believing in old men's lies" and was repeated in a more mundane fashion both in soldiers' letters and in journalists' prose and photographic captions. To a degree the frequency of its use helped turn "hell" into something more than a metaphor, since it provided a set of very old images to describe the indescribable features of the war on the western front.

The otherworldly landscape, the bizarre mixture of putrefaction and ammunition, the presence of the dead among the living, literally holding up trench walls from Ypres to Verdun, suggested that the demonic and Satanic realms were indeed here on earth. Once this language had a foothold in everyday parlance, it became easy for ordinary men to imagine that hell was not some other place, some exotic torture chamber under the trapdoors leading to the nightmare worlds of Hieronymous Bosch or Roger van der Weyden. To all too many English men and women, hell was indeed just across the Channel.

Apocalyptic legends marked the first two years of the war. As the casualty lists lengthened and the war dragged on, the realm of the supernatural was dominated more by ghostly apparitions than by divine or demonic ones. Again this is hardly surprising, since the problem of coping with a war of annihilation through legends and tales had been eclipsed by the problem of mass bereavement in a war seemingly without end. Here too we inhabit the perimeter of pagan beliefs, in that conventional Christian modes of burying the dead and commemorating them were simply irrelevant in this war. The dead were literally everywhere on the western front, and their invasion of the dreams and thoughts of the living was an inevitable outcome of trench warfare. Lieutenant George Goddard of the Royal Garrison Artillery spoke for many soldiers when he wrote: "In a world of Death one would expect to penetrate the veil when it hangs so constantly before one!"[39] Both during and after the war, tales of the return of the fallen were common, and produced a form of popular literature linking front and home front in a kind of spiritualist embrace.[40]

The link between the spiritualist world and the experience of the First World War is evident in the commemorative art produced after the war. This was perhaps more prominent in France and Germany than in Britain. Different romantic and religious traditions informed British developments, but they shared with French and German popular and commemorative art the same tendency to envision the dead as part of the landscape or the lives of postwar society. German romanticism drew heavily on classical images, and especially on motifs of heroic masculinity.[41] British romanticism emphasized the pastoral, perhaps best exemplified in the English country garden ambience chosen for the thousands of small British cemeteries scattered throughout France and Flanders and looked after to this day by the Commonwealth War Graves Commission.

The man who chose the biblical phrase that dominates the approach to these cemeteries was Rudyard Kipling.[42] "Their name liveth for evermore" had a particular meaning for Kipling, the poet of empire. His 18-year-old son was severely wounded in the face, and then was lost, presumed killed, at Loos in September 1915. His poem "En-dor" brings out the mood of bereavement and the spiritualist temptation that he, like so many other grieving men and women, had felt during and after the war:

The road to En-dor is easy to tread
  For Mother or yearning Wife.
There, it is sure, we shall meet our Dead
  As they were even in life.
Earth has not dreamed of the blessings in store
For desolate hearts on the road to En-dor.

The reference is to the Book of Samuel, in which Saul asks the witch of En-dor to call up the ghost of Samuel. This is a terrible sin for Saul, who thus violated Jewish law, which treated witches as pariahs, and their practices as anathema. For this sin (and others), Saul dies in battle. The biblical reference to spiritualism and to the fate of Saul gives a somber ending to Kipling's poem:

Oh, the road to En-dor is the oldest road
  And the craziest road of all!
Straight it runs to the Witch's abode,
  As it did in the days of Saul,
And nothing has changed of the sorrow in store
For such as go down on the road to En-dor!

Kipling explored the spiritualist world with the same ambivalence in a number of his short stories. A positive and gentle spiritualism may be found in "The gardener." Here he tells the story of Helen Turrell, a woman who has selflessly raised her brother's illegitimate child, who is killed in the war. Helen travels to his grave in France. After an unpleasant encounter with a half-deranged Englishwoman secretly visiting the grave of her illicit lover, Helen goes to the vast cemetery where her nephew lies. Unable to find the grave, she is helped by a man she "supposes" to be a gardener, who "with infinite compassion" shows her the spot.

  More negative and less Christian in its treatment of spiritualism is Kipling's story "A madonna of the trenches." This is a tale of a soldier, Clem Strangwick, who goes mad after the war because he witnessed a few years earlier a ghostly trench encounter. Serving in the same unit was a friend of his family, Sergeant Godsoe, who one night sees an apparition of his Aunt Armine, to whom Godsoe was engaged. In the trenches, the lovers reach out for each other, but he stops, saying: "No, don't tempt me, Bella. We've all Eternity ahead of us." He invites her into a dugout, wedges the door shut, and is found dead the next day. Strangwick goes completely mad when he receives a telegram saying that his Aunt Armine has just died. All this is told in a spiritualist or Masonic lodge, full of people who seek some kind of spiritualist truth, and "go down the road to En-dor."[43]

  Kipling's tales drew on wartime legends,[44] and tell, in a highly ambiguous manner, of the spiritualist way of remembering the dead after the war. In a host of ways, other writers did so too. Poetry conjured up the dead in metaphors common to all languages. In later years, the publication of soldiers' writings, both fiction and autobiography, created a new genre of "war literature." Much of this prose was in itself a kind of war memorial, a ritual entombment of and separation from those who had fallen by those who had survived.[45] In both ephemeral and more enduring works by ex-soldiers, the presence of the dead, both as metaphor and myth, was acknowledged. This literature recreated the uncanny world of the soldiers and brought home, as Kipling had done, their mixed language of irony, humor, and superstition. If the war created "modern memory" as Paul Fussell has claimed, it was a very traditional, even archaic, kind of memory to which the war gave birth.[46]

The best instance of the mix of the archaic and the spiritualist in English commemorative art is that of Stanley Spencer. Born and raised in the Berkshire village of Cookham, Spencer studied at the Slade School of Art, exhibited in Roger Fry's second postimpressionist exhibition in 1912, and in 1915, at the age of 24, joined the Royal Army Medical Corps.

Spencer was part of the British army that never got into war literature: the men who also served, as orderlies, porters, cleaners, launderers, and the like. No glory here. Spencer, like thousands of other forgotten men, inhabited the vast underbelly of the British army, and did so in very unheroic settings. The first was Beaufort War Hospital in Bristol, where the sick and wounded were cared for alongside civilian lunatics. The second was Macedonia, where he was attached to the Seventh Royal Berkshire Infantry, a unit that had turned him down as physically unfit (too small) when he had tried to enlist in 1914.

After demobilization, Spencer returned to Cookham, and to religious art, but of a very unconventional kind. His was a spiritualism with marked similarities to that of Blake, albeit on a less powerful and certainly less beautiful plane. Nevertheless, Spencer followed Blake into the figurative world of the everydayness and the normality of the spiritual life. The war did not create this interest; it gave him the material and memories to extend it in striking ways.

Spencer spent the early postwar years on many different projects, but among the most important were a series of paintings on the Passion of Christ, begun in 1920 and continued intermittently throughout his life. These paintings show clearly how Spencer's prewar fascination both with the Pre-Raphaelites and with Gauguin's rounded portraits developed after the war. The painting of Christ carrying the Cross (now in the Tate Gallery) was executed in 1921 while Spencer was living at Sir Henry Slessor's home in Bourne End, near Cookham. In this work, the obscurity of the Christ figure, masked and hidden by the local people of Cookham, echoes Breughel's compositions, and shares a positively Flemish taste for the particularism of local settings.[47]

Much more unusual, and arguably more original, is the cycle of frescoes on the resurrection of soldiers, designed in the early 1920s, and realized in a specially constructed chapel in Burghclere, near Newbury in Berkshire. Spencer's benefactors, Mr and Mrs J. L. Behrend, gave him the chance to realize his vision, and then dedicated the chapel to the memory of Mrs

Behrend's brother, who had died of illness contracted while on military service in Macedonia during the First World War.[48]

Again, the traditional character of the project is clear. The form of the enterprise recalls Giotto's frescoes in the Arena Chapel in Padua, or, more likely, John Ruskin's description of them. But both in its evocation of the entirely ordinary and unheroic world of military life, both at home and abroad, and in its treatment of the Resurrection, Spencer's work is unique within the corpus of war art. A series of side panels take us through scenes of Spencer's war, in the drab and dreary corridors of Beaufort Military Hospital, to the brown and dusty hillsides of Macedonia. In these paintings, no one fights, no one kills, no one dies. There are some wounded men portrayed, one being painted with iodine, and one whose apparently frostbitten legs we see protected from contact with his sheets. But there is no pain in them. There is as well no joy in the faces of the soldiers carrying on their mundane lives. It is as if they are all in a trance, stuck in a dream world of onerous tasks, avoided where possible, or simply endured. There is only one officer, sitting astride a blanket that only after careful scrutiny we discover is actually covering a horse. He is either trying to teach his men map-reading or simply telling them where they are. In either case, none of his men appears to take the slightest interest in his words. In its unromantic, unmilitary, unofficered normality, Spencer's war memorial is like no other in Britain or (to the best of my knowledge) on the Continent.[49]

The most remarkable feature of Spencer's chapel is the central panel portraying the Resurrection. Just as in his painting of Christ carrying the Cross, here the Savior is hard to find. He is near the top of the wall above the altar, seated, receiving from a group of risen soldiers the crosses that presumably marked their graves. The center of the painting is dominated by two horses, fallen down, craning their necks around to see why the cart they have pulled has collapsed. Above them, and below the Christ, is a young soldier, staring at the wooden crucifix on his cross, seemingly oblivious of the risen Christ by his side.

All this takes place on a Macedonian hillside, where animals graze and soldiers sleep, rise from their graves in fur jackets, polish epaulets, unwind their puttees, cut the wire fallen on another soldier's head and body, and generally go about their business. As Spencer later recalled, the painting is Resurrection as Armistice, when soldiers rise and hand in their crosses as they would hand in their guns when the need for them ended.[50] There are soldierly handshakes in one corner of the painting, but there is absolutely no joy.[51]

Most of the men in Spencer's frescoes share the same dark features, rounded heads, and stubby figures. Either in menial tasks or in military routine, their bearing and manner have none of the marks of the abstraction or cubist features of Nevinson's war art or of the individual portraiture of Muirhead Bone. It appears that Spencer chose his own way, remote from both the avant-garde and the rearguard of British art, in the exploration of spiritual realities.

It should be clear, therefore, that the image of the rising of the dead of the Great War that graces the Sandham Memorial Chapel at Burghclere was in no sense simply a reflection of Stanley Spencer's eccentric religiosity. He spoke a spiritual language many contemporaries used and adapted to their particular circumstances. The more extravagant forms of Catholic popular art provided a reservoir of images for spiritualists on the Continent (and in Ireland). Protestant iconography in England was somewhat more restrained, but both Blake and the Pre-Raphaelites provided ample artistic material for spiritualists like Spencer. When he came to paint his frescoes at Burghclere between 1927 and 1932, he testified both to the robustness of the English spiritual imagination and to the capacity of the spiritualist temperament to see transcendence even in the carnage of war. None of this needed the war to establish; it was all there for those like Stanley Spencer who believed in the incontrovertible imminence of the spiritual life,[52] and who maintained that belief in the decades following the 1914–18 conflict.

The period of the First World War was in some ways the apogee of spiritualism in Britain. By the 1930s its appeal had waned, and it had relatively few prominent adherents during and after the Second World War.[53] The reasons for its decline go beyond the purpose of this essay. My intention here is simply to suggest the powerfully conservative effects of the First World War on one aspect of English cultural history. The upheaval of war led not to a rejection or recasting of attitudes about spiritualism, but to the deepening of well-established Victorian sentiments and conjectures concerning the nature of the spiritual world.

Some of these practices and beliefs were superstitious. Others entered the realm of the uncanny, the paranormal, the necromantic, or the mystical. All shared a tendency to slide from metaphors about remembering those who have died to the metaphysics of life after death. The 1914–18 conflict certainly did not create these modes of thought, but neither did the war discredit or destroy them. Those bereaved – and they numbered in the millions – needed all the help they could get. The magical and mythical realm flared up at a time of mass death and destruction to help illuminate a world darkened by the catastrophe that today we call the Great War.

NOTES

1 S. Hynes, *A War Imagined: The First World War and English Culture* (London, 1990), p. xi, for the latest (but certainly not last) formulation.
2 For a recent formulation, see Modris Ekstein, *The Rites of Spring: The First World War and the Birth of the Modern Era* (New York, 1990).
3 Among them are: A. Wilkinson, *The Church of England and the First World War* (London, 1978); S. Mews, "Religion and English society in the First World War," (PhD, Cambridge University, 1973); A. Marrin, *The Church of England in the First World War* (Raleigh, NC, 1974); K. W. Clements, "Baptists and the outbreak of the First World War," *Baptist Quarterly*, Apr. 1975.

4 L. Barrow, *Independent Spirits, Spiritualism and English Plebeians, 1850-1910* (London, 1986).

5 N. Edelman, "Les tables tournantes arrivent en France," *L'Histoire*, 75 (1985), pp. 16–23; and N. Edelman, "Allan Kardec, prophète du spiritisme," *L'Histoire*, 98 (1987), pp. 62–9.

6 Marion Aubrée and François Laplantine, *La Table, le livre et les esprits* (Paris, 1990), pp. 87–8.

7 J. Pierrot, *The Decadent Imagination 1880-1900*, trans. D. Koltman (Chicago, 1981).

8 Aubrée and Laplantine, *La Table*, pp. 47–8.

9 R. Haynes, *The Society for Psychical Research 1882-1982: A History* (London, 1982), pp. 183–94; J. Oppenheim, *The Other World: Spiritualism and Psychical Research in England, 1850-1914* (Cambridge, 1984).

10 D. Cannadine, "War and death, grief and mourning in modern Britain," in J. Whaley (ed.), *Mirrors of Mortality* (London, 1980), p. 227.

11 L. Lambert, "Les mystères d'Outre-Tombe," *Art funéraire et Commémorative*, 12 (Apr. 1920); see also Aubrée and Laplantine, *La Table*, p. 274.

12 A. Conan Doyle, *The History of Spiritualism* (London, 1926), Vol. 2, p. 226.

13 A. Conan Doyle, *The New Revelation and the Vital Message* (London, 1919), preface and pp. 77–8.

14 R. Brandon, *The Spiritualists: The Passion for the Occult in the Nineteenth and Twentieth Centuries* (London, 1983), pp. 168–9.

15 J. Arthur Hill (ed.), *Letters from Sir Oliver Lodge, Psychical, Religious, Scientific, Personal* (London, 1932), letter of 31 Aug. 1923, p. 181.

16 Oliver Lodge, *Past Years: An Autobiography* (London, 1931), p. 187.

17 For example, his two articles "Personal appearances of the departed" and "Effects of light on long ether waves and other processes," *Journal of the Society for Psychical Research*, XVIII (Feb.–Mar. 1918), pp. 32–4, 213–20.

18 R. Blatchford, "My testimony," in Sir James Marchant (ed.), *Life after Death according to Christianity and Spiritualism* (London, 1925), p. 118.

19 Oliver J. Lodge, *Raymond or Life and Death: With Examples of the Evidence for Survival of Memory and Affection after Death* (London, 1916), p. 128 (for Mrs Leonard).

20 Ibid., p. 85.

21 Ibid., p. 99; Eustace Miles, "Britain beyond the grave," *Occult Review*, XXIII, 1 (Jan. 1918), p. 39, as cited in D. Jarrett, *The Sleep of Reason: Fantasy and Reality from the Victorian Age to the First World War* (London, 1988), p. 196.

22 C. Richet, *Thirty Years of Psychical Research: Being a Treatise on Metaphysics*, trans. S. de Brath (London, 1923), pp. 216, 610.

23 Charles A. Mercier, *Spiritualism and Sir Oliver Lodge* (London, 1917), pp. 4, 5, 6, 10.

24 Viscount Halifax, *"Raymond": Some Criticisms* (London, 1919), pp. 7, 11, 12, 39, 41.

25 J. N. Figgis, *Hopes for English Religion* (London, 1919), pp. 181–2, 183.

26 W. D. Geare, *Letters of an Army Chaplain* (London, 1918), p. 84; D. MacFadyen, *Our Mess: Mess Table Talks in France* (London, 1920), pp. 124–6. I am grateful to Ms Laurinda Stryker of Newnham College, Cambridge, for drawing these references to my attention.

27 F. W. Worsley, *Letters to Mr Britling* (London, 1917), p. 69.

28 G. K. A. Studdard Kennedy, *The Hardest Part* (London, 1918), pp. 185–7.

29 B. Mathews (ed.), *Christ: And the World at War* (London, 1917), p. 42.

30 T. W. Pym and G. Gordon, *Papers from Picardy by Two Chaplains* (London, 1917), pp. 188, 201, 202.

31 The Département de la Somme has some splendid examples in its collection for the Historial de la Grande Guerre, a new museum to be opened at Peronne in 1992. In France the business of providing plastic Virgin Marys, ivory colored, or gold- or silver-leafed, flourished during the war. See, for example, advertisements in the *Almanach du propagation des Trois "Ave Maria"* (1918).

32 I am grateful to Dr Joanna Bourke for bringing this point (and some striking artifacts) to my attention. On continental Catholic popular piety, see David Blackbourn, *Populists and Patricians: Essays in Modern German History* (London, 1987), esp. p. 9.

33 Eric J. Leed, *No Man's Land: Combat and Identity in World War I* (Cambridge, 1979).

34 Arthur Machin, *The Bowmen and Other Legends of the War* (London, 1915), pp. 11–12, 66.

35 Harold Begbie, *On the Side of the Angels: The Story of the Angel at Mons: An Answer to "The Bowmen"* (London, 1915), pp. 21–44.

36 "Notes of the month," *Occult Review*, XXII, 1 (July 1915), pp. 7–10.

37 Phyllis Campbell, *Back of the Front* (London, 1916), pp. 31–2, 84–5, 94, 98, 100, 112–13, 119. See also her article "The angelic leaders," *Occult Review*, XXII, 2 (Aug. 1915), pp. 76–82.

38 Ford Madox Ford, "Arms and the mind," *Esquire*, 94 (Dec. 1980), p. 80, as cited in Hynes, *War Imagined*, p. 106.

39 Lt George Goddard, "Orthodoxy and the war," *Occult Review*, XXVII, 2 (Feb. 1918), p. 84.

40 For two examples among many, see J. S. M. Ward, *Gone West* (London, 1919); and *A Subaltern in Spirit Land: A Sequel to "Gone West"* (London, 1920). Another well-known example is the appearance of the ghost of Wilfred Owen to his brother in Nov. 1918.

41 G. Mosse, *Fallen Soldiers: Reshaping the Memory of the World Wars* (New York, 1989).

42 On Kipling and the war, see Frank Field, *British and French Writers of the First World War: Comparative Studies in Cultural History* (Cambridge, 1991), pp. 153–76.

43 The two stories may be found in C. Raine (ed.), *A Choice of Kipling's Prose* (London, 1986), pp. 369–81, 404–12.

44 See the strikingly similar story of a woman's ghost coming to fetch a soldier about to be killed, in Elliott O'Donnell, "Hauntings in Belgium," *Occult Review*, XXI, 4 (Apr. 1915), pp. 223–31.

45 J. M. Winter, *The Great War and the British People* (London, 1986), ch. 9.

46 P. Fussell, *The Great War and Modern Memory* (Oxford, 1975).

47 *Stanley Spencer: The Passion* (no ed.) (Edinburgh, 1986).

48 G. Behrend, *Stanley Spencer at Burghclere* (London, 1965), p. 62.

49 For the distinct tradition of war memorials in France, see A. Prost, "Monuments aux morts," in P. Nora (ed.), *Les Lieux de mémoire*, Vol. 2: *La République* (Paris, 1984); and A. Becker, *Les Monuments aux morts* (Paris, 1988); for Germany, G. Mosse, *Fallen Soldiers* (New York, 1989); for Australia and England, the forthcoming studies of Ken Inglis and Catherine Moriarty.

50 R. Carline, *Stanley Spencer at War* (London, 1978), p. 184.

51 Samuel Hynes calls the scene "joyous," an emotion remote from the faces and postures of every single figure in the cycle. See Hynes, *War Imagined*, p. 463.

52 Behrend, *Spencer at Burghclere*; Arts Council, *Stanley Spencer 1851–1859* (London, 1976); Carline, *Spencer at War*.

53 Air Marshal Lord Dowding was one of them, claiming to have spoken with fallen pilots during and after the Battle of Britain. See Louis Pauwels and Guy Breton, *Nouvelles histoires extraordinaires* (Paris, 1982), pp. 111–30. In more recent years, Arthur Koestler and the Cambridge Nobel-prizewinner Brian Josephson have helped keep the tradition alive.

Index